BEHIND EVERY SUCCESSFUL MAN
Wives of Medicine and Academe

BEHIND EVERY
SUCCESSFUL MAN
Wives of Medicine and Academe

Martha R. Fowlkes

New York Columbia University Press *1980*

Library of Congress Cataloging in Publication Data

Fowlkes, Martha R   1940–
Behind every successful man.

Bibliography: p.
1. Wives—United States.   2. Professions—United
States.   3. Physicians' wives—United States.
4. Teachers' wives—United States.   I. Title.
HQ759.F68   301.42'7   79-24901
ISBN 0-231-04776-2

Columbia University Press
New York   Guildford, Surrey

To My Father
David G. Richmond

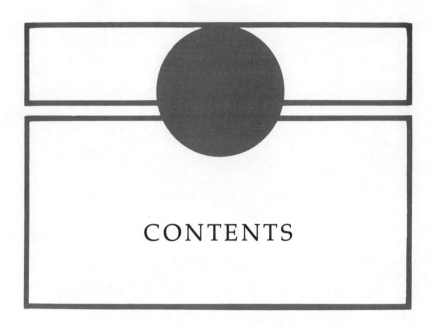

CONTENTS

TABLES

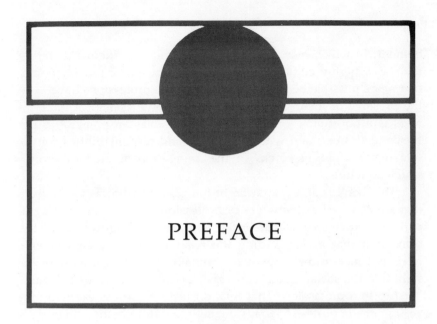

PREFACE

This book is about the lives and marriages of forty women; twenty wives of university professors and twenty wives of doctors. Professional careers and professional life are its broader subject. For there are some peculiar incongruities in the sociological study of professions and professional participation. Most sociologists will readily acknowledge that it is a woman's role in the family that keeps her *from* work, but they seldom, if ever, make note of the ways in which that same role enables her husband *to* work. Possibly because most sociologists who have studied the professions have themselves been male, little attention has been given to the functional interdependency of family and career structures, of male work roles and female roles at home, and of how this interdependency contributes to and facilitates the professional roles of men, and, indeed, sustains the organization of men's professional careers.

The structure of American professional work and rewards is typically viewed sociologically as an inevitable and efficient development, in which men happen to be the main participants, rather than as a highly culture-dependent, historically-bound phenomenon made possible because, in the main, the professions have been the preserve of men. Central to the traditional system of male careers is a traditional wife at home whose roles are integral to her husband's career, and whose existence and responsibilities constitute major building blocks in the foundation of modern professional structures.

This book is an exploration of how and in what ways the lives that women lead as the wives of professional men form an integral part of their husbands' careers. It is a book that grows out of the conviction that understanding the relationship between women's roles and male careers opens up a vitally important avenue of insight into the social construction and conditions of successful membership in a profession. That relationship, in turn, is explicitly revealing of the professional advantage inherent in being a man with a certain kind of wife and implicitly revealing of the disadvantages to women, who, lacking wives, aspire nontheless to equality of career participation and success with men. Moreover, through the lives of the women under study in this book, it is possible to catch glimpses of a changing social order, as that is manifested in the workplace and reflected in family roles and relationships.

In an academic sense, this book can be viewed as an expansion of the sociological analysis of Becker and Strauss (1956) regarding the interdependence of careers and the role of "important others" at various stages of the career—although as the life patterns of the women in this book suggest, a wife is, in many instances, not merely an important other, but *the* important other. In a more popular sense, this book is an empirical investigation of the proposition—seldom taken very seriously except for brief moments at testimonial banquets—that "behind every successful man there is a woman."

Personal Note

All research has a personal and an intellectual history and constitutes to some degree an exploration and expression of self as well as of others. For this reason it is important that any account of the formulations and perceptions that shape a piece of research and its attendant conclusions not discount the subjective aspects of the research process. No social science research is truly "untouched by human hands" in the sense of being utterly devoid of any relationship to the researcher's own values and interests, though research is frequently presented in the most bloodless manner possible as if to assure the reader of its utter trustworthiness as science. It seems to me to be far more scientific to put squarely before the reader the salient facts about a researcher's experience and reactions which, together with those of the actual research subjects, have contributed to the development and presentation of a piece of research, thus enabling the reader to make a full and knowledgable assessment of the research. For all of these reasons I end this preface and begin this book with a brief personal note.

No doubt one's intellectual bent has its origin, as does one's emotional bent, in a variety of early life experiences and in the social and psychological features of one's life course over time. The origins of the particular study contained in this book are far less obscure and more immediate, however. As a woman who attended college at the juncture of the 1950s and 1960s, it is probably not surprising that I found my way only haltingly and over a period of several years to a full-fledged career commitment. By the time I returned to graduate school in 1972, I had married and raised children, and I had also been affected by the prevailing spirit of social reform of the 1960s. I had held jobs relating to the evaluation and delivery of health and mental health care services, and I had been active in the early years of the women's rights movement.

I carried these interests with me into my doctoral work in sociology. As a student, my interest in medicine shifted from a focus on services to the structure and organization of medical professionalism itself. My commitment to the women's movement led me into the sociological study of sex roles and to a consideration of the distortions that tend to result from sociological constructs and inquiries that overlook the existence of women altogether or disregard the importance of sex roles as factors in shaping social institutions and interactions. The application of these ideas to the study of professions and career structures paved the way for the formulation of the research that appears in this book.

However, it was not only the intellectual but the social experience of graduate school that played an important part in shaping my research interests. As I began to make the transition to thinking of myself not just as a student but as a professional, I saw that the organization of my life course was seriously at odds with the organization and requirements of career structures. Compared to other students who were younger, unencumbered by family ties, and whose uninterrupted chronology of academic study provided indisputable evidence of their singleminded dedication to the sociological enterpirse, I was at a distinct disadvantage.

Although I realized that this disadvantage had its source in the choices and roles I had felt were appropriate to my life as a woman, it was not until one day during a brief encounter with a fellow graduate student and his wife that I saw with stunning clarity the inherent advantage that belongs to a man who is free to pursue certain choices and roles in his life precisely because his wife does not.

The scene was a photographer's waiting room filled with mothers waiting to have bargain-priced pictures taken of their children. I was one of the mothers and so was the wife of the graduate student. She waited with her two young children somewhat more patiently than I did, because as always, I was feeling the press of the demands on my time of my combined work and family routines. She clucked sympathetically and said something about not knowing how I did it all and that she herself had her hands full with just caring for her children. Then she began to talk about life after graduate school and wanted to know what sort of future job I envisioned for myself. I answered quite honestly that I had no idea what was ahead, and that any career plans I made would certainly have to consider my husband's professional needs as well. In reply she noted how much easier things were for her and her husband because she was willing to go anywhere there was a job he would be happy in.

Just about this time her husband walked in expecting to find her ready to leave. When he saw that she had some time yet to wait, he became impatient and remarked with obvious irritation that this was all a waste of time and that he had counted on being home earlier so she could begin typing his field notes. With that I saw how vastly different and unequal were the terms of our supposedly mutual graduate studenthood. It was very simple: he had a wife and I did not. And although I did not conceptualize this experience in any depth at the time, in thinking about it later I realized that his wife had, in just a matter of moments, delineated for me the double-duty, supportive, and adjunct features of the wife's role. This encounter stayed with me, and at some point personal experience and intellectual inquiry were conjoined and a research project was born—and this book was written.

There is irony, of course, in setting out to study the very structures and processes of which one feels in some ways a victim. And there is danger too—that victimization may engender a bitterness that obscures objectivity, and that one's own personal rejection of certain aspects of the wife's role may block full understanding and appreciation of the different content and expression that other wives have given to their roles. It is true, there were days when the fatigue of caring for infant twins—who arrived quite surprisingly in the midst of my research—gave way to anger as I confronted my data about forty men whose professional success and the conditions upon which it was achieved seemed to make a mockery of my own attempts at professional achievement under the circumstances.

On the whole, I have felt far more rewarded than deprived by my full participation in family as well as professional life, though it is often difficult not to regret the attenuation of career that is the nearly inevitable result of dividing time and attention between the two commitments. I can only hope that the frank recognition of that regret has acted as a safeguard against loss of objectivity as a researcher. And although I have come to define my own role as a wife quite differently from the women I interviewed, I lack neither respect for nor familiarity with the circumstances of their lives. Nor—as I hope is abundantly clear throughout the book—do I feel that those lives are lived in unimportant ways. Indeed one of the major gratifications for me in this research was in giving the wives the opportunity to be seen and heard as the truly central figures that they are both inside their families and in relation to their husbands' careers.

That is not to say that I lay claim to this research as the work of an "insider" in the sense that Merton (1972) has discussed that term, though the ideas and perspectives of the research are clearly interwoven with my personal and professional experience as a woman. Certainly the interviews themselves could just as easily have been conducted by a man. Perhaps I was able to establish rapport more easily and quickly than a man who was not a wife and mother might have been able to do. But I was, after all, talking to these women not in the capacity of my domestic roles but as a professional sociologist, a role that is task—but hardly sex—specific. The sense of sympathetic identity that the interviewee comes to feel with the interviewer during the course of a successful interview depends far less on actual likeness between interviewer and subject than on the question-asking and listening ability of the interviewer. Some women, I felt, would have been more relaxed in the professional presence of a man whose role conveyed no threat or challenge, however implicit, to the traditional wife's role, as I sometimes felt that my own did. Of course, no one interviewer can be all things to all subjects, and it is inevitable that some interviews will yield more "complete" results than others.

While the primary purpose of the interview, or any research technique, is to yield data for analysis, discussions of research methods all too often overlook the fact that the research process affects not only the subjects of research but the researcher as well. Along with other professionally motivated women, I have been guilty of the tendency to disassociate myself from the traditional roles of women, to stereotype them with a kind of negative simplicity, to judge them, in other words, in the manner that men have judged them, in order to gain acceptance and approval in the workaday world of men and their values.

What I have gained from my brief but in-depth excursion into the daily lives of women at home is an enormous respect for the complexity of those lives, a great appreciation for the sensitivity to the needs of others that is built into women's family roles, and a new understanding of the initiative required of most women who must find ways of putting order and cohesion into their own and their families' days without the advantage of predetermined career structures to guide and direct them along their adult course. For women at home to be judged inferior to men at work is to assume that the instrumental world is necessarily superior to the world of intimate relations; for women themselves to make those judgments is to contribute to the very inequality that they decry. Through evaluating the lives of these forty women, I have come to revalue a part of myself. For that I am grateful.

In addition to the wives who were the central contributors to the content of what is written in this book, I wish to thank the following persons who made unique and invaluable contributions to the context in which it was written: The Women's Studies Committee of the Woodrow Wilson National Fellowship Foundation, Alice S. Rossi, Robert Faulkner, the late Ely Chinoy, Peter H. Rossi, Sherry Marker, Miriam I. Leveton, Patricia Y. Miller. Each in his or her own way helped to sustain both my sociological faith and my sense of humor at one or another (and sometimes several) of the important turning points that occurred from the time the research for the book was first conceived until it was set in print.

I am also indebted in less immediate but no less relevant or meaningful ways to Alfred Harris and Raymond Firth whose dedicated teaching many years ago laid the foundation of my ongoing enthusiasm for the study of the social world in all of its many forms and manifestations.

Barbara Kirouac, Andrea Cohen, and Claudia Kahn assisted with typing, often going way beyond the call of duty to do so. Thanks to them, as well as to the editorial staff of Columbia University Press for clear and conscientious communications and advice.

The most special thanks of all are due to my husband, Oliver Fowlkes, and my daughters, Lisa and Anne Bladen, whose hearts, help, and homemaking were so steady and true that I scarcely knew I did not have a wife. I am grateful, too, to the twins, Abigail and Margaret, who have delightfully introduced me to a world where everyday is lived altogether naturally as a partnership of true equals.

PERSPECTIVES on FAMILY and CAREER: CONVENTIONAL WISDOM and UNCONVENTIONAL QUESTIONS

It is the particular cultural bias of Americans (including the sociologists among them) to view career achievements in highly individualistic and meritocratic terms. There are essentially two major approaches to the sociological study of elite occupational careers, commonly known as professions. One is in the tradition of Everett Hughes and Howard Becker, which emphasizes the subjective, experiential and particularistic aspects of the career venture; the other is in the tradition of Talcott Parsons and Robert Merton, and stresses the organization, structure, status, and formal role behavior of professional life. Regardless of the approach adopted, however, most writings on occupational careers take the shape of the specific lines of mobility in a particular occupation as given. They are rarely studied as a topic in their own right; rather the "models" of appropriate career lines to success are taken for granted as a resource for. investigation.

Thus the analysis of professional career lines focuses on the extent to which participants emerge as products of career systems, a perspective that overlooks the theoretically more important question, namely, to what extent are career systems the products of the people—that is to say, the men—who participate in them? Insofar as high-ranking occupational careers—those in law, medicine, university teaching, science, engineering, corporate management—are male dominated, the standards for career training, mobility, and success contain a host of assumptions about what is primary and what is secondary in the pursuit of the professional career. As Hochschild (1974:22) has noted, professional structures have developed to "suit half the population in the first place."

While the ultimate test of an occupation's professional status may be, as Freidson (1970a, ch. 4) suggests, its autonomy, or freedom to control the terms of its work, the individual aspirant to a professional field is far from free to control the terms of his recruitment, training, participation, or ultimately, his success within the profession. Holmstrom (1973:29) puts this in a slightly different way in her comment that the "trouble with having a profession today is that if you have one you are expected to pursue it in a certain way—and it is a very rigid way."

For each profession there is a characteristic model of the appropriate career lines to be followed en route to the successful outcome, beginning with and including a "prolonged specialized training in a body of abstract knowledge." (Goode 1960:903) Each profession, moreover, has its own timetable for advancement, based on a combination of age and specified kinds of productivity and experience. To be sure there may be several routes to posts of high prestige and responsibility within any one occupation, but Becker and Strauss' (1956) references to these routes as "escalators" is telling. Whatever the route chosen by the professional participant, the expectation is that there will be a continuous and uninterrupted journey from the bottom to the top. The ability, furthermore, to steer a course through the "stretches of maximum opportunity and danger," as Becker and Strauss call the critical junctures of a career, depends heavily on doing the right kind of work in the right place at the right time. Any discontinuities between timing, place, and work experience or output are likely to put the career aspirant at a competitive disadvantage.

The continuous, uninterrupted career is by definition a full-time career. The genuinely professional commitment is an expression and investment of self, measured not in the number of hours worked but as a "calling" in which the work of the profession stands as a kind of higher goal and in which one's major identification is with professional peers and the profession as a whole. The deeply personal and abiding nature of the professional commitment is summarized sociologically by Hughes:

> These characteristics and collective claims of a profession are dependent upon a close solidarity, upon its members constituting in some measure a group apart with an ethos of its own. This in turn implies a deep and lifelong commitment. A man who leaves a profession once he is fully trained, licensed and initiated, is something of a renegade in the eyes of his fellows. (1971c:376)

Opportunities for salaried part-time professional work are rare, and where such positions do exist, they are not part of the career escalators for a given profession. Lacking developmental sequence and opportunities for advancement, part-time professional work constitutes a job and not a career. Rapoport and Rapoport, for example, make this distinction between work and career:

> The term "career" is sometimes used to indicate any kind of work, but in its more precise meaning in social science it designates those types of jobs which require a high degree of commitment and which have continuous developmental character. The individual develops a career by moving from one job or stage to another, continuously gathering and applying relevant experience for improved performance in a more senior position or in a more expert role of some kind. (1971:18)

In a related point, Rossi (1972b:146) argues that the institutionalization of a pattern of interrupted work for college-educated women depresses the creativity and development that are the prerequisites for career participation in the top professions. Even in the entrepreneurial professions, in which the practitioner is supposedly free to arrange his schedule of work to suit his personal preference, neither colleagues nor clients are likely to give much credence to the commitment to service of a part-time practitioner. The result is likely to be that in situations where commitment is less than full time, clients will be steered elsewhere by the lay and colleague referral system. Then, too, the evaluation of successful achievement in the entrepreneurial professions is closely connected with money earned. Full-time work means more money, which in turn means more success.

Inside each professional career there are occupational pressures for specific kinds and chronologies of geographic mobility and immobility. Professional work quite frequently occurs outside the confines of the everyday workplace of office and institution. For besides working in a place, professionals also work in a field or a discipline or a corporation whose boundaries are not local but national and, increasingly, international. In addition, certain policy-formulating and decision-making responsibilities fall to the professional in precisely those areas in which he is free to control the terms of his work. Therefore, service on committees and attendance at meetings, conferences, lectures, doing consulting work, taking research-related leaves and sabbaticals comprise—and are expected to comprise—an important part of professional life. Professional work is thus potentially quite irregular and open-ended in its time demands, and at certain times, and under certain circumstances, there may be a distinctly peripatetic quality to the pursuit of professional success.

Quite clearly certain assumptions are firmly embedded in the present structure of professional careers—that commitment to a professional career is a central, if not the overriding commitment, in a person's life; that the career is the major source of one's personal and social identity; that whenever necessary, the career has priority over all other life involvements; that the career is the major determinant of the chronology and geography of one's life and the central organizing feature of a given day. When seen in light of these assumptions, it is obvious that professional life is neither incidentally nor coincidentally a male way of life. It is *intrinsically* a male way of life in which there are no heroines, only heroes.

The heroic male professional is characterized by zeal for his work—an internalized devotion to its tasks and demands independent of pay rates or the work week. Indeed, his work is the most important thing in his life. Self-motivated, he assumes complete responsibility for his work and routinely turns in a superior performance. He has high standards and ethics. Conversely, the male professional's career is so demanding as to preclude other major commitments. . . . The heroic male professional sacrifices "selfish" concerns like personal and family life to the demands of his career. An invidious judgment concerning the worth of career and family is central to the implied comparison between the assumed motivation of the female worker—divided, uninspired, venial—and that of "the" male worker. (Laws 1976:36)

High-level careers have been built by men for men. In a fundamental sense they are occupational extensions of the male role and reflect the freedom and norms of that role. Perhaps it would be more accurate to say that the male role is an extension of the occupational world. And if women cannot themselves meet the conditions of professional success, they nonetheless make it possible for men to do so. For married professional men, who have always been the majority group in professional life, the ability to measure up to their own set standards in their professional roles depends in a variety of essential ways on the roles of the women who are their wives.

Sociological theory has emphasized the segregation rather than the interconnectedness of family and work, unless, of course, it is the work of women that is being considered. Indeed there really are no sociological studies of women's occupational participation that do not emphasize the interconnectedness of women's work and family roles. (See, for example, studies by Myrdal and Klein [1968]; Epstein [1971]; Fogarty, Rapoport, and Rapoport [1971]; and Knudsin [1974].) Where men are concerned the sociological segregation of family and work contains an implicit judgment that "real" professionalism is an entity in itself; that it stands *sui generis* as a reality; that it is not contingent upon, intertwined with, or even compatible with other social institutions, particularly those which embody affective rather than instrumental or goal-oriented values.

This emphasis on segregation that is apparent in sociological analysis is reinforced (or perhaps even caused by) the sex-typed division of labor that grows out of the male dominance of the discipline of sociology itself. In sociology, as in many academic dis-

5

ciplines, the study of what men do and of the concerns that men have in the world of cash and power tend to be considered the most intellectually worth-while topics, with the result that more prestige accrues to the study of work than to the study of family, which is often thought of as the "women's work" of the discipline. Yet as Rossi notes, the judgment as to the merit, and therefore the prestige, of one or another area of sociological inquiry is at once arbitrary and highly personalized.

> One wonders if the generation now enjoying prestige in graduate sociology departments has forgotten their own youth. The middle-aged sociologists who rule in academe today studied Navy boat crews, waitresses and watchmakers, authoritarian personalities, anti-Semitism, printers' union workers, TVA projects, social mobility, stratification, bureaucracy. This upwardly mobile generation of survivalist young Turks of twenty years ago built their careers on topics which had their deepest roots in these men's personal histories—and then they went on to train several generations of young sociologists on the mystique of "value neutrality," super-science, and super-theory. (1973:127)

Pahl and Pahl (1971:14) have commented that the separation of career and family as fields of study is synonymous with the separation of the "tough-minded industrial sociologists" into one corner and "tender-minded students of the family" in another. Since the world of work is peopled largely by men and the world of family by women, the sex composition of the two worlds is taken for granted rather than seen as offering theoretically significant insights into those worlds and the connecting links between them.

Classical macrosociological perspectives (e.g., Smelser 1959; Ariès 1962) stress the tailoring down of family size and the rearrangement or loss of family functions as a consequence of the organization of work in industrial society. In her study of the housewife role, Oakley (1974) examines the attenuation and involution of the role of the wife that followed from her exclusion from the occupational structure of industrial society. Studies of two-career families by Poloma (1970) and Garland (1971) pay great attention to the social norms that underpin the roles of women in the family and of men in the workplace, without much consideration of the in-

terrelationship of those roles and of their origins in the social structure.

The few studies that have made a point of examining male careers in conjunction with family life place the most emphasis on the
ways in which a wife is acted upon by a man's quest for career success. Seidenberg (1975) focuses primarily on the mobility requirements that are built into the career of the corporate executive and
on the strain that those requirements impose upon a wife and family. In a more journalistic vein, MacPherson (1975) discusses the
special restraints on and toll taken on the wife whose husband
makes a career of running for high public office. Finally, Pahl and
Pahl (1971) complement their study of managerial careers with a
good deal of descriptive material about wives' responses to and
views of the way of life entailed by those careers. Their approach to
the study of family and career has more to do with the way the two
coexist than with the ways that they are actually conjoined.

None of these perspectives comes to grips with the interdependency of family and career roles. Nowhere are the questions posed
about what a wife does in behalf of her husband's career and of the
ways in which family life and roles mesh with and sustain professional life and roles. Absent too are questions about how well men
can perform or meet their own set criteria in professional life except
as family life itself is professionalized and the wife's role is tailored
to the occupational system.

Yet it is clear that as he goes about the business of establishing
and maintaining a successful professional career, a man has three
distinctly different kinds of needs, each one of which has a potential counterpart in the wife's role. In the first place there is the need
to do the actual work of his profession in a way that will establish
him in a favorable competitive position vis-à-vis those who are in a
position to influence the direction of his professional life. Second,
there is the need for a sustained achievement drive, which implies
the need to be able to give his best to his work and to cope with the
particular stresses of the career commitment. Finally, there is the
absolutely crucial need for time in which to accomplish the work at
hand.

In response to the first need—for the realization of career

goals—a wife may act as an *adjunct* and make an active contribution to the status or content of her husband's work. In response to the second need—for a sustained achievement drive—a wife is able to offer her husband both active and passive kinds of *support* that not only nurture and revitalize his career ambitions but also ensure that he is untroubled and unhampered in his quest for career success. And a wife can respond to her husband's need for time by doing *double duty* as parent, homemaker and organizer of family life, thereby leaving her husband free of the interruptions and distractions of home-based responsibilities and routines.

This role classification is not static and there are a number of factors that may contribute to variation and change in the wife's role. The wife's own background prior to marriage may affect her sense of herself and her roles in her marriage, for example. There may also be patterns of interactive effect, so to speak, that derive from the coincidence or overlap of particular stages in the family cycle with particular stages in the development of the man's career. It is to be expected that different women will seek and find different gratifications in their roles as wife. Depending on the nature of the transactions between husband and wife, some activities and orientations may be defined and enacted more explicitly than others by the wife. The most likely correlates of variation in the wife's role are the specific features of the different kinds of professional careers and the personalities of the kinds of people who choose to have, or marry into, those careers. And just who those people are—both professionals and spouses—may also be related to changes in the work settings and work roles of professional life.

Professional Careers and Male Roles

For convenience, it is possible to refer to professions as a general category of occupations. In reality, however, the individual professions differ markedly from one another with respect to the kind of work done, the organization of that work, the values and self-concept embodied in the professional role, the audience for the work of the profession, and the shape and content of a typical career for that particular profession or career track within the profession. To the extent that the professional endeavors of men vary along these lines, it is likely that the lives and roles of the women who are their wives will also vary. The interdependency of occupational and family structures as a general social pattern is best illustrated by depicting the common and distinct ways that the wives of men in a given profession are affected by and drawn into the structure and values of the profession itself. The wives who appear in this book are married to men who have careers in the fields of university teaching and the practice of medicine, professions that well exemplify many of the contrasting features of high level occupational life.

The Profession of Medicine

Among the elite occupations commonly known as professions, medicine is perhaps the most prestigious. This prestige is accompanied by a high degree of autonomy. The medical establishment controls not only the scientific and technical content of its work, but the economic terms of its work as well. The practice of medicine in the United States is typically entrepreneurial and competitive—a full-blown expression of rugged individualism. A doctor's success is measured by and reflected in his income; the high socioeconomic standing of medicine adds to the prestige of the occupation and of the individual practitioner within it.

The entrepreneurial role of the practitioner is perforce a highly other-directed role. The doctor must be attuned to his standing in both the medical community and the wider local community if he is to attract—through the lay and the colleague referral system—the clients on which his income depends. In the primary care specialties especially, the physician needs to maintain a secure and stable patient population and must work to ensure that his clients do not go elsewhere. The client's needs come first and those needs may be urgent and difficult to schedule, with the result that the working hours of the physician may be open-ended and highly unpredictable.

The medical professional role confers a great deal of authority upon the practitioner. This authority has its source in the structure of the doctor-patient relationship itself as well as in the institutional position of the medical profession in the medical division of labor and among other health-related occupations. (See Freidson's discussion of medical authority, 1970b, chs. 4 and 5.) The physician delivers services to clients who rely on the expertise of the physician to solve their health problems. Precisely because the lay person lacks the skills and knowledge that the physician possesses, the client is in a position of dependency on the doctor; the doctor-patient relationship is inherently a relationship between subordinate and superordinate. The physician's authority is reinforced by the fact that a doctor need not persuade a client of his technical competence because that competence is imputed by the medical role itself. Moreover, in most instances the inequality between doctor and patient rests not only on the differences between them in technical expertise but in social status as well. Freidson comments that "the very character of the distribution of status through the population is such that the upper middle class practitioner will in most cases be treating his status subordinates . . ." (1970b:114).

The physician's authority is not only the authority of expertise but the authority of institutionalized power. The medical profession enjoys a virtual monopoly on the delivery of health care. The physician's perspective on the nature of health and illness determines which occupations will be included and which excluded from the medical division of labor and which kinds of human services will be considered health services and which not. The profession, not the state, controls the political and legal terms of medical work and entry into and training for the profession.

Within the medical division of labor, medicine is the dominant occupation and the only occupation that is fully autonomous and not subject to the direction and evaluation of others in the paramedical hierarchy (Freidson 1970a, pt. 1). The physician stands at the top of the hierarchy and all other medical occupations are integrated around, subject to control of, and subordinate to the work of the physician. No other occupation in the larger societal division of labor has ultimate authority over its own work to match that in medicine, a profession that holds fast to its prerogatives and is reluctant to work cooperatively with or relinquish authority to paraprofessional workers in matters of diagnosis or treatment. Even in their own practices, doctors may share business and "on call" arrangements and may consult with one another on some aspects of patient care, but they are careful to preserve territorial rights where authority for patient care is involved.

Medical dominance is largely synonymous with male dominance. The medical role carries with it an explicit connotation of maleness. Subordinate positions in the medical hierarchy typically are occupied by women, particularly in the field of nursing, which is the most prominent of all the paramedical occupations. The nurse is more than a functional subordinate of the doctor; she fulfills the traditional female functions of housekeeping and nurturing. Even more importantly, she does this in the context of recognizing and depending upon male dominance and authority. The hierarchical structure of the profession translates into a social statement of the appropriateness of men occupying the most prominent positions, with women acting as assistants and handmaidens to men.

Freidson has described medical training as "unparalleled by any other in its duration, its detail and its rigidity" (1970b:84). The main goal of medical training is the acquisition of technical competencies and skills that enable the practitioner to solve the health problems that are brought to him by individual clients. The clinical mentality is a pragmatic mentality; to the practitioner the application of knowledge rather than the creation of knowledge is of paramount importance. The doctor is trained to view the patient as a beneficiary of his expertise, not as a partner in an interpersonal relationship. His education has taught the physician to place the greatest value on the complicated and unusual cases that offer the greatest challenge to his expertise; more routine and commonplace health problems are devalued for their lack of interest, and problems that do not have an apparent medical solution are often dismissed as irrelevant. The existence of a clinical value system by which the relative worth, that is to say interest, of a case is measured has been noted by several authors, among them Fox (1957); Merton et al. (1957); Becker et al. (1961, esp. chs. 14, 16, and 20); and Mumford (1970, ch. 8). Apparently the stress of practicing in the high-risk specialties—those in which "responsibility is symbolized by the possibility of killing or disabling patients in the course

11

of making a mistake" (Freidson 1970b:87)—is compensated for by the challenge that they offer.

The practice of medicine can be summarized as representing a quintessentially male role—dominant, individualistic, authoritative. Mastery and control are the prevailing values of medical work. Inequality is structured into almost all of the doctor's working relationships, be they with patients or with persons working in the paramedical occupations. Both within and outside the medical world, the physician's role assures him of high status and the deference that goes with it.

The Profession of University Teaching

Every academic has a dual set of loyalties—one toward his professional field of knowledge and one toward the university in which he practices his profession. Although academic prestige to a large extent derives from scholarship, academic pay and rank derive from teaching and institutional responsibilities as well. The dual task orientation of the academic—to the creation of knowledge on the one hand and the communication of knowledge on the other—tends to result in a dual time orientation also. The daily schedule of the academic is organized around both immediate day-to-day teaching and departmental responsibilities and the long-term goals of research and writing. Very often there is an inherent tension between the two roles, such that the academic is pulled in several directions at once within the space of the workday. The teaching role is the only component of academic life that is publicly visible and determined by others. In his endeavors as a scholar and researcher, much of the determination of effort is left to the faculty member himself. The so-called flexibility of academic life is a function of its inner direction.

But the most important decision of all is that involving professional ambitions and standards. How hard the faculty member works at his field of specialization, whether he gives primary attention to teaching or to research, how and what he desires to write and publish, how much he reads, how much he participates in professional activity and association, how rapidly he seeks to advance himself professionally—these are largely decisions the individual faculty member makes for himself with a minimum amount of pressure from the college or the university itself. To be sure, there are salary and status incentives to encourage the faculty member, not to mention of course any family considerations. Yet by and large the faculty member determines his own career. (Millett 1962:69)

Self-determination notwithstanding, the academic career is an organizational career; the academic earns his salary from the university that employs him rather than from clients on a fee-for-service basis. Entrepreneurialism is not completely absent from academic life, however, for many academics, especially those in the sciences, find it necessary to compete for outside sources of funding in order to be able to support the research upon which their scholarly reputations are built. In the university setting (as distinct from the college) the academic is judged and rewarded, with tenure and promotion, primarily on the basis of his accomplishments in and contributions to his discipline.

The academic does not establish his career on the basis of assumed expertise; his career is built upon a continual process of demonstration and proof of his expertise in his discipline. The main audience for academic work is not the layperson but other experts, the community of scholars in his field. Academic rank is largely a reflection of the quality of one's scholarship and every academic begins his career as a subordinate in relation to those who are the "consumers" of his work—the senior members of his department and those persons of established reputations in his field. The hierarchy of academic life is not a hierarchy of functional subordinates to the dominant academic, but it is a hierarchy through which the academic himself moves as his own scholarship matures and gains recognition.

Although student and teacher differ in the credentials and amount of learning that each brings to the classroom, the academic teaching role does not carry with it the same sort of "authority of expertise" that the medical professional role does. In the first place the teacher functions as instructor, not as problem solver; by and large students enroll in a class not because they feel they need to but because they want to. Whether they want to be there or not depends a great deal on how appealingly a professor is able to communicate his subject and relate to his students in interpersonal or advisory ways. Furthermore, as a teacher an academic is subject to formal student evaluations, which have some influence on his standing in the department and ultimately on the success of his career.

The expertise that separates student and teacher is one of degree rather than kind. The student, by virtue of being taught, comes closer to, and may even become, the teacher's equal in expertise. As the student acquires the knowledge that the teacher imparts, his student status is less and less a subordinate status, and on the graduate level of education the lines between student and teacher may become blurred to the point where the two are working together in essentially collegial rather than hierarchical fashion. By comparison, in the doctor-patient relationship the doctor is always the expert, the patient always the novice. No matter how frequently or extensively a patient receives medical care, he is no closer to acquiring the status and authority of the physician than is the person who has received no medical care at all.

Lipset and Ladd have written that "the greatest source of influence of academics may stem from their control of the process of certification as to competence for virtually the entire range of elite occupations" (1975:3). It follows from this that academic autonomy is located primarily within the disciplines and the departments and professional schools in which those disciplines are taught. Academics do not have the power to organize and control the entire system of education as such; academic freedom is the freedom to determine what constitutes the legitimate subject matter of a field or discipline, in what form that subject matter shall be taught, and to what standards on the part of faculty and students. Obviously higher education has no reason for being apart from its faculty, and as Millett notes "there is no other justification for the existence of a college or university except to enable the faculty to carry on its instructional and research activities" (1962:65). Nonetheless, the faculty is but one of several constituencies who share power and together comprise the community of authority which is the organizational basis of academic life.

Academe is committed, in principle anyway, to an avoidance of a hierarchy of power, not only in the overall management of its affairs, but within the individual departments as well. Everyday academic life is centered primarily in a department whose official business is the provision of education in its special subject. Faculty members, who share a common commitment to a subject, decide collectively and cooperatively on matters of course offerings, major field and degree requirements, hiring and promotion of personnel, admission of graduate students and the academic aspects of interdepartmental relationships. As an educator the academic never functions exclusively as an individual practitioner. The topic and quality of individual instruction, as well as general issues of educational policy, are areas in which the department as a whole collaborates in making decisions and assessments. This is not to say that departmental life is necessarily harmonious; factions as well as friendships are likely to spring from the interaction of colleagues and the intensity of feeling engendered by certain issues.

The central values of academic life are intellectual. Whereas professionals, such as doctors, are users of knowledge, intellectuals are seekers of and creators of knowledge. "The goal of the academic community is to provide an *environment* of learning, not a product of learning" (Millett 1962:62). The intellectual approach to the world is inherently critical or skeptical; the academic quest is a quest for new forms of understanding. The mandate of the scholar or the researcher is to create and to innovate, not to be bound by the status quo and the established order. "Intellectuals . . . are more likely than those in other occupations to be partisans of the ideal, of the theoretical, and thus to criticize reality from this standpoint" (Lipset and Ladd 1975:13). Politically, academics are associated with the politics of change and protest; the more intellectual a discipline or field, and the less closely it is tied to the economic interests of the business world, the greater the liberalism of its faculty.

American academics have stood further left politically than any other major occupational group for a long time. It should be evident, however, that there are deep divisions within the faculty. . . . Apart from the sheer magnitude of the variations, the most striking discovery bearing on faculty political attitudes by discipline is the rather neat progression from the most left-of-center subject to the most conservative, running from the social sciences to the humanities, law and the fine arts, through the physical and biological sciences, education, medicine, on to business, engineering, the smaller applied professional schools, such as nursing and home economics, and finally agriculture, the most conservative discipline group. (Lipset and Ladd 1975:55, 60)

Aside from their shared status as elite occupations, the professions of medical practice and university teaching differ in many important respects. In contrast to medical professionalism, academic life is characterized by the lack of hierarchy in its structure and the lack of authoritativeness attached to its roles. Communication and cooperation are essential to academic relationships with colleagues and students alike. In his teaching and in his scholarship, the academic is always in process; in a fundamental sense neither he nor his knowledge is ever a finished product.

In a very general way Bakan's (1972) distinction between the *agentic* and *communal* approaches to tasks and relationships may be applied across professions to the distinctions between academe and medicine. Notwithstanding the variation that may be found within professional life as to role definition and value orientation, in general medicine may be characterized as essentially agentic, while the more collegial and process-oriented life of academe is closer to the communal end of the continuum. Bernard elaborates on the differences between the two approaches as follows:

Agency tends to see variables, communion to see human beings. . . . Agency has to do with separation, repression, conquest and contract; communion with fusion, expression, acceptance, non-contractual cooperation. Agency operates by way of mastery and control; communion with naturalistic observation, sensitivity to qualitative patterning, and greater personal participation. . . . The specific processes involved in agentic research are typically male preoccupations; agency is identified with a masculine principle, the Protestant ethic, a Faustian pursuit of knowledge—as with all forces toward mastery, separation and ego enhancement . . . men [prefer] the agentic, women the communal. (1973:22–23)

The extent and kind of the differences between what is involved in a commitment to university teaching and a commitment to the practice of medicine suggest very strongly that different kinds of people find their way into each of the two professions. It is not a new idea that there is a process of self-selection into occupations, and indeed it stands to reason that people are attracted into professional fields on the basis of modes of thought and interaction, interests and values that are consistent and compatible with their own. Hughes has written on "Personality Types and the Division of Labor" (1971b) and Rosenberg's study (1957) notes a link between the values of those attracted into a discipline and the values of a discipline itself. Personality and work setting and experience are mutually reinforcing and result in the formation of occupational subcultures—

> And once formed, such subcultures apparently become more than the sum of their contributing parts. A set of characteristic styles, concerns, values and traditions, and general orientation to the social and political world takes shape. (Lipset and Ladd 1975:69)

Although both medical practice and university teaching are male dominated in a statistical sense, medicine far more than university teaching is also an expression of male dominance in the social sense. The agentic approach of medicine is stereotypically male, while the collegial expressive orientation of academe represents a deviation from conventional male norms; the sort of man who feels at home inside one profession is not likely to be the same sort of man who feels at home inside the other. Insofar as a similar process of selective recruitment operates in the choice of a marriage partner as in the choice of profession, it would not be surprising to find certain likenesses between the roles and relationships of a profession and the marriages and life styles that go with it.

2

LIFE CYCLES AND
LIFE STYLES

Successful Professional Men

We turn now from the ideas that shape the inquiry of this book to the people who are at its center. The forty professional men whose wives have the lead part in the pages to follow are successful in ordinary ways in the mainstream career tracks of their professions. (A full description of the techniques used in sample selection, data gathering and analysis is contained in the Appendix.) They are men of solid accomplishments, and they enjoy the respectable reputation and secure professional status that have traditionally been the reward for competent men who have applied themselves with diligence and energy to their careers. The careers of these husbands are not marked by the extraordinary or prodigious achievements and elite reputations that are the province of only a very few in a given professional field. The professors and doctors in this book are not men who have "made it" in any absolute sense, but rather, they are successful in the context of a particular career track in a particular place or institution. Most of these men, furthermore, are at or nearing the peak of their careers; they are neither neophytes nor in decline so far as their professional work is concerned, nor do they represent a model of success that might be considered outmoded or irrelevant to younger persons presently in training for or aspiring to professional careers in the fields of medicine or university teaching.

Within their professions, these men work in different fields or specialties, and their careers, therefore, represent some of the variation in organization, content, and approach to work that is to be found within university teaching and medicine—variation that may, in turn, be reflected in the roles of their wives. The twenty academic husbands are tenured, full or high-ranking associate professors. Ten of them work in the disciplines of the natural sciences, such as biochemistry, zoology or microbiology and the other ten have careers in the humanistic disciplines of English, history, philosophy and classics. Though none of these men are unusually prolific as scholars or can lay claim to truly national reputations in their fields, they have been steadily productive, and their research and writing are known to colleagues who work in the same subspeciaality. At the present time all but two or three of these professors are actively engaged in scholarly research in addition to their teaching, and in the case of the scientists, most of their research is supported by grants.

These professors are all members of the faculty of a large New England state university, which has a better reputation academically than most state universities, but is certainly less prestigious than either the top-of-the-line state universities or the well-known private educational institutions. Many of these men, however, did their graduate training at some of the leading public or private universities in the United States. The university where they are presently employed has been in existence for decades. Its current academic standing, particularly in the liberal arts disciplines, is the product of a policy decision, made only about ten years ago, to expand the size and upgrade the quality of its departments. At present the university has a nearly full complement of graduate departments and professional schools, and in most of them, competition for admission is moderate to high. There are now nearly

25,000 undergraduate and graduate students at the university, with a total faculty of about 1,500. These professors work in departments which may have as few as twenty faculty or as many as one hundred.

The medical husbands have analogously middle-range careers. They are all Board Certified specialists, either in the primary care fields of internal medicine or the major surgical specialties, such as general surgery, orthopedics or neurosurgery. They are all practitioners (as distinct from academic or research physicians), although four of the twenty men work in salaried hospital-based practices rather than in private practice. (The differences in practice setting, while unintended in the sample selection, proved to have quite interesting sociological implications, which will be considered in later chapters.) These men are well-established, either because they themselves built up the practices in which they are now the senior physicians, or because they are the younger members in just such a thriving and settled practice. Although none of them have national or even statewide prominence, many of these physicians and surgeons would be seen as *the* doctors to go to in the particular corner of the state in which they practice. These medical professionals are not publishers, but a number of them have held responsible posts on a variety of hospital committees and in the local medical society; they are not without influence, therefore, in shaping policies for health care delivery in their community.

That community is a middle-sized New England city, with a population of some 160,000, which is not unusually distinguished as a center of political, cultural, or other activity. Like many cities of its kind throughout the country, it serves as a regional center of business, commerce, and law. So far as the scope of its medical services is concerned, the community falls between the relatively uncompetitive small town medical setting with one community hospital and several dozen practitioners in various major specialties, and the highly competitive setting of the major metropolis, replete with renowned specialists, major teaching hospitals and medical schools and centers of medical research.

There is lively but not unusually intense competition among the 350 to 400 practitioners who practice in the medical district in which the city is located. They represent the full array of standard medical and surgical specialties, and also many of the subfields of the specialties. Three of the four hospitals in the city have recently consolidated into a regional medical center. Like the university described above, medicine in this community has undergone a growth spurt in the past ten years, with a resulting increase in the population of doctors, as well as in the range of medical facilities and services available in the hospitals. Some research, teaching, and training does take place in the hospitals and the medical center itself is affiliated with a medical school in another (larger) city some distance away. However, these hospitals do not, either separately or together, constitute a major center of teaching or research with a full-time community of medical educators. As ideal types, the hospitals in this city fit most closely the "community" rather than the "university" model of hospitals as depicted by Mumford (1970). The great majority of doctors in the city work only in the private sector and practice medicine in the traditional entrepreneurial mode.

For many of these doctors—as for the professors—the setting of their own education and training was more high-powered and distinguished than their present work setting. Perhaps the comparability of the career status and setting of the two groups of medical and academic professionals is best illustrated by the fact that though they reside not so many miles apart from one another in real life, they would be unlikely to call upon one another's professional services with any frequency. The doctors' families, in search of the "best" education for their children, would be apt to pass over the nearby state university in favor of more prestigious institutions; similarly, the academics would be likely to travel considerable distance to major metropolitan areas for diagnosis and treatment of any unusual or highly specialized medical problem. The irony of the consequences of the professional value system, by which an individual is judged more by the company he keeps, so to speak, than by his own background and individual accomplishments, should not go unnoticed, though the temptation to elaborate further will be resisted.

Life Together

The vital statistics of the academic and medical marriages that are under study in this book are similar in many respects (see table 2.1). The average couple in each group has been married for about sixteen years and the marriage has existed and persisted alongside the husband's career down through the years. All of the medical marriages are first and only marriages. Two academic husbands were married and divorced prior to their present marriages; the wife of one of these men also had had a previous marriage—overall an impressive record of marital stability, at least in its formal sense.

For most of the couples the chronologies of their marriages and the husbands' careers have not only been intertwined but coterminous as well. All of the medical couples and fifteen of the twenty academic couples were married during the time of the husband's career education and training (see table 2.2). The greater length of time required for the completion of medical education and training (table 2.3) probably accounts for the fact that all the doctors were

TABLE 2.1 MARITAL DATA

Average	M.D. Families (N = 20)		Ph.D. Families (N = 20)	
Number of years married	15.9 (7–25)		16.2 (7–23)	
Number of children	3.7 (2–10)		2.8 (0–6)	
Number of moves in marriage*	3.6 (2–6)		2.5 (0–5)	
Age at marriage	*wife* 23.7 (19–27)	*husband* 26.7 (22–31)	*wife†* 25.1 (17–33)	*husband†* 27 (18–35)
Age now	39.6 (29–47)	42.7 (34–50)	41.3 (28–49)	43.2 (36–46)

NOTE: Summary of averages (actual range in parentheses).

*Does not include first place lived in marriage unless the marriage was followed by a move together to a new place for both spouses; includes only moves to new geographical locations, not moves to different residences in the same geographical location.

†For one wife and two husbands, the present marriage is a second marriage.

TABLE 2.2 STAGE OF HUSBAND'S CAREER AT TIME OF MARRIAGE

Career Stage	M.D. Husbands (N=20)	Ph.D. Husbands (N=20)
Pre- or early career education/training	14	11
Late career education/training	6	4
Early career	0	4
Career established	0	1
Percent married during husbands' career education/training	100	75

NOTE: Definition of career stages
Pre- or early career education/training:
M.D.—through and including medical school and internship.
Ph.D.—through and including master's degree, Ph.D. coursework and examinations.
Late career education/training:
M.D.—through and including residency and other specialty training and military service (if residency and other training still to be completed at the time).
Ph.D.—through and including dissertation research and writing, nontenure track (i.e., instructor level) teaching position, postdoctoral research.
Early career:
M.D.—in first three years of medical practice.
Ph.D.—in teaching position at assistant professor level.

TABLE 2.3 AVERAGE YEARS OF TRAINING

M.D. Husbands	Ph.D. Husbands
9.3 (8–11)*	6.3 (4–9)

NOTE: Actual range in parentheses; excludes bachelor's degree.
*Does not include years spent in military or public health service, which, though required, did not constitute education or training as such.

married by the time they were ready to launch themselves as independent professionals.

Aside from the obvious fact that, for the upper middle class, the usual age of marriage and the usual age of career preparation, especially for men, are the same, there are factors about careers themselves that tend to precipitate both the desire and decision to marry during the period of early career education and training. One is the intensity, with its attendant loneliness, of career preparation. In *The Making of a Surgeon,* William Nolen describes the young doctor's need for a domestic refuge, away from the pressure and confinement of hospital routines:

We felt if we were going to run ourselves ragged for five years it would be nice to do it not only for ourselves but for a wife and family. We also wanted a life away from the hospital. Bellevue was all right when we were working, but it was no place to live when we were off duty. We needed a change. We needed a home. (1970:146)

For many of the professional couples—academic as well as medical—in this book the decision to marry and the early marriage relationship were similarly forged out of the husband's need for support and companionship during his career training.

He was thrilled when we married. He had lived in a tiny room in the hospital for the first year of his internship. Now he had a one-bedroom apartment and me. *(17)**

I was not anticipating getting married at the time and I never planned to get married at such a young age. . . . We talked about it to a certain extent; he was anxious to get married and very lonely. He was also twenty-seven and ready to get married. He was a really great person and it was a real dilemma for me. *(7)*

We were very young when we began dating. I never went out with anyone else. He was very lonely in medical school and wanted to get married. After dating him for four years I knew he was all-important. I thought there was no reason why I couldn't continue school, but I never went at all. *(15)*

In addition, the period of career education and training and the early years of settling into a career are marked by turning points which frequently involve geographic mobility. Many of these marriages occurred at just such a turning point, when career requirements forced the choice to marry.

---

*The number in parentheses following a quotation is the number assigned to that particular interviewee.

He went underground to study for his orals and we were both living in New York at the time. He was always a very conscientious student, but I was there when he finished his orals. We got married when we did because of the fact that he had this job here—it was either get married or separate. (24)

Our marriage was timed around his training. We had to get married before June when he had to leave to get to [Canada] for his residency. (4)

Most of these wives are the conventional few years younger than their husbands, and at this time the average couple in each professional group is on the young side of middle age. In their professional lives the husbands are in the mid-career phase. On average they are in their early forties, their careers a proven success, with at least a decade and a half remaining until retirement. Family life too is at mid-cycle. The childbearing years are behind; the postparental years are yet to come. (See table 2.4.) Though the average medical family is larger in size than the average academic family, the majority of families in both groups have by now seen all of their children off to secondary school. One academic couple is

TABLE 2.4 AGES OF CHILDREN

		No. of Families	
Children's Age Range*		M.D. (N = 20)	Ph.D. (N = 20)
0–5 years	(no children in school full time)	0	1
0–18	(at least one child in school; at least one child still preschool age)	6	2
6–18	(all children in school full time)	10	12
6 upwards	(all children of school age; at least one post-high-school age)	4	4
18 and over	(all children post-high-school age)	0	0
No children		0	1

SOURCE: Table format adapted from a similar table in *Managers and Their Wives*, by Pahl and Pahl (1971:116).
*The above categories are mutually exclusive.

TABLE 2.5   PRESENT INCOME OF MEDICAL AND ACADEMIC
HUSBANDS

Income (in thousands)	M.D. (N = 18)*	Ph.D. (N = 17)
11–20	—	1
21–30	—	15
31–40	1	1
41–50	5	—
51–60	2	—
61–75	6	—
Over 75	4	—
Percent of all husbands earning over $50,000 a year	67	0

NOTE: Income figures for M.D.s refer to take-home income or salary, not total income earned by an individual physician or surgeon in his practice.

Income figures for Ph. D.s include basic academic salary and any additional income earned from royalties, consulting, guest lecturing, extra teaching, etc.

*In tables where N equals less than twenty persons in each professional group, it reflects the total number of responses to a particular item on the questionnaire forms, which were filled out and returned separately after the interviews had taken place.

(involuntarily) childless and another academic couple has only one child; all other families have more than one child.

Despite the similarities in the configurations and chronologies of the medical and academic marriages, there are pronounced differences in the ways of life of the two groups. After a while certain clues to these differences become so apparent that an alert observer would find it possible to descend, like Mary Poppins, without introduction and unannounced into a household and know almost immediately whether it belonged in the medical or academic world. The income differential between the two groups (table 2.5) is readily visible in the home setting. The medical home is in almost every case larger, more expensive, and more lavish than the academic home. Moreover, the residential setting is suggestive of the tastes and values that characterize each of these professional worlds. The medical home often has a feeling about it of being on display, with furniture, interior decoration, and even landscaping being picture-perfect. These houses often seem to have been self-consciously "outfitted" with a view to pleasing and impressing the public, as well as the occupants. The carefully matched and arranged rooms conform to standards of conventional good taste as defined by the model rooms of good quality furniture houses.

The medical homes come to seem interchangeable, although in one the accent might be French provincial, and in another Colonial. But the academic homes are very different, not only from medical homes, but from one another. Their similarity is in their individuality. None of the academic homes is opulent, but they vary greatly in style and character. They include farms, bungalows, tract houses in small subdivisions, old, rambling Victorian affairs, and lodge-type homes of wood and glass in wooded settings. It is rare for an academic house to contain any distinctive or even identifiable style of furniture, unless it is Scandanavian modern. There is the inevitable abundance of books found in almost every academic household, and it is not uncommon to see musical instruments that give evidence of regular use, and/or elaborate sound systems for playing recorded music. Artwork is unusual and varied and often relates either to the husband's academic interests or to places where the family has traveled during sabbatical years. In many of these houses there are signs of the husband's hobby projects—furniture refinishing, carpentry, and gardening. It is fair to say that while these academic houses do not conform to conventional standards of taste and decor, they are conformist in their nonconformist emphasis on taste that bespeaks culture and learning, and, one might add, cleverness, rather than on taste which is a clear proclamation of material affluence.

Not surprisingly, the medical residential pattern is far more geographically cohesive and socially homogeneous than is the academic. Sixteen of the twenty doctors live in the same small suburb, the most fashionable and well-to-do of any of the towns within close commuting distance of the urban center where they have their practices. Aside from its few boutiques clustered together in a small whitewashed brick colonial-style center, it is a town with no business or commercial enterprises. It offers abundant recreational and educational amenities for children, and for the adults there are a number of private country clubs and socially active churches and temples to which many of the doctors' families belong. This is known locally as *the* town for the established, successful professional to live in, and the doctors apparently seek out this geographic statement of their professional standing. In a very real sense the medical life style and the suburban life style are indistinguishable from one another.

The academics of this study, in contrast, live in a variety of locations scattered in all directions within a ten-mile radius of the university. The nature of the academic value system is such that academics tend to be less engaged in (or even sympathetic to) established social and community institutions than are doctors, whose profession gives them a strong sense of their group identity as well as of their social standing. Academic life exists somewhat apart from the upper middle-class mainstream, as do academics themselves. They do not, therefore, live together as a community within a community and in their choice of residential setting, they are far more varied and individualistic than are the doctors.

There is also considerable difference between professors and doctors in the rhythm of life overall and the uses of leisure time. The routines of medical husbands are sharply demarcated into regular and recurrent patterns of "time off" and "time on." The doctor is either hard at work or not hard at work and the kinds of time are quite distinct and separate in his life. Among medical couples leisure time is highly organized, usually centering on specific, scheduled activities that occur outside of the home—most commonly, regularly scheduled games of golf or tennis, attendance at booked-in-advance cultural events, social gatherings with other couples, or travel. One medical wife describes how this pattern works in her own life with her husband.

We play tennis together every Thursday night. He's always off on those nights. He is on call every three nights and every third weekend. When he is not on during the weekend, he does not go in at all. His weekends off start at seven-thirty on Friday. When we're off, we have a lot of interests. We sometimes leave town and go skiing or plan trips to Boston. (7)

Academic life, on the other hand, does not have such clear boundaries of beginning and ending, nor are the dividing lines between home and work settings as clear-cut, since a great deal of academic work is portable. Few academics set aside regular periods of time that are designated for leisure; leisure time as such is seldom scheduled, it just happens. Academics also tend to use their leisure time together in more casual and private ways than medical couples, often working together on home or garden projects, playing music or reading or socializing on an impromptu basis. In general, academic leisure time is best described as time spent *away* from work rather than time spent *at* certain activities or events.

About half the weekends there will be one social get-together of some sort that comes up. Other than that we work on our vegetable garden and my husband works on his greenhouse or does home repairs or works on his book. The children help with the housework and the older two mow the lawn. We go to things like the town fair. We might take the children on a nature walk; sometimes my husband will come along, but he likes quiet walks in nature and the children are noisy. About half the weekends he will spend some time working on Saturday and Sunday mornings. (*38*)

Medical and Academic Wives—Past and Present

Among the medical wives there is a marked similarity in the ways that they put their days together, and their present routines and activities are essentially variations on a theme. There is considerably more variety in the lives of the academic wives, whose days take them in very many different directions so far as their own interests and endeavors are concerned. The proportion of medical wives who presently have paid work or academic credit-earning commitments outside the home is exactly the reverse of that for academic wives. (See table 2.6.) Only five of all the medical wives interviewed are now working or studying in any fashion, compared to fifteen of the academic wives. Not only in the present, but throughout the years of their marriages, medical wives as a group have shown far less commitment to academic or work achievements

TABLE 2.6 PRESENT WORK/STUDY COMMITMENT OF WIFE

Paid Work or Credit-Earning Study	M.D. Wives (N=20)	Ph.D. Wives (N=20)
Full-time	0	3
Regular part-time	3	10
Minimal (less than 6 hrs. work a week or no more than one course) or intermittent (e.g., substitute teaching)	2	2
None—but feels positively toward possibility of work or study, specific plan formulated for forseeable future	1	0
None—but feels positively toward possibility of work or study, no specific plan formulated for forseeable future	7	3
None—no firm desire or plan for work or study in forseeable future	7	2
Percent of all wives with paid work or credit-earning study	25	75

than the academic wives. (See table 2.7.) Only one doctor's wife has maintained a regular work or study involvement for more than half of the years she has been married, whereas half of the academic wives have been active in these ways for at least half of the years of their marriages.

Although a few of the medical wives who are currently at home full time have some idea that they might like to work or go back to school at some future date, only one woman among them has laid the necessary groundwork and made the plans to do so. For most the possibility of work is vaguely formulated and often in the realm of wishful thinking.

In six years all the kids will be gone and its overwhelming to me. I think I will have to make some decisions for myself. It's not the boredom, it's the lack of structure that bothers me. I like being at home and doing what I want to do. But when I wake up in the

TABLE 2.7 PERCENT OF YEARS MARRIED DURING WHICH WIVES
HAVE HAD REGULAR PAID WORK OR CREDIT-EARNING STUDY

Percent of Years Working or Studying	M.D. Wives (N=20)	Ph.D. Wives (N=20)
Less than 25	13	5
25–49	6	5
50–74	0	6
75–100	1	4
Percent of all wives working or studying for half or more of the years of their marriage	5	50

morning and it's raining and I know I won't be golfing, then I think, "What am I going to do?" (9)

However, the homogeneity of the daily routines and activities of the doctor's wife does not reside in what she does *not* do with her time. The simple fact of not working or studying does not in itself imply likeness among women. Rather, the similarities among medical wives are to be found in how they do spend their time outside the home in the absence of structured or formal work or academic commitments. Outside the home the doctor's wife is active primarily as a community volunteer, a role that she performs together with other women in a variety of women's organizations and groups. Her volunteer activity is typically centered in or channeled through the Junior League, the League of Women Voters, the local schools, churches, hospitals, art museums, theater or symphony or one or another social agency. Many women are active in several of these areas, so that there is a high degree of overlap in the activities and acquaintances of medical wives. In many respects the service groups to which they belong are social groups as well, and women very often join organizations as a way of meeting people and expanding social contacts.

When we first came here, I loved having the house and babies, but that first year was a tremendous separation from my past relationships with other girls. The next year I got involved in the Junior League and that was a place where I met people with similar inter-

ests and the volunteer aspect appealed to me. I ran the thrift shop
and that was a barrel of fun. (3)

I found my way into the community by joining the Junior League
and [my college] club and then the tennis club. I met a lot of people
that way. I also worked for [educational television] through the
Junior League and coordinating volunteer services. I worked on day
care too. Then I had a baby. Then the next year I was on the Board
of the Junior League and edited the magazine. This year I'm doing
education and planning all the meetings. I'm also president, now,
of the PTA. We belong to a temple, but we're not very active. (17)

These volunteer activities are usually interspersed throughout
the week with more specifically leisure or social sorts of activities—luncheons, shopping trips, golf or tennis games. A few wives
have either left behind or eschewed altogether the community volunteer role and spend their time outside the home primarily in
social or leisure pursuits. Even the few medical wives who work
tend to stay involved with community activities and plan space in
the day for recreation and social get-togethers with friends.

The academic wife is not the sociable joiner that the medical
wife is. Her community activities, to the extent that they exist, tend
to center on social protest and social change rather than social service. A few academic wives have been active in the women's movement, another few in partisan political campaigning or the antiwar
movement and one or two in town government. Mostly though, the
academic wife's outside activity or time left over from family is
focused on her own work or academic course commitments, which
she pursues with seriousness of purpose, though often within narrow time constraints.

I go to school three mornings a week. I have two courses. My
courses begin at ten and I stay there and eat lunch. I get home
about one-thirty. The children are not here until three-thirty and
what I do next depends on my mood and what day it is. If I'm feeling tired I may lie down and listen to a record or do some writing
for my English course. (37)

I realize now that I have a block of time from nine to two-thirty
most days. I try to paint every day. If I start in the morning, then I
will usually continue right on through. (25)

The academic wives display a wide range of specialized skills and interests and have long-range commitments to the fields in which they are working or studying, even though most do not have full-time involvements, and many are still earning credentials or are working outside mainstream career tracks as such. Because of the diversity of their outside involvements, academic wives make friends and social contacts inside their own world of work or special interest groups and do not join together with other faculty wives in common activities or have highly overlapping ties among themselves. Among the academic wives interviewed, there are students in the social sciences and fine arts, a musician, a studio artist, a linguist, a scientific illustrator, and several academics in as many disciplines. Two of the stay-at-home women are managing small farms in a rather unusual and specialized version of the housewife role.

Quite clearly the doctor's wife is much more traditionally female in both personal achievement motivation and the kinds of activities that do occupy her time than is the academic wife, who is more individualistic and achievement-oriented. The differences between the two groups in the extent and kind of their outside involvements is not a reflection of differences in their level of educational achievement per se. To be sure there are four more women with degrees at the M.A. or higher level among the academic than the medical wives (see table 2.8), but a number of the academic wives who are presently working or studying do not have advanced

TABLE 2.8   EDUCATIONAL ATTAINMENT OF WIVES

Educational Attainment	M.D. Wives (N = 20)	Ph.D. Wives (N = 20)
High school only	1	
Education past high school, no B.A.	3	2
B.A. and/or R.N.	9	7
M.A., M.S., M.S.W.	6	6
M.D. or Ph.D.	1	5
Percent of all wives with B.A. and/or R.N. or higher degree	80	90

degrees and some of those with advanced degrees are not employed or otherwise committed outside the home. Overall the medical wives, sixteen of whom have at least a B.A., are as well-educated as the academic wives, eighteen of whom have earned at least B.A. degrees.

However, when the achievement backgrounds of the wives are assessed qualitatively rather than quantitatively, the connection between past history and present way of life becomes somewhat clearer. (See table 2.9.) At the time they met and married their husbands, the majority of medical wives had educational and occupational backgrounds in the traditionally female fields of nursing, secretarial work, social work, secondary-school teaching and the like. These jobs are occupational extensions of the female role and in them women perform the supportive, maternal, and housekeeping functions of the occupational world, and are status subordinates to men. These occupations typically attract women with a highly tradi-

TABLE 2.9   ACHIEVEMENT STATUS OF WIFE AT TIME OF MARRIAGE

Achievement Status	M.D. Wives (N = 20)	Ph.D. Wives (N = 20)
The Uncommitted		
B.A. or less, no substantial work experience, no specific educational, work interests or goals	4	4
The Traditionally Female		
Education, training (completed or ongoing), or employment in traditional female occupations of secondary school teaching, nursing, or other paramedical fields, social work, secretarial work	13	4
The Collegials		
Advanced professional or academic degree (completed or ongoing), or high-level work experience, or specific educational, work interests—all in other than traditional women's fields	3	12

tional definition of the female role, who view work as inimical to that role, and who seek their major life rewards in nonoccupational family roles. Relatively few women enter into these fields with the idea of making any sustained and serious commitment to a career, even in the nonclerical fields which require considerable effort and time in education and training. Women seldom enter into these occupations on the basis of any highly specified interests, nor do they seek long-term gratifications from their work; instead they usually drift into the women's fields either as a way of marking time until marriage and family roles are open to them, or as a kind of contingency planning in the event that the marriage fails them in some way.

> Whatever else motivates and sustains women in these pursuits, it is rarely that aim of furthering a career. Or, to put the matter somewhat more circumspectly, it has in general been noted that whereas large majorities of women in these fields are genuinely attached to (that is, neither alienated or disaffected from) the day-by-day work of their field, such attachment only rarely embraces a deep career commitment to the profession *per se*. (Davis and Oleson, 1972:67)

In their own study of nurses, Davis and Oleson found little evidence of long-term career commitment among even those women who had been trained in a program that consciously attempted to inculcate a strong professional and leadership orientation in its students and eschewed the more traditional definition of the nursing role. The researchers conclude that the problem of lack of professional commitment among those who choose traditionally female professions has less to do with the content of the training than with the values and role definitions of those who enter into these occupations. They speculate that "girls who choose the female professions are perhaps even more feminine (in the conventional sense), even more committed to traditional values, than are their vocationally indifferent peers. . . ." (1972:69)

Vocational indifference was characterstic of most of these medical wives with backgrounds in the traditionally female fields of work. At the time they married they had little more than a passing or vague interest in their fields and saw their work as something that might occupy their time for a while, but would readily be exchanged for marriage and family, with no particular thought of going back to or building on their background or experience at a later date. When asked about the place of work for themselves at the time they married the wives, with few exceptions, answered succinctly and interchangeably: "I suppose I really didn't think about it. You work till you get married or have children. That's all." It is not surprising that the present involvements of these women outside the home are oriented primarily toward volunteer work and community service rather than toward their own individual achievement. In this they are joined by the "uncommitted" wives who had no substantial work experience or work interests to build into marriage in the first place.

Interestingly, the academic wives with "traditionally female" vocational backgrounds have proved to have a more enduring commitment to work than their medical counterparts. Two of the four academic wives in this group had had many years of varied kinds of secretarial experience when they married, and though they had formed no particular attachment to the content of their work, they found a great deal of gratification in the social world of work. The other two women did have a substantive interest in the fields in which they trained, and one wife switched from one occupation into a woman's occupation because of its greater appeal to her. All four of these women are working in some manner now.

The majority of academic wives, however, entered into marriage on what may be considered a more "collegial" basis with respect to their view of the place of work for themselves in their married lives and their fields of interest. This is not to say that these wives envisioned having full-time uninterrupted careers for themselves alongside their husbands, nor that they had reached (or even aspired to) the same level of education or work accomplishments as their husbands at the time they married. But their backgrounds were not in the traditionally female fields, and where the doctors' wives seemed as young, unmarried women virtually unable to imagine or look ahead to any but marriage-and-family-defined adult roles for themselves, the academic wives more often had dual self-images—one which projected them into the world of work and achievement (though not with reference to specific career goals) and one which projected them into the world of marriage and family.

Before they married, these women had taken their own work-related accomplishments and satisfactions quite seriously and consequently entered into marriage with a reserve of skills, credentials and experience based on other than transient interests or considerations of mere expedience. Invariably, family roles took precedence over work roles and once married, all of these academic wives modified, forestalled or even suspended their own commitments. Nonetheless, most of them have built on their early interests and achievements and have maintained some outside work involvement which, however modest when judged by conventional standards of career success, has provided them with a much-valued avenue for self-expression and independence.

Professional Lives and Wives:
A Comparative Introduction

The introduction to the people of this book is an introduction to the different worlds of medical and academic life, to the marriages that are a part of those worlds, and to the wives who are a part of those marriages. The academic marriage began more often than not as something of a partnership of equals in terms of the achievement status of the husband and wife, and over time most academic wives have reserved a small corner in their marriages for themselves in which to pursue their self-defined interests and commitments. The doctor in most cases married a woman who was not his equal in education or achievement, and whose educational background bespoke a highly traditional definition of the female role and willingness to defer to and subordinate herself to a dominant male. Unlike the academic wife, the medical wife has not built independent accomplishments of her own into her marriage, but has, together with other women, focused her interests and activities in the community, meshing the service orientation of the traditional female role with a volunteer role.

It is true that most medical as well as academic wives have backgrounds that are at least somewhat, and usually closely, related to their husbands' fields of work. (See table 2.10.) However, the

TABLE 2.10   RELATEDNESS OF WIFE'S FIELD BACKGROUND TO HUSBAND'S
WORK

M.D. Wives (N = 20)	Number
Extent of Relatedness	
Same or close: education, training, work experience in medical field or medical setting	10
Some: education, training, work experience in human services	5
None	5

Ph.D. Wives (N = 20)	
Extent of Relatedness	
Same or close: education, training, work experience in same or closely related discipline as husbands	12
Some: advanced academic degree in another field or some background in husband's field but not in same or closely related discipline	6
None	3

presence of field-relatedness between husband and wife is not in itself an indication that the marriage is forged on common bonds of shared work interests or incorporates an acceptance of equality between husband and wife in the area of work. In Hacker's words:

> The presence of love does not in itself argue for either equality of status nor fullness of communication. We may love persons who are either inferior or superior to us, and we may love persons whom we do not understand. (1972:136)

Indeed, the prevalence of traditionally female occupational backgrounds among medical wives suggests that the medical marriage is structured on role distance and status inequality between partners. In this connection it is interesting to note that most medical couples (fifteen, as compared with only five academic couples) first met in a strictly leisure or social setting (usually on a blind date) having no connection with the world of work. Medical marriages had their beginnings, therefore, in the segregation of marriage and work, and intimacy, like leisure, was set aside from the occupational world and the relationships in it. Thirteen academic couples, in contrast, first met in a common work or academic environment—only five M.D. couples first met in a medical setting. Thus the academic couples began their relationships with the integration of work and intimacy, each one an aspect of the other. In addition, the collegial background of many academic wives contributes to a rough equality of status in the academic marriage and foretells the possibility of some mutuality of achievement and of shared communication about that achievement.

Clearly, the woman who marries a doctor is not in general the same kind of woman who marries an academic. The differences between them are readily apparent, not only in data about their work and educational backgrounds and the activities and endeavors that frame their daily lives, but also in their physical and verbal self-presentations. The doctor's wife is attractive by conventional standards, well-groomed and fashionably dressed. There is evidence that her looks are important to her and that she pays more than passing attention to her appearance. The academic wife is not inherently less attractive, but the characteristic plainness of her appearance and attire suggests that she puts little stock in the cultivation of traditional female allure.

In conversation, the academic wife tends to be reflective and intense, concerned with her relationship to her work as much as to her family. She seems to be actively asking questions about the direction of her life and is responsive to, and eager for, change. The style of the medical wife is chattier, and her world, as she describes it, is one that is settled and not subject to change, at least not by her. The parameters of her own life are not easily distinguishable from those of her husband and children, and often she gives the impression of someone who has stepped off to the sidelines in

39

order that there will be enough room on center stage for the important persons in her life.

The following sketches, written originally as private field notes to jog the memory about the context of an interview, serve well, though quite unintentionally, as a comparative personal introduction to the wives of medicine and academe.

Mrs. ——— is . . . tall, slender with graying hair, cut in a short, rather severe style. She is a neat, plain person (kind of like her house), not unattractive, but not seeming to wish to emphasize that aspect of herself. At first she appeared to be rather prim and stern in her demeanor—later I decided she was just self-contained. I suspect this is a person given to a great deal of introspection and self-examination, and in fact, much of her concentration in her life seems to center on examining the quality of her life. She . . . is obviously drawn toward the ascetic, monastic qualities of her religion. She goes on retreats by herself at regular intervals throughout the year. She is a person who evaluates herself and her involvements with such intensity that that alone consumes a great deal of energy. (The wife of a professor in the humanities, in her mid-thirties.)

She is a casual person in demeanor and appearance. She wears short, loosely styled blonde hair, no make-up and a sweater and blouse combination with slacks. She does not appear to put emphasis on being any sort of a fashion plate. . . . She is invested in her own work . . . for the pleasure and gratification it gives her rather than because she wants any official career recognition. She would be more than willing to work full time if interesting work within a reasonable commuting distance were available to her. She emphasized that she has never been bored and that she expects herself and others to develop their own resources and to find their own way to interesting involvements. Indeed she has shown a great deal of initiative over the years . . . in finding ways not only to keep alive her own disciplinary interests but also to expand on them as well. She works very hard at various pursuits and spends several hours a day on her language study. She is quite willing to have her husband's career come first because it gives her the space and flexibility in her own life to work in ways that interest her: (A scientist's wife in her late thirties.)

She is a woman of thirty-six who looks somewhat worn for her age, muted in affect, though she was pleasant in conversation. She has short brown hair, no make-up and wore blue jeans and a cotton jersey top. . . . Her own ambition before she married was to be a

medical illustrator. Her professional interests are highly overlapping with her husband's. In many respects, he has facilitated her
career by providing her with exposure to his own field. She reads
and edits his work. . . . The real trade-off for her support of his
career is the chance to expand her own knowledge in areas that
interest her. She describes herself as a loner and does seem quite
withdrawn and introverted. (The wife of a scientist.)

Mrs. ———— is a tall slender woman with loose, almost shoulder-
length blonde hair. She wore a dress, stockings and heels, bright
lipstick and some green eyeshadow as well as a few expensive
rings. Overall the effect was attractive and tasteful, but a bit
like a throwback to the fifties. . . . Talking with her, I was overwhelmed by the impression that I was interviewing a contestant for
the Miss America pageant. She smiled and was demure and a bit coy
throughout. She was always cheerful and composed. She is not really happy living in the area, but she smiles again and says, "Well,
what can you do? I've adjusted, that's all." (A surgeon's wife in her
late thirties.)

Mrs. ———— is an attractive, fashionably thin woman who describes
herself as very diet- and weight-conscious. She is well-groomed
with short, carefully styled hair. She told me during the interview
that her husband had been quite suspicious of the interview
and wanted her to be sure to check on exactly what I was doing.
She emphasized throughout the interview that her marriage and
their family life were affected more by her husband's personality
than his profession. She obviously never expected that her husband
would have a major involvement in child rearing, and prior to her
marriage, she had defined that role as a central one for her. Her
main disappointment is with his interaction as a husband. He
sounds to be very passive. (An internist's wife in her early forties.)

Mrs. ———— looked like a middle-aged version of models in *Seven-
teen* magazine in the fifties. She had blond hair in a pageboy
cut. She wore light make-up and was dressed in a plaid skirt and
tights. She discussed her life and marriage in the manner of an enthusiastic team backer, cheering the victories and smiling through
defeat. She sees homemaking as her main role and asks little for
herself outside that role. That has left her free to absorb the stress
that has been part of the ups and downs of his practice over the
years. (An internist's wife.)

She is a slender woman who was dressed casually but fashionably
and expensively in slacks and a shirt. She wore light make-up
and her medium-length dark hair was loosely curled. She was very

friendly during the interview. She is a woman who lives very much within a traditional woman's role, though not specifically in a doctor's wife role. Her life fits into and around his life, and in many ways, she expands his horizons and range of acquaintances by the diversity of her activities in the community. The general shape of their lives and their closest friendships are definitely molded by his profession and her priority, for now, is with home and children, with a goal of a part-time job in the vague future. (A surgeon's wife in her mid-thirties.)

As these wives differ, so do their husbands. The doctor who marries a woman with a traditionally female background is not the same kind of man as the academic who makes a collegial marriage. These differences in personal style and life style hint at a compatibility between the male professional role and the marital relationship, with the conventional male role of medical practice matched by conventional patterns of marriage and life style overall, and the less conventional male academic role correlated with greater diversity of life style and a less traditionally sex-typed marriage in terms of the status and activities of the wife. The hierarchical structure of medical work—male dominant, female subordinate—and the role distance of medical practice is reflected in the medical marriage, while the more collegial emphasis of academic life shows through in the academic marriage. In keeping with the agentic orientation of medicine, intimacy and work are exclusive of one another and develop as separate spheres of activity and commitment, while the more communal style of academic life is built into the origins of the academic marriage where work and intimacy occur side by side. The life of the medical wife is embedded in the local community, as is the practice of medicine itself, whereas the academic wife is more inner-directed and, like the academic world, places a premium on individual accomplishments and personal growth.

This suggests that men in academic and medical careers make marriages that reinforce the roles, relationships, and values of those careers, and that the wife's role itself takes on the coloration of the profession. The likelihood is, then, that the kind of man who is attracted to a particular professional role marries the kind of woman who shares the values associated with that role and who is prepared to reinforce and uphold that role in her own role as wife. The specific features of that role and the patterns of their enactment are the subjects of the chapters that follow.

3

BEING AN ADJUNCT

Dear God, please grant me a full awareness of my responsibilities as helpmate to my physician husband. Help me to cultivate, practice and love the virtue of unselfishness that he may see in me the perfect wife and helpmate. . . .
(*From "A Physician's Wife's Prayer" of the Women's Auxiliary of the American Medical Association*)

Finally, and most importantly, my greatest debt is to my wife——who carefully read, perceptively criticized, and edited everything I wrote.
(*From the preface of a sociologist's first book*)

It is as a career adjunct that a wife contributes most directly, visibly, and tangibly to her husband's career success. Expectations of what is involved in being the wife of a male professional are frequently so clearly stated and institutionalized in the work setting that Papanek (1973) has referred to elite careers as "two-person careers." Certainly these medical and academic wives have had a wide range of obligations and opportunities both to solidify and enhance their husbands' career progress. So far as the status and interpersonal aspects of the husbands' careers are concerned, the wives have worked to promote a positive public and social image of their husbands and their work. These women have also performed a variety of helpmate activities, which relate directly to the management of the work setting or to the performance or completion of the work itself. In this chapter, the wife's contribution both in enhancing her husband's reputation, and in directly helping him, will be examined.

The Public and Social Role of the Wife

It is difficult to measure precisely the extent of a man's need to be socially well-received by those who judge him professionally, but the importance of that acceptance should not be underestimated. The doctor, especially, who is in the business of selling his services in a competitive market, stands to benefit by any positive advertisement of the quality of his product. Handling one case poorly can involve the loss of old patients and reduce the number of new patients in a man's practice. Social channels are important for establishing a good local reputation that will override these unavoidable cases with a poor outcome. However, a successful medical practice is not built and maintained on the basis of a large and loyal clientele alone. As Freidson points out, "dependence on colleagues in one way or another is the rule today in the United States because consultations, hospitals and capital equipment are essential to modern practice" (1970a:92). With varying degrees of emphasis, according to the mode of practice, the physician performs for the twin audiences of colleagues and clients. So, in turn, does his wife.

While present trends in medical practice clearly point to a future increase in group practice, for a very long time the typical mode of medical practice in the United States has been the solo practice. This phrase, "solo practice," is as often used in an ideological as in a descriptive sense (Freidson 1970a:91). The notion of medical practice as an all-encompassing commitment to patient care has its roots in part in the social and economic realities of solo practice. Solo practice is inherently precarious; the risk of losing patients and the threat of competition are always present. "In answer to the threat, one keeps his patients to himself, but to do this involves a deadly grind of perpetual availability for service" (Freidson 1970a:93). As a result of the profession's carefully contrived doctor shortage, however, a physician's availability for service is, these days, more an ideal than a reality. Patients are more likely to have difficulty gaining access to a doctor than a doctor is to have gaining access to patients.

Nonetheless, as a set of ideals, the solo practice of medicine has typically and of necessity involved a man in a special sense of mission or calling in which he ministers to the physical needs of his patients with the same attentiveness and devotion that a clergyman ministers to the spiritual needs of his congregation. Like the minister's wife, the doctor's wife has traditionally been expected to share in the belief system of the professional commitment, which is thought of as transcendent of personal self-interest and in the service of a higher good. She is also expected to display her support for her husband's service to the community (most especially where the doctor's residential community overlaps with his patient and colleague community) in ways that will reflect back on the seriousness and centrality of his work commitment; her identity becomes an extension of his and as his adjunct she proclaims his good work through her own.

This is undoubtedly the founding spirit of the women's auxiliaries attached to the American Medical Association, district medical societies, and local community hospitals. Membership in these organizations is based on the ascribed status of doctor's wife, and activity centers around volunteer work, causal socializing, fundraising and research on legislative and policy issues that might affect the status of the medical profession. In essence, a woman's participation in any one or all of these organizations is tantamount to an expression of her commitment—and subordination—to her husband's professional commitment. In effect, then, the medical profession has, through its auxiliaries, institutionalized an official, though unpaid, adjunct status for the doctor's wife, just as it has institutionalized a similar status for women in general in their paid positions in the medical division of labor. Traditionally the adjunct commitment of the medical wife—as that is summarized by the lines from "A Physician's Wife's Prayer" quoted at the beginning of this chapter—has differed little in concept from the role of the nurse, who in the context of a traditionally perceived female role "serves sacrificially . . . supports and protects a dominant male" (Mauksch 1972:215–217).

The extent to which the derived status of doctor's wife can become the basis of a comprehensive and formal role definition is illustrated by the existence of the magazine *MD's Wife*, published by the Women's Auxiliary of the American Medical Association. The underlying assumption of the magazine is that doctors' wives constitute a special interest group with a highly traditional female role definition. The format of the magazine is similar to other women's magazines and emphasizes food, family, fashion, and the volunteer roles and social concerns of women. The notion that the woman who is a doctor's wife has a special identity is apparently not in any danger of becoming outdated, for in 1977 a new magazine called *Medical Mrs.* appeared on the scene and is offering lively competition to the older, established *MD's Wife*. The new publication, slicker and glossier than its counterpart, also views the medical career as a two-person career in which the wife fulfills specified responsibilities and obligations. *Medical Mrs.*, though, speaks more directly to the strains inherent in the medical marriage and is more frank in accepting the pleasurable life style wrought and bought by the doctor's affluence than is *MD's Wife*, which tends to have an altruistic and self-sacrificing tone.

In those situations where the medical colleague community also functions on some level as a social community, the medical wife is likely to be inducted into a public role in her husband's behalf. Of course, the medical profession doesn't offer the only, nor even the most obvious, example of a wife's induction into participation in her husband's career.

[One] type of two-person career emphasizes the man's public image. These [occupations] include some where the wife's participation is almost, but not quite formally institutionalized—the ambassador's wife, the mayor's wife, the wife of a company president, the First Lady and so on. All of these women are expected to give acknowledged public performances, as are also the wives of political candidates. . . . The

47

rejection of such public roles by the wife requires considerable effort and is generally seen as injuring the husband's work performance. (Papanek 1973:100)

Every doctor's wife interviewed mentioned having been contacted by and invited into active membership in the auxiliaries of the district medical society and the local hospitals, when her husband arrived in the medical community. The extent and kind of participation that the wives have had in these groups shows considerable variation, however. It is not surprising to find that those women who have involved themselves in auxiliary work most automatically, willingly, and actively are those for whom the identity of doctor's wife is most salient. Almost always they are women over forty, married to men who are closely identified with the tradition of solo practice. The husbands in this group (about half of the medical sample of twenty) are either presently in solo practice, began their careers in solo practice, or have worked closely throughout their careers with a man who himself had been in solo practice up until the time he formed a two-person partnership with one of the husbands in the study. The wives of these men are quite at home with the image of themselves as doctors' wives, and they felt little, if any, schism between those activities that would be gratifying to them personally and those that would extend and favorably promote their husbands' service orientation. These wives were glad of the opportunity to establish themselves socially in the company of other doctors' wives, at the same time that they fulfilled what they saw as their rightful obligations to their husbands' practices.

I was new here and he wasn't. . . . In a way it was more of a problem getting me established. I did volunteer work to get out of the house. . . . I think I felt it would have looked bad if I had not been in the auxiliary. (11)

I guess we both felt it was something I should do. I don't know why I felt that way. I have no idea what is going on now. . . . In the past it formed a kind of cohort of newcomers. I was called for some of the hospital auxiliaries and a few people reached out because they were nice. (9)

You have that sense of "you should." . . . To my way of thinking it would be wrong not to do your part. It's possibly helpful to your husband's work—it seemed like the appropriate thing to do. He works at the hospital and if you can help, you really should. I wasn't really doing it for his practice. (3)

I tried to be friendly and hospitable, but he didn't need that. People like me but [he] has made it on his own. I'm not a clubwoman and haven't joined many things. The auxiliary was my main way of getting into the community when we came. . . . I've always been active in the auxiliary. They're always looking for new, young, enthusiastic volunteers and they nailed me right away. My husband thinks I should be involved, yes. He thinks every doctor's wife should give time to the auxiliary. If there's a newcomer in the neighborhood, I try to interest them in the auxiliary. But this new breed of doctor's wives doesn't want to get involved. They have this hang-up—they don't want to be known as doctors' wives. (15)

While the women just quoted express positive feelings toward their auxiliary work, the concluding remarks of the final quote indicate that this uncritical attitude is by no means shared by all the wives interviewed. There is indeed a "new breed" of doctor's wife, whose repeated assertion echoed a clear theme throughout the interviews: "I'm not a doctor's wife, I'm just a wife." These women are irritated by, even scornful of, the idea that their participation in the community should be predominantly or even at all shaped by the kind of work their husbands do. The wives who express these feelings tend to be in their thirties and are married to men who constitute, in effect, a new breed of doctors, who have never touched base at all with the tradition of solo practice. These physician husbands have worked only in group- or hospital-based practices, both settings where the financial base of the practice is secure and stable, and patient coverage is shared with other members of the group or with supporting staff (residents and fellows) of the hospital.

It seems likely that in these situations where the financial risk of medical practice is either diminished or nonexistent, the notion of medical practice as an all-encompassing commitment to patient care is attenuated as well. Friedson's research confirms that doctors in solo practice are more likely to emphasize service, in response to the patient's need for personal interest, while doctors in group practice are more likely to emphasize technical competence in diagnosis (1961:152–68). In a group or hospital practice setting, the practitioner enjoys the authority and status of the physician role, without the inconvenience and uncertainty of solo practice. Far more than the solo practitioner, the man in group or hospital practice is in a position to consider what he wants to get out of his medical practice, in addition to what he should give to it. It is likely that a different sort of person than the sort who identifies with the solo practice model is attracted to group or hospital practice—the new breed being more medical executives, compared to the medical preachers of the solo practice tradition.

Similarly, the new breed of doctor's wife does not closely identify with the service tradition of medicine and does not see her role as one to be tailored in that respect to her husband's calling. She views her husband's work more as a life style than as a way of life. She sees his doctoring more as a set of work demands that have an impact on her life and the life of the family than as demanding work which she is called upon to share, and she thinks of herself not as a doctor's wife but simply as the wife of a doctor. It is not that she has no sense of identity as a doctor's wife, but that she eschews the older, more traditional identity associated with the more traditional form of practice and the more traditional man in it. She—this new breed—is undoubtedly the audience for the new *Medical Mrs.* magazine, whereas *MD's Wife* would appear to appeal more to the old breed of doctor's wife. There is also a high degree of overlap between the wives of the new breed and that group of medical wives who expressed positive feelings about the possibility of work for themselves at some point in the future. (see table 2.6.) It seems clear then that just as the doctor in group or hospital practice has redefined and circumscribed his role in comparison to that of the solo practitioner, his wife has changed her approach to her role also.

On the other hand, this distinction as to the shape and orientation of medical practice should probably not be too sharply drawn; it is most likely a matter of degree and not of kind. Even though the group- or hospital-based physician may not face the problem of building a solid patient clientele and has scaled down his service commitment accordingly, good rapport with colleagues in the medical community remains vital to his effective practice. It is also in the best interests of the profession for practitioners to promote a favorable public image through their espousal of selfless dedication. In the face of ever-increasing competition from within the profession and Kennedy-style criticism of current modes of medical practice from without, the individual practitioner can hardly afford to appear detached from or indifferent to his patients or colleagues—nor can his wife.

And, indeed, it was a rare wife who did not feel obligated for the sake of appearance to have at least some minimal affiliation—if only by joining and paying dues—in one or another of the medical or hospital auxiliaries. To be sure, the young wives were reluctant participants at best and often felt torn between their own preference not to have any medically related involvement at all and the fear that their husbands' professional standing would suffer if they did not. One internist's wife articulated this dilemma with special clarity:

They are very quick to call you. The first year I had the excuse of the house and the baby. That was wearing thin, so I did relent and do a few things at the hospital. I did it out of obligation. I was annoyed and disappointed in myself for doing it. They do some good things, but they put pressure on you when you first come and you do feel obligated. You feel you owe it to your husband. [And the consequences to your husband?] Well indirectly I suppose. This is a small town and people talk. I don't know how drastic it would be, but I wouldn't want to be unfair to my husband especially with his being new in town and just starting practice. It was important for him, I thought, to have a good reputation. (17)

Another woman found an interesting way to conform with the behavioral expectations that others might have of her in her doctor's wife role without compromising her sense of the principles involved.

I did not join the ——— hospital auxiliary, but I did do volunteer work in the hospital through the Junior League. I did what I wanted to do. I felt that I owed the hospital something and I enjoyed doing the sort of work I did there. Sure I've been criticized for this but I

51

don't care. I've made a contribution and I've done it in a way that's comfortable for me. (19)

Older men and their wives who come out of the solo practice mode are also in a position to keep the tradition of the old breed alive and to impose and perpetuate the values of that tradition on a younger, up-coming generation of doctors and their wives, thus ensuring that the new breed will not deviate too far from the norms of the old. In this way, tension and incompatibility between the two are minimized. The following remarks of one older wife are interesting in this connection. She is commenting about the wives of men whom her husband and his partner were interviewing as possible candidates to become the third partner in their practice in internal medicine. Her husband began the practice as a solo practitioner.

Now we are interviewing and thinking—we saw this young couple last night. The wife's interests are paramount, and I don't think that they care for the way this young man is looking at the community. They feel this man should be looking more at their practice of medicine and evaluating them at the office. But they are spending their time looking to see if there is English riding in the community, what kind of opportunities there are for his wife, who teaches natural childbirth classes, and they had already been to real estate people looking at houses before they were even offered the position. Another young man came a couple of weeks ago; I had his wife and children here at the house for coffee in the morning. They felt that he was more of a physician. He talked about cases. And I felt that his wife was more concerned about her children and her home. This is where I can help [my husband] and I relate back to him what I see. (3)

In a similar vein another wife talks about a woman's need to find satisfaction in the traditional wife-mother role if she is to be happy and contribute, in turn, to her husband's happiness, and thereby to his effectiveness in practice.

It used to be that a woman took pride in this sort of thing—sending her husband out neatly and properly dressed. Young wives now are different—these women are left with nothing if they can't take

pride in turning their husbands out to go to work and they can't go
to work themselves and they feel raising children is demeaning.
Then they are left with nothing. . . . When my husband took an associate, I was involved in some of the hiring procedures. I would
have the candidates to dinner. The first time a candidate came he
came alone and after that we pretty much insisted he bring his
wife. This is a hard community for someone to live in unless they
choose this kind of community. When associates leave it's usually
because the wife doesn't like living here. I got involved in sizing up
the wife and giving advice. (9)

Thus, for the women just quoted, being an adjunct or helpmate
to their husbands' careers consists in part of making a judgment
about a man's suitability for entering into medical practice in the
community in terms of the appropriateness and adequacy of his
wife's definition of her role. Perhaps when the community setting
of medical practice is larger and more heterogeneous, and a man's
professional life is geographically and socially unconnected to his
personal life, such judgments lose their force, if indeed they exist at
all. But the new breed of medical wives who have come with their
husbands into this particular (and not at all unrepresentative) community are not so much untraditional, but neotraditional. If they
express their impatience with some of the expectations imposed on
them, they are at the same time eager not to offend. If they express
some opposition to being described as "doctors' wives" they nonetheless acknowledge the primacy of their identity as wives. And
they have complied fastidiously and courteously with expected role
behaviors, even if they have not always believed in what they were
doing.

Only one doctor's wife, whose husband practices out of a hospital, expressed any real outrage at the prevailing norms of medical
wifehood. Her protest is also interesting as a depiction of some of
the value differences between the world of private practice and the
world of hospital-based practice.

Yes, I just went off the board of the [district medical auxiliary]. Do
you want an honest opinion? This is where it gets tacky. Some of
the wives are nice people, but their style of being a doctor's wife—
they're all private men's wives. They're all in the Dark Ages—living

through their husbands for their husbands and they don't do anything that would reflect on his practice. Even the laypersons here are backwards; doctors are still gods on pedestals. . . . I just don't fit in. I don't have to be competent; I don't have to be a paragon. Our children are not doctor's children—they're just children. If what we do makes him not have patients—they should go to him because he's a competent physician. They should care less what I'm like. (1)

It is interesting to note that for all her protest, this wife, like most of the wives, "did her time" with the auxiliary even though there is no practice more secure—in terms of salary and patient population—than the hospital practice in which her husband works. With regard to colleagues, however, the hospital practice is quite insecure, because private practitioners are often resentful of and threatened by the hospital physicians who might siphon off patients from the private community. Hospital physicians have a special need, therefore, to build trust and rapport with the private men and their wives are sensitive to this need.

[Do you come with a feeling of being already established when your husband is in a hospital practice?] It's true you do get a salary but it is also necessary to build a rapport with the doctors in the community. A lot of getting settled is contingent on how much they like you, so you do have to establish yourself. I do think my joining helped him, but my primary purpose was not to build his reputation. That was more as an offshoot. (8)

In all only three of the twenty doctors' wives in the study have had no auxiliary affiliation of any sort. One is the wife of a man in a junior-level hospital position, who works in a unit that delivers highly specialized medical service that depends on the facilities and equipment that hospitals alone have. His position is, therefore, both nonpolitical and noncompetitive. Another wife, who is in other respects of the old breed, centered her outside volunteer and service activities in the Catholic community from which her husband drew (to begin with anyway) most of his patients. The third wife is herself a physician, and although she was actually invited to join the women's auxiliary of the district medical society, she understandably declined the invitation, preferring to join the medical society itself.

Regardless of the strength of their affiliation with the various medical and hospital auxiliary groups, both the new and old breed of doctors' wives participate in the wider community in a way that certainly serves to maintain, if not actively promote, their husbands' professional and social status. As a group the doctors' wives have been far more active in the established civic, educational, religious and cultural lives of their community than have the academic wives. (And unlike the academic wives, none of the medical wives have been partisan political campaigners or antiwar activists.) Through their group membership in the various community activities, doctors' wives are invariably brought into contact with other women who, as wives of businessmen or lawyers, for example, enjoy a high social standing similar to their own. Of course most women sought out these groups and activities on the basis of their own interests, but insofar as a husband's reputation is built in the community, it certainly cannot hurt for the doctor's wife to be well- (and noncontroversially) regarded as a participant in community life. Several women readily acknowledged that their community activities had benefited their husbands' careers.

Yes, I guess I did help him to get established. I did feel I had to get out with the medical ladies. . . . As far as my other activities, they were not specifically in the interest of his practice, but it does help anyway. People mention that they are having [a certain kind of problem] who don't even know that there is someone who does that special surgery and then I can mention what he does. (14)

To some extent I helped him get known. I joined things to help him get known. Otherwise you are a name in the phone books. . . . I was aware of the fact that his name should be around and people should know of us pleasantly. I joined things on that basis. (9)

In another context it would be interesting to explore the relationship between the elite status of medicine, its sense of itself as a professional special-interest group, and its apparent need to function socially as a cohesive community. Whatever the reasons, patterns of social life and entertaining in the medical community are highly ritualized. On the most uncomplicated level, of course, a woman is likely to want to entertain and be entertained, as a way of making new friends and finding a social niche for herself, when she arrives with her husband in a new place. Since a woman's most immediate access to the community is through her husband's work and through his colleagues and their wives, it is not surprising that most wives reported that much of their social life is centered in the medical community. Now that their own husbands are established, many wives make an effort to welcome the wives of newcomers to the community.

A fair amount of our social life has been centered in the medical community. That was purposeful in the beginning. Then it got so the men in medicine began talking about medicine and the women would migrate to the other side of the room and end up talking about recipes, so we sought out friends in other fields. Our bridge and tennis friends are M.D.s and I do think there is a stronger bond in the medical profession than in some professions. There are a lot of big parties where we are invited to come and meet new partners. Occasionally I will call a friend and say there are so many new people, let's throw a coffee for the wives. It's difficult to come into a new community. (8)

Although simple hospitality and courtesy are genuine aspects of what is involved in medical social interaction, they are not the whole story. Although no wife seemed able to specify precisely what is at stake in medical social life, it is clear that behind the affability lies a politics of entertaining, which is directly linked to the colleague network where concerns of competition and cooperation loom large. One wife, for example, discussed the significance of the *absence* of certain social overtures to her on her husband's arrival in the community.

You always have a lot of competition between surgeons. Even in the association that's true. Maybe it's because they're egotists. When a new surgeon comes in, it means a smaller piece of the pie for the others. . . . At the beginning I was contacted by a lot of medical wives, but not by surgeons' wives. I think that's the competition. (18)

Many wives commented rather disdainfully about the tendency of wives whose husbands are newly set up in private practice to entertain lavishly in a way clearly calculated to build their husbands' contacts. Only rarely did a wife admit to entertaining specifically in her husband's behalf; more typically she disclaimed any such motivation on her own part.

We didn't entertain specifically with that in mind. We were trying to find a place for ourselves in the community. Some people come to town and do things that look like they are designed. (9)

We were invited a lot when we came and I've always done my share of entertaining. For a number of years we had an eggnog party during the holiday season, but I don't think that had anything to do with my husband's relationships to his colleagues. (16)

Nonetheless, the social calendar of the medical community is punctuated by the regular occurrence of parties given on a grand scale, sometimes for as many as two or three hundred people. Whenever a group takes in a new partner or associate, for example, it is the occasion for major entertainment. When the dozen or so physicians who are new to the community each year is multiplied by the number of persons in the groups that they have joined—often, apparently, each partner and his wife take their turn at introducing or entertaining the new person—it adds up to a considerable number of social events. Social gatherings also occur on a seasonal basis, and professional life is mixed with personal and family life on the occasions of weddings, bar mitzvahs and so on.

The entertaining that goes on is in the whole medical community. Every medical person eventually knows the other one. Most of the medical people tend to move [here]. It is the general tendency of the medical people to try to go all out and it's more intensified here because of the large numbers of medical people. There is a tendency to have large parties where everybody comes. (7)

Although the wives interviewed may not be the ones who are giving these parties, somebody obviously is, and the wives, for their part, just as obviously feel obliged to attend or otherwise account for themselves because of some real or imagined consequence to their husbands' reputations if they do not.

You do get a report card. If you don't show you're on the list. Both his partner's wife and I wondered at the same time why we're still doing this. I have started giving excuses and not going. I was called to task once by an older doctor's wife. I had given as an excuse for not being there that we had plans with the children. She told me that was not an acceptable excuse. I told her that it wasn't even an excuse, that's the reality of it and it's none of your business. From then on I stopped giving reasons. But a wife does notice who doesn't attend and then she tells her husband who doesn't come to her party. (1)

We don't have the private practice pressure on us of "better be friendly with the other doctors in order to get referrals." But I think you have to be fair and impartial as head of the department. I try to make sure if it's a cocktail party where a new partner is being introduced that we do show up. I always call and say we can't make it because—and then give some excuse. To be perfectly honest, I do "regret" some of them even when I know we're going to be here. (19)

Insofar as the new breed of medical wife rejects the identity of doctor's wife, she also tends to reject participation in a formal hostess role. As is her wont, however, she sustains this new image of herself not through nonparticipation, but through conforming in a new guise and style. Her social life with her husband continues to be centered heavily, though not exclusively, in the medical community.

I find them [the large parties] worthless. I hate it and you can't meet anyone there. I enjoy having people for dinner because I enjoy cooking. But I have held my own. When the new associate came I . . . did a different thing and had several small parties of six or eight people. It kind of set a new trend. (7)

I entertain who we would like to. I do make sure that we see some doctors that we like who [he] might not see too often. Just to keep in contact and for fun. . . . I try if I hear of someone who is full time in the department with [him] or connected with him to go and meet the person if they live in [town]. (19)

Yes, we do have a social life built to some extent around the medical community. I had a dinner party here and our best friends were definitely medical and some close friends on the street came too. My friend and I thought once that we might do it and looked into the possibility of renting a hall, but we never have gotten around to it. (17)

The social and public activity of the academic wife is less institutionalized than that of her medical counterpart, and its connection to her husband's career advancement is less explicit. To be sure, academic life is not without its own women's auxiliaries in the form of faculty wives' groups. But the sense of duty that a woman feels regarding her membership in such groups probably varies a great deal according to the size of the university and the shape of the political process that determines the upward mobility of individual faculty members. It is a safe guess that the participation of the faculty wife is most salient in the small and/or elite institution, where faculty members are expected to make a specific commitment to the life and traditions of the wider academic community, over and above their commitment to their departments and disciplines. In any event the professor does not have to conscript a clientele, although there may be instances in his career when it is to his advantage to have well-placed contacts among people in the university system. However, for the academic men in this study, where the university setting is large, public, and nonelite, the most relevant community of colleagues has not been university-wide but department-bound. Only a few men, for example, have had any active committee life outside of their departments.

Formal affiliation with the university women's association has not seemed particularly necessary to the academic wives interviewed. Most women mentioned that when they arrived at the university they were called and invited to join the university wives' group. Very few women did, and those who did not felt no hesitation in turning down the invitation. The few women who did join said that they were interested in the chance to meet women whose husbands were in other departments (and whom they might not meet otherwise) and to participate in the various social activities of the association—including golf lessons, bridge playing, antique study groups, or volunteer work. They expressed no feeling of obligation to join, and indeed, it is difficult to see how a wife's membership per se in a group comprised of women whose husbands were but a few of several hundred faculty members from a wide range of departments could have had any significant impact on her husband's reputation and progress within his department.

Esteem, and therefore meaningful colleague relationships, are built on the department level, and social life does occur there. On the basis of interview data from wives alone, it is very difficult to get a clear picture of the strength of the relationships between department social life, an academic husband's career mobility, and the specific role played by a wife in that social life. Even within the department, organized social life is probably less important to the fate of the academic career than to the medical career for two reasons. One is that the academic work setting provides opportunities for casual social interaction with one's relevant colleagues in the context of the workday itself that are not present in the medical setting, where if colleagues meet it is only in passing over the specific issues of a case in the midst of a heavily booked appointment schedule. The second reason is that there is in academe a strong ideological commitment to the notion that academic career success does not rest on the strength of interpersonal loyalties, but on productivity and merit. The reality of the situation may frequently differ from this ideal, but the fact remains that the truly outstanding scholar does not need to attend overmuch to social niceties if the quality of his work speaks for his worth. Clearly it would be foolhardy to press this point too far, since it is not uncommon for so-called objective assessments of scholarly work to be permeated with subjective judgments. It is worth noting, though, that the two academic husbands (one humanist and one scientist) who have an unusually high investment in their research and writing and who have earned substantial national acclaim in their fields, have been noticeably less active in departmental social life than have the other academics who appear in this book.

Academic social life is neither as large-scale, formal, nor institutionalized as it is in the medical community, with the result that the clues to the precise meaning of departmental social life probably reside less in its organizational than in its interactional features. Without direct observation, we can only guess at the kinds of indirect communications that permeate the social setting and their subtle and diffuse effect on a man's standing with his colleagues and his consequent progress through his deparment. (Hochschild [1969] found, for example, that the ambassador's wife serves an unofficial but vital function in the communication of social and political messages.) Furthermore, most wives saw no connection at all between their after-hours departmental social life and their husband's day-to-day work situation in the department, though one wife offered some penetrating insights into general benefits that accrue to a department directly and perhaps to its individual members indirectly when the department has some social sense of itself.

I think entertaining does help. . . . A lot of social things ease tensions. If you know what a good story teller someone is, or how nice they are with their children, it doesn't bother you so much what their habits are at work. When the social part of the department fell apart, there was nobody left. The other wives are all liberated and don't have time to entertain. I wonder as more and more women are not at home if there may not be more tensions in other departments too. Either a wife plays an important role in easing those tensions or she frees him to do that sort of thing by having time to spend with people at work. (29)

Because most of the wives interviewed felt that the extent and kind of their socializing with their husbands' colleagues and their wives has been both generally nonintrusive and socially comfortable, the possible professional utility of the social life is more hidden from view than it is in the medical community, where social events are self-consciously and conspicuously staged and carry a bold, unwritten stamp of obligation on them. This does not mean that academic social life has no utility, however, for some suggestion of the nature of that utility is revealed by the characteristic shape and chronology of the wife's experience with departmental social life.

Virtually all of the wives reported that they and their husbands had been drawn into some social life with other colleagues and their wives at the time when their husbands were newly arrived in their departments. The usual pattern was that newcomers would be entertained at least by the department chairman and very often by the other older and more senior members of the department as well. In this way the new man and his wife eventually came to know all the other members of the department and their spouses.

Wives vary in the extent to which they either felt obligated or interested to pursue a departmentally based social life, once they had been officially welcomed. Some of the younger wives preferred from the beginning to do no more than attend the one or two department-wide events held each year, and their lack of social participation apparently carried no penalty.

He doesn't have any friends in his department and we don't socialize in his department at all. . . . I found it easier to opt out from most things. I didn't feel any penalty attached to that. There was never any question of [his] not being promoted. (23)

I was pleased to find this place different from what I had expected and that very little was expected of me in a faculty wife sense. I have always been conscious that it is terribly demeaning to a man to think that a wife is supposed to help him in his career—the idea that for a man to get ahead he has to have a certain kind of wife. It's a terrible insult to his abilities and a man ought to be able to get ahead on his own without a little helpmate type. I haven't done anything like that and it hasn't been expected of me. (23)

More often, however—particularly if the department was small (under forty or fifty) when she and her husband arrived—a wife found herself caught up in a round of entertaining and being entertained for the first few years of her husband's life in the department.

One felt one should be involved socially, but I like it too. The department was small when we came—friendly and hospitable. We have always enjoyed social life; we come from a background of entertaining and being entertained, so we fit in very easily. We have done a lot of socializing with my husband's colleagues over the years and some of our best friends are people in the department. (30)

Almost from the first year—not quite the first year—we didn't know people well enough or have the money—certainly by the third year if not the second we were trying to entertain people and most of the people here then also did some entertaining. (22)

In general, the humanists seem to have been more gregarious throughout their careers than the scientists—an observation that prompts speculation as to whether there is a link between academic discipline and the style of personal-social interaction. Furthermore, as indicated by the nostalgic remarks of the woman quoted earlier on, there is some evidence of the existence of a traditional faculty wife role definition and social style that is reminiscent of the old breed of medical wives. Several of the older faculty wives, now in their middle or late forties, mentioned that they had been personally taken in hand when they arrived by the wives of their husbands' department chairmen. It was apparently the understood function of the chairman's wife at that time to help settle the wives of newcomers, specifically with respect to their tasks as wives and mothers, and the new women were given information about schools, shopping, activities for children and so on. It was also well understood that the young wives themselves were expected to meet certain social obligations in the interest of promoting their husbands' careers.

I think I had an image of what the academic instructor's wife should do. . . . Our difficult periods came when we were young and struggling and had little money. When the children were young I felt a good deal of personal harrassment. After all, I had degrees and they were all going down the drain. It was a typical female frustration. I don't think it was connected to his career except that his career came first. I had the feeling that if the chairman's wife in his department had a tea, then I should get a sitter and go to that tea. (27)

Yes, I did feel cast in the role of a faculty wife—very much so. I think I did not think that much about it. I just did it. I had a very strong sense of obligation. I was his wife and it was his position and therefore those things followed. It's hard to know what the consequences would be of not getting involved; now we are very little involved with social life at the university. . . . We have some friends in his department, but not terribly close. There's been a tremendous shift. We used to give parties where everyone was [in his field] but now our closest friends aren't even university people. (21)

But all this is in the past. If the academic wives of twenty years ago bear a strong resemblance to the medical wives of the present, the old breed of academic wives is now truly a dying breed. Even those wives whose social participation in their husbands' departments was substantial in the early years of their husbands' careers felt that their departmental connectedness has diminished considerably over time. In part this is a consequence of the greatly expanded size of many departments, which has led to an increasingly depersonalized departmental social life.

We used to have a great deal of department social life when everyone was on friendly terms. The department head and other members invited each other over. But some members of the department have never been here. We don't entertain much now. (35)

The first year the department was not big and they entertained everyone; the second year it was much bigger and they stopped doing that. (24)

As the department grew larger and larger I tried for a long time to keep this up. We had dinner parties and had new people out. It just got to be too much, too much work and I found that many of the new people were not persons I particularly wanted to ask back a second time. They never asked us anywhere and then we were both terribly busy, and I noticed that other members of the department were also doing less entertaining. So now we are not deeply involved in departmental social life. (22)

Also, academe has been more responsive than medicine to affirmative action policies and more adaptive to the demands to allow women access to professional life; academic departments now are less likely to be exclusively male domains in the way that they used to be and that medicine continues to be. The result is that there is a growing awareness of the unfairness of imposing social obligation on a woman simply on the grounds of her status as a wife. As some of the women quoted earlier indicate, younger faculty wives are bringing new norms of wifehood into academic life, and unlike the new breed of medical wives they have not met with resistance from the older wives. It is in the nature of academe to be more open to ideological changes and innovations in life styles than medicine, which is typically a defender of the status quo. Whereas medical wives retain an essentially traditional image of themselves and their roles as women and wives, many once traditional faculty wives are eager to follow the lead of younger women and to shed the older version of the faculty-wife role and some of the responsibilities that went with it. Since many academic wives are now pursuing their own independent interests and activities, they prefer the flexibility of the present to the constraints of the past.

The way it has gone for the last two or three chairmen, the chairman gives a cocktail party on campus. He organized it. It's not the same as having to have everybody out to one's home. That's the way it used to be. The last couple of the department chairman's wives have paved the way for this, so I feel relatively relaxed about it all. (24)

When I first started teaching . . . I was too exhausted to do entertaining. I worked all day at school and then worked here with my private students and would have to do all kinds of housekeeping chores at night because the children were too young to take that kind of responsibility. . . . So I would work until 11 at night and get up and do it all over again the next day. It's no way to live so I stopped entertaining. . . . Every once in awhile, he'll say we should have so-and-so to dinner. I prefer it that way, because when the urge is strong enough, he'll say it enough so that I'll do it. (26)

We haven't entertained lately. I just decided I don't want to anymore. We had been entertaining regularly—twice a month or so we would have a big gathering with ten to twelve people. I want to be quiet now. Everything kept snowballing, and I was getting more involved in everything. After I started working, it gave me more confidence to decide to do what I wanted to do. . . . I decided by golly I've done all these things and now I know just what I want to do and don't want to do. (39)

The whole department has cooled socially because women are liberated and they realized that the women had the whole ball game—all the burden of entertaining fell on her shoulders. (25)

Although academic wives portray academic social life currently as being very casual, even laissez faire, this should not be taken to mean that socializing has been of no consequence to their husbands' careers. In the first place virtually every academic couple has taken care to be at least minimally involved in departmental social life. However great or small the flurry of social activity in the lives of these couples, it inevitably occurred at the time when the husband was becoming established in his department and making his way up the tenure and career ladder to the senior ranks. The falling off of social life that has occurred in more recent years very likely reflects more than just factors of department size and composition or even changing norms of women's roles. The timing of the slackening of social life appears to coincide quite directly with the timing of a husband's promotion to the top ranks of his department. He has reached a point where he can afford to "let go" socially. And then there is the fact that in recent years most departments at the university, as in many colleges and universities, have stopped growing in size and are adding few, if any, new members. Therefore, there is no longer much occasion or need for the kind of cross-rank socializing that once took place when these now senior professors were junior members of their departments.

The wife of the department chairman is still caught up in a certain amount of obligatory and self-conscious socializing. Departments continue to have at least a formal sense of themselves as communities of colleagues, and one of the functions of a department head or chair is to keep alive that sense of community. To do this he relies on his wife's services as a hostess. Five of these academic wives are married to men who have held a chairmanship in their departments. Though the wives have not felt the need to entertain in a particular style or with any specified frequency, they have felt it imperative to entertain in some manner, on an impartial basis, rather than not at all.

The first year we took them out—we had done nothing to that point and it was easier to take everyone out somewhere. We figured that was the whole year's batch and that was that. After that, we have entertained everyone in small groups. (36)

Over the years I tried to have the new members over to dinner and look like I was not favoring anyone. (27)

The Wife as Girl Friday

Both academic and medical wives have assisted directly in the completion of their husbands' work tasks and/or the management of the work setting through performing a wide range of semiskilled "women's work" sorts of services. The "girl Friday" contribution, like the social and public participation of a wife, is nonspecialized activity and does not depend or draw on any base of field-re-latedness or shared expertise between husband and wife. Since most of the medical marriages are non-collegial in character, it is not surprising to find that most doctors wives have developed their adjunct contribution most elaborately along the girl Friday and so-cial dimensions. However, acting as girl Friday is not confined ex-clusively to those women who have no background of field-rela-tedness to their husbands' work or no work commitments of their own. In both professional groups in marriages where the wife has training and expertise that is related to her husband's field, she is just as likely to function as a girl Friday as she is also to act in the more specialized and collegial capacity of professional assistant or advisor. (These latter contributions will be discussed in the section to follow.) Indeed some wives who have training in medically re-lated fields have worked with their husbands only as girl Friday and not as professional assistants at all. One wife with high-level nurse's training and considerable work experience in the field made the following comment.

I would love to be involved in his office, I really would. . . . I would be willing to do anything, even secretarial work. (13)

In such instances a specifically subordinate female role definition has taken precedence over a self-definition centered on work and achievement, even as that might be expressed within the context of the traditional wife role.

The kind of work that women do as girl Fridays reflects the dif-ferences between the work task and work setting of the medical and academic professions. As office decorator and human relations ex-pert the medical wife functions to lend the "woman's touch" or perspective to her husband's work. The majority of medical wives, whose husbands are in private practice, have extended their home decorating skills to their husbands' work setting. On one level of course this is simply a courtesy a wife extends for her husband's convenience because it is a task for which he has little time or interest.

However, according to an article in one issue of *Medical Mrs.*, when a wife undertakes to decorate her husband's office, she should see her work not merely as a time-saving convenience to her husband but as making an important psychological contribution to the doctor-patient relationship and by extension, to the marriage relationship.

> Now why go through all this trouble and soul searching to decorate the doctor's waiting room? Because if patients have been made to feel they are "serving time" while awaiting their appointments, they'll enter the office and treatment room in a nervous, angry and possibly belligerent state which can make them difficult and downright unpleasant to deal with. So take a minute to analyze your husband's waiting room and see if it's a happy place. Remember, a tranquil setting that calms patients will make life a lot easier and more pleasant for the man treating them. And that can make him a happier, easier and more pleasnat man to live with. (Sept/Oct 1977:35)

And of course for the wife there are the additional gratifications of knowing that her homemaking skills are on display to a wider audience than just her family and friends, and of gaining some public recognition for her work.

> I have decorated his entire office—all six rooms. He had a staff meeting at the hospital last night and he told me I was the hit of the party, meaning the job I had done with the decor of his office. The other offices are much below his opinion of what his is. (10)

Many medical husbands look to their wives to supply judgments or insights of an interpersonal sort in a variety of situations, clearly drawing on the idea (quite possibly true) that women are more skilled in the area of human relationships than men. As one wife said:

A woman feels different vibrations from people and sees them differently and I will recommend ways of handling people. He doesn't look for my advice but he will consider what I say quite seriously. . . . Once one of the secretaries left—she had been with them for quite awhile and they missed her terribly. I was the one who finally reached her and asked her to come back. (15)

Some wives do address themselves specifically to problems that their husbands might have relating to patients, but it is much more common for a wife to act as a kind of unseen personnel manager, dealing at a distance with intraoffice tensions among the "girls" there (as they were invariably referred to), which seem to be a perpetual thorn in the side of the doctor, especially in group and hospital practice. It may be that in contrast to the solo practice man, the group or hospital physician is prepared to deal with people primarily in problem-solving rather than interactional terms. Also, of course, there just *are* more personnel around in the group and hospital setting, and a greater likelihood that staff-to-staff difficulties will arise in addition to physician-to-staff difficulties.

There are periodic upheavals in the office. It's a typical situation with groups of females and the interactions that go on in the group. Stress is among the personnel, not among the doctors. They're really busy and pushed and they can always manage. The problem is with the women. I hate to characterize it as being a problem of women, but that's how it is in that office. They can't seem to cope with stress—there's a lot of crying and weeping and name-calling. (7)

For personnel problems he uses me as a sounding board. He's in charge of all the . . . technicians and over 100 . . . unit nurses. That's the part of his job that he dislikes the most. Females come and cry. He hates catting. . . . I tell him that some of it's natural and they just have to blow. Essentially he'd like to relax and forget it. (1)

Yes, sure I get involved. I will tell him what I think about how something was handled. Not necessarily the medical part, but how a person was handled. . . . There were problems involving the nurses and their personal problems. I was trying to make a decision as to how this could be handled—how the nurses could be helped with their problems so they wouldn't interfere with their work. (5)

It is not uncommon for the wife of a doctor, in solo practice especially, to refer to the practice as belonging to both of them—as "ours." A few wives have acted on this conceptualization to become not unseen but actual office managers in their husbands' practices for substantial periods of time. One wife, for example, was helping her husband to manage the transition from group to private practice (along with caring for a two-week-old baby) by answering all patient calls and booking appointments. Throughout her marriage, she has also spent a part of every evening entering information into patient records. Another wife worked together with her husband to establish the business and personnel aspects of his practice on a firm footing in order to leave him free to attend to patient care without being distracted by other considerations.

I worked in my husband's office fairly routinely. I handled the books and the personnel. I don't do that any more now that he has an associate. I feel now that I should stay out of it, but I used to work three or four days a week. . . . It's been a month now since I've been at the office. . . . He would like me to work there so we could cut down on help. I do save him money. Also I handle things differently. We had a slow day Monday and I brought thirty-three patients into the office. People would call and be undecided about whether to come in and I told them to come right in. The secretary doesn't do that. She asks him to make that decision. He likes to do his thing medically and doesn't like to be in the business end. I'm the office manager and stay in touch with the girls every day. I don't want them to bother him—he only gets excited. (4)

Several other wives have worked as secretaries, bookkeepers, or receptionists in their husbands' offices on an occasional or ad hoc basis when office help has been in short supply or absent for the day.

The girl Friday work of the academic wife has consisted almost entirely of typing and more generalized secretarial work. The combination of a student budget and doctoral dissertation writing provided the major impetus for the assumption of these tasks by wives. More than half of the twenty academic wives typed their husbands' doctoral dissertations and their husbands have, for the most part, continued to rely on them for a great deal of professional typing since that time. As one wife noted rather wryly, "Yes, I typed his dissertation. I set my own precedent." These ongoing typing services reflect in part the fact that the secretarial help available is very limited. Many departments make no provision for typing professional correspondence or personal manuscripts, grant applications or research reports. Over the years many women have become quite skilled at rather specialized manuscript or scientific typing, and their husbands' reliance on their wives' services has tended to increase rather than decrease. Not infrequently a woman's secretarial commitment is reinforced by her husband's compliment that she is the best person for the job.

I've typed a lot of papers for him and still do it if it's something very very important that he feels no one else can do. (35)

I typed his Ph.D. dissertation and got so good at typing that I typed all his friends' books for money. I'm still typing his articles—I'm awfully good. (26)

Though most academic wives confine their girl Friday services to typing, one humanist's wife has provided her husband with much more comprehensive assistance in the management of his work. Although she has a Ph.D. herself, it has never been put to active use, and she has related to her husband's work less as a colleague than as a handmaiden.

I typed his M.A. thesis and his Ph.D. and also did some research for him. It was more or less my idea to start with. I had had that relationship with a person in [my major] department when I was an undergraduate. I was very good at research. But my husband had smarter ideas and was better at writing than I was so we sort of combined things like that. . . . I do a lot of reading and he sort of depends on me to give him the gist of a long article or to show him what to read in the [newspaper] or other periodicals that don't pertain to his field but that he ought to know about or that impinge on his field in some way. . . . He works very hard in his courses. I get to correct the papers. It's an awful chore. It is something I can do so that we have something in common. I learn things from it because he uses new material every year. I don't go to his classes. There's only been one year since he was here when I haven't been involved in grading or reading. Then he had a graduate student paid to do it. Usually I only do the objective questions. This year I did the essay questions too. I don't know how much he respects my competence; I don't know how much I respect it. All I know is if the person is writing good English and I can see the more blatant mistakes. He doesn't usually talk to me about his course preparation. Sometimes he might ask me to get books for him, but he's not looking to me for feedback. (29)

The Wife As Professional Assistant, Advisor and Collaborator

The typing services of the academic wife frequently occur within the broader context of her contributions to the actual substance of a finished piece of writing or research. The wife as unseen colleague, as critic, editor, researcher, and scholarly analyst is, of course, the stuff of which the acknowledgments are made that appear in the prefaces and forewords of academic publications. These familiar brief statements are testimony to the link between a wife's own labors and expertise and the content of her husband's work. Below, some examples from books by social scientists:

> And once again, . . . my wife . . . shared the pleasures and burdens of research; her training in psychiatric social work was particularly important for [certain] sections. . . . That the book was not finished earlier is not her fault. . . . Rather its appearance testifies to her sustained interest and participation.
>
> ———, to whom I was then married, helped in the field work and a number of observations in the book are hers.
>
> My wife, ———, contributed many insights in the course of my work, some of which I have been able to incorporate in the book.

Even wives who have not done any typing for their husbands have frequently provided other sorts of professional assistance to their husbands in their work. This is especially true of the wives of men who work in the humanities, because those are fields that are more intelligible and accessible to the lay person than the scientific disciplines and ones in which the wives are apt to have some general, or even specialized, backgrounds of their own. And a few scientists' wives have advanced degrees in fields related to their husbands' work, and have lent a helping hand in their husbands' research.

Sometimes a wife's advisory function consists of talking in an informed and thoughtful way about whatever work her husband has in progress; at other times she is called upon to give more explicit feedback and suggestions or even to help with the research process. Many wives enjoy being drawn into their husbands' work in these ways and find their rewards in the feelings of professional worth and expertise that result; other wives make their contributions more from a feeling of obligation to conform to the helpmate norms of the wife role.

After we were married in June I left [my graduate work] and stayed in a rooming house with him and went out to the field with him. I couldn't do much with my own data. That time was pretty much lost for me. I could have saved myself all the hassle of doing my work under very stressful conditions if I had stayed behind another four months. . . . But it never occurred to us that once he left . . . that there would be any point in my staying on there on my own. You know, the wife always follows the husband. It never occurred to us to do otherwise. So in the fall I got a job as a technician and went along with [the research team] to the field. In the short run it was interesting and I made a little money; in the long run it was useless to me professionally. . . . I did read his dissertation and helped him with some of the data analysis . . . I also read over his material. (34)

Yes, I do read his papers and articles. Usually as he writes he always asks me to read it afterward. I do have some knowledge of the field because I have an M.A. in it. So I read it not just to read it but with a critical outlook. I can suggest certain things to him and we talk it over. (28)

What I like is when I helped him on the anthology. He has always shown me anything he writes first and I'm his first critic. Which is an honor. I like that. I didn't know I could do it. . . . [He] used to show me his poems, and I would be terrified I would hurt his feelings, if I didn't say anything. I would always work up enough courage to say "well, that didn't work" if I thought that. And I was shaking inside and I've gotten over that. He was grateful and so he has reinforced me. So I feel I have worked and given him a great deal on the anthology—it's been very intense work. (25)

This sort of professional advisory role is rare among doctors' wives, partly because medicine is not easily understood by the nonexpert. But even those with medical backgrounds of their own (including the one physician wife) tend to downplay their own skills and information as being rather simple and therefore irrelevant to the content of their husbands' work, which is perceived as highly esoteric.

Sometimes I will offer criticisms or feedback in areas where the medical and the interpersonal blend since my specialty is what it is. It's far too difficult to read in his field—it's very very specialized. (12)

No, I don't really share the medical details of his work. In all honesty a nurse's education is really very narrow—just scratching the top of the surface. I have friends who like to think that they know more than they do. (3)

Some women with a background in nursing enjoy hearing their husbands discuss some of their cases, but more because it sustains their own interest in medicine than because they feel they are able to offer any contribution to the work.

Only a few medical wives have had a more professional relationship to their husbands' work. Two wives who are nurses have worked with their husbands in an active (though unpaid) nursing role. While this is clearly helpful to their husbands, their assistance as nurses is not without gratifications for the wives as well.

He will discuss medical aspects of his cases. I enjoy it and put in my two cents worth. I give advice and suggestions and so on. . . . I thoroughly enjoyed nursing and the challenge of it and I'm glad he's an internist. He thoroughly loves medicine. He shares more with me because of my nursing background and interest and he is glad to have my feedback. (6)

One wife, with an advanced degree in a medically related field, has kept in unusually close touch with the subject matter and the content of her husband's work. She reads in his medical journals and will occasionally criticize or summarize articles that pertain to his work. He shares his interesting cases with her and, as she noted, "he has even been known to bone up on his basic physiology talking to me." She also attends all the conventions that her husband does and hears papers on new techniques in his field —one in which she herself has research credentials. Indeed it is often difficult to tell where her interests leave off and her husband's begin; she is far more of a collaborator in her husband's work than an assistant or advisor to it. Thus she has been able to keep her own training alive and up to date through her connection with his work, and sustain a kind of informal career of her own until the time when she feels she can return to further study or paid work.

In this respect she resembles a few of the academic wives, who, as collaborators in their husbands' careers, have kept their own careers afloat. These women have all worked on books together with their husbands and have received credit as coauthors, although they do not have full-time or permanent institutional affiliation of their own. In fact, one of the wives, with a Ph.D. of her own, gave up the search for an academic position for herself, and has started a writing project in collaboration with her husband in order to give herself a professional focus.

He started thinking of writing a book and talked of writing it on his sabbatical. . . . I said why wait—I'm not doing anything and I write fairly well and I think we work all right together. He found that idea just fine. . . . I really do want to continue to work on this book and feel confident that we can put out a better-than-average book. I think this will occupy me intensely for two years and I'm already beginning to think of directions to go in after that. (34)

Balance and Reciprocity in the Adjunct Role

Overall the adjunct contribution of the doctor's wife has been heavily weighted in the areas of public and social participation and girl Friday services; the professional advisory or assistant function has been noticeably underdeveloped among these wives. As adjuncts, therefore, medical wives have served their husbands' careers in quite rigidly sex-typed and subordinate ways. Like the services performed in the highly stratified medical division of labor, the adjunct tasks of the medical wife flow upward toward the top to support—and reflect—the work and status of the physician. The practice of medicine is competitive and where it is locally based, it is very difficult for a doctor's wife to escape substantial involvement in social and public life. Almost every medical wife has been quite heavily involved in some combination of auxiliary work, community activity and social life, which serves to promote and/or maintain her husband's professional status.

In contrast, the adjunct involvement of the academic wife has been marked by somewhat more collegiality and flexibility. Her public role in the academic or wider community has been virtually nonexistent and her social role on the departmental level has taken shape easily to fit with her own needs and preferences. As typist and, more importantly, as professional assistant, editor and collaborator, the academic wife contributes directly to the content of her husband's work, though the scientist's wife has done less in this respect than the humanist's wife. Because academic social demands need not loom large, it is possible for the academic wife who neither types nor has the background nor interest to contribute to her husband's work to have virtually no adjunct function at all. This has been true for a number of professors' wives, whose social involvement has been kept to the barest minimum and who have no other adjunct relationship to their husbands' work.

The semicollegial status of the academic wife in her adjunct role is reinforced by the fact that her husband is not merely a recipient of her services, as the medical husband tends to be, but in most instances he has been an active commentator on or contributor to the substance of her own work and interests as well. To be sure, no academic husband has typed for his wife, nor has any academic wife pursued career or other interests in such a way as to compete with the centrality and importance of her husband's career. Although a wife's status has been secondary or subordinate to her husband's in those respects, it is nonetheless true that in other respects the academic husband frequently returns to his wife a good deal of the adjunct support that he receives from her. Most academic wives interviewed did not discuss their interest in or input into their husbands' work without also volunteering comments about their husbands' reciprocal response to the wives' own work or activities. The following quotations show clearly the pattern of easy give-and-take and mutual consultation and support that has grown up between these husbands and wives:

In the past I read less in his field than I do now. I have read what he has written, but I didn't edit it. I would do that now. I used to type his papers and we both worked on his doctoral dissertation, typing around the clock. He reads most of what I write and gives me some feedback. He's just learning how to. He was my best painting critic finally. He said he didn't know anything about painting, but he's turned out to be the critic I listened most to. With my poetry it's more difficult. He's not really motivated to do a lot of reading to train himself. (21)

I don't get involved with typing, but he might ask me to read things that he has written—passages of books. He's looking for advice and he listens. He does the same for me when I write things that are hard for me. We consult with each other. (38)

We have shared some of his reading . . . and we talk about selections for the course together. I certainly have not read all the [literature] that he teaches. Neither does he read all the things about [the field] that I'm involved in, but he does read on occasion, and I do tell him about my experiences. . . . We consult each other a lot. Yes, he has read my things—not so much as I've read of his—but he was very proud of my work when I was a student. . . . (30)

From the very beginning [he] has been a tremendous support of my painting. Once . . . when I was pregnant . . . he just gathered up all those watercolors I was doing and went to the . . . public library and got me a show. I never would have done that for myself. (25)

In some families, an increased or intensified work commitment on the part of the wife has meant a decrease or alteration in the amount of the wife's adjunct participation in her husband's work.

I don't read so much of what he writes any more. I hear less about it since I've been working. . . . I helped my husband a good deal with his work when he was in graduate school—I typed his papers and helped edit. I still help him now but only occasionally. (30)

It was my decision. I really didn't enjoy doing it—typing his papers and technical letters and exams. It really wasn't my function to do that. I raised this issue with him. Yes, it was difficult, but I decided it wasn't the way I wanted my life to be. I was going to live my life a bit more the way I did want it to be. . . . I hadn't been working to mental capacity. . . . It was my decision to go to school. . . . Yes, I do talk about my work. I've gotten very involved in my courses and find them interesting. Oh yes, he is interested. (37)

It is true, of course, that the academic wife is much more likely than the medical wife to have a separate work life and/or well-developed interests of her own that may be pursued in conjunction with her husband. But that fact is not in itself an explanation of the greater reciprocity that exists in the adjunct role of the academic marriage. From its very start the academic marriage was predisposed toward greater mutuality than the medical marriage, and the collegially oriented adjunct participation of the professor's wife grows out of the structure of the academic marriage relationship. The shared professional context within which the adjunct activity of the academic wife frequently occurs is both a congenial complement, as well as contribution, to the academic work role itself. Given the nature of the academic value system, the intellectually accomplished and achieving wife is bound to reflect positively on her husband, perhaps far more so than the woman who lives primarily within the world of social hostessing and civic activities.

On the other hand, the very structure and values of medical work are reflected in the hierarchical, other-directed, status-oriented adjunct role of the medical wife. The way was paved for the development of that role by the very terms of a wife's entry into marriage with her doctor husband. Furthermore, as medical work roles change, the adjunct participation of the wife undergoes a shift in emphasis as well, and there is a new breed of wife by the side of the new breed of doctor, lending further support to the idea that changes in marriage roles and relationships keep pace with changes in professional roles and relationships.

4

LENDING SUPPORT

The instrumental function . . . keeps a group at work and the emotional-expressive
function . . . keeps the group at peace. The person performing the positive
emotional-expressive function does it in these ways—[s]he shows solidarity,
raises the status of others, gives help, rewards, agrees, concurs,
complies, understands, passively accepts.
(*Bernard, 1971:88*)

The man who takes hold of his professional commitment most fully
and most effectively is the man who is free to give his best to his
work. The ideal wife, then, is one who provides her husband with
a support system that enables him both to maximize his professional opportunities and goals, and meet the day-to-day demands
of professional work in a trouble-free state of mind. Unlike her adjunct work, the supportive contribution of the wife is diffuse and
pervasive, consisting more of a generalized stance and set of attitudes and responses that simultaneously sustain, nurture, and bolster her husband's career commitment. Moreover, a wife supports

her husband both actively and passively; at the same time that she reaches out to sympathize and encourage, she also holds herself back and does not hinder.

The functional interrelationship between the support provided by a wife and the occupational role of a husband has been described by Slater:

Having created a technological and social structural juggernaut by which they are daily buffeted, men tend to use their wives as opiates to soften the impact of the forces they have set in motion against themselves. (1970:73–74)

Epstein makes a similar observation—that it is the "job of the woman, the wife and the mother, to provide the safety valve that the family's members require for revitalization in their occupations" (1971:112). Finally, Whyte (1971) elaborates specifically on the wife's role as a nonrole: that is to say, what a woman does not do in support of her husband's career is as important as what she does do, and often, more important. This chapter will explore the connections between the characteristics of a man's professional role and the various ways that his wife lends support to that role.

Patterns of Accommodation and Noninterference

Medical wives experience and perceive medical work as primarily consisting of a set of unalterable givens, which derive from the immediacy and unpredictability of patient needs and, in the case of the private practitioner, the reality of financial considerations. As these wives know it, the work of the physician involves high status and great responsibility. It is largely shaped by external and nondeferrable imperatives to which wives adjust by tailoring their own activities, needs, and preferences to fit into the space and time left over once their husbands' work requirements have been met.

The essentially nondeferrable nature of medical work is illustrated by the response of medical husbands to questions posed (in questionnaire form) to them about the balance of the time in their lives. Only a very few of the men who responded to the questions reported that they were spending less time professionally than they wished. (See table 4.1.) Two of these men have some research ambitions in addition to their work in practice and a third feels that his practice is somewhat precarious financially, with the result that he feels considerable pressure to put in as much time at the office as he can. Even though half of the men feel that they are spending about the right amount of time in their professional work, they are in their own eyes doing so at the expense of their personal time.

Since most medical marriages occurred while the husband was in medical school or doing his specialty training, medical wives were familiar from early marriage with a rigidly imposed schedule of work. For many a medical couple the very timing of the marriage itself was an accommodation to the time requirements of the husband's work.

His chief told him that that day in April was the only day free for him to get married. And I had always wanted to be a June bride. (20).

TABLE 4.1 PERSONAL AND PROFESSIONAL TIME

Use of Time*	M.D. Husbands (N = 13)	Ph.D. Husbands (N = 16)
Spending more time than I wish professionally and less time than I wish personally	2	1
Spending about the right amount of time professionally and less time than I wish personally	7	3
Spending about the right amount of time professionally and personally	1	3
Spending less time than I wish professionally and personally	3	9

*Husbands were asked to indicate whether they are spending *more* time, *less* time, or *as much* time as they wish in each of nine professional and personal areas. Interest here is in the overall use of time in the two areas and the balance between them; therefore, only the summary of individual responses to all items is presented.

He took off his first ten days of residency for our honeymoon. That was his vacation for the year. (17).

We were always moving in July on our anniversary and it was always a disaster. We got married then because it was the end of the medical year. (2)

In deference to what they viewed as the magnitude and importance of doctoring, many wives entered into marriage having already accepted a position of second-class citizenship in relationship both to the status and the time demands of their husbands' work. This self-image is especially prevalent among the old breed of doctors' wives, whose husbands are primarily identified with the traditions and values of solo practice. These wives are resigned to being losers in the contest for their husbands' time and attention, and they express this accommodation in a vocabulary of sexual rivalry:

I knew I would mostly be the second-best thing in his life; medicine would always come first. (18)

He said early in the game that his first love was medicine and I would always have to play second fiddle. (11)

The marriages that work are the ones that understand that when you say "I do" it's to Madame Medicine. (1)

[He] is very devoted to medicine. I've never been threatened by this because I knew when I married him that this was going to be the way he would practice. (15)

I thought he needed me then but he didn't. His pathology exam was more important. I understand, but even sex has always played like tenth place. Everything else came before that. It's been a big, big problem and disappointment. That's a really big put-down for a woman. I never came first, never. A doctor I worked for once told me before I got married that until you learn that your husband is married to two women and one is a very demanding wife, you'll never be happy. So I figured medicine was number one and that was it. . . .(2)

I don't think there are any rules about how a doctor's wife should behave. She might have to exercise a little more patience than another woman with respect to time. If a woman needs a lot of tender loving care it's a profession to stay away from. (16)

Many of these women of the old breed, who see their roles as wives as extensions of their husbands' service commitment, place a positive valuation on their uncomplaining acceptance of the stringent and companionship-depriving medical work schedule, particularly during the years of internship and residency. Self-sacrifice is worn like a badge of maturity.

The army people were very nice to us and it was a good experience. I found the army wives per se very interesting. They had lived in so many places and they were unspoiled in that they'd known hardship with their husbands being away so much. (15)

I was the world's worst service wife. I hated it when he went off on maneuvers. I was also not good—I was miserable—during his residency and I was miserable on the days he was home knowing that he would be gone the next day. I gradually matured through that. . . . It was a painful growing-up process. (6)

The new breed of doctor's wife, whose husband works in a group or hospital setting, is apt to find the language of submission less congenial and is more likely to express her accommodation in the language of independence. It is a paradoxically subordinate independence, however, for what the new breed wife is really referring to are not her own autonomous achievements, but the ways in which she keeps busy in her husband's absence, thereby reducing her dependence on his companionship. In this respect she is little different from the old breed of medical wife and the distance between the two groups is more verbal than behavioral. Whether a woman expresses her accommodation to her husband's career in terms of independence or passive acceptance, the functional consequences are the same. Either way, compliance and noninterference with the professional commitment result.

My expectations for what being a wife meant were a little shattered initially. When I arrived he was on—it was during the end of his internship. He was living with one single bed in one room. He worked for twenty-four hours plus eight during that time. The living quarters were very close and I never saw him. I was really very depressed. I took some courses and kept pretty busy. I'm a fairly in-

83

dependent person and I did make an effort to get out and explore the city. (7)

I knew our whole life would revolve around his work. . . . I need to get out a few hours a day and really don't mind being home. I don't want a relationship where I am dominant in work. . . . The most important thing for a doctor's wife is to be independent. You have to have a life not of your own, but your own interests. (4)

You have to be an independent person but not to the point where you're separate. (3)

In the beginning I was very irritated by it [his hours] and you just adjust. But I think it would be hard if I were sitting home doing nothing; it would be terrible. I'm not that kind of person. I like to be doing things. . . . This year is a great year for me because I'm busy and have a lot of energy. When I'm happy he's happy. I get depressed when I'm not busy. . . . He simply does not function in a disturbed environment; equanimity is very important to him. (19)

I think my husband would have expected that I would have been involved with my career—much more than I am now. But I also think he wouldn't like it to be too interfering once he got home. (12)

It helps to be independent. I wouldn't be very happy waiting to see my husband three hours a day at the most. (17)

Within the overall framework of passive or subordinate accommodation that a medical wife makes to her husband's work, there are a host of more specific and daily ways in which she sets aside her own plans and preferences in the interest of not interfering with her husband's professional commitment. Repeatedly wives talked of meals delayed and gone cold, social engagements called off at the last minute or attended alone, the need to travel in separate cars on "on-call" evenings, birthdays celebrated in the absence of husband and father. One wife, whose husband has spent his entire career in solo practice, eloquently described her "lifetime of interruptions":

I thought it would be Utopia. About fifteen years ago I had a conversation with another doctor who had a nine-to-five-job in medicine and didn't know what it was like to be doctor's wife. He was talking about what a great life it was and I told him it stunk. It's pretty bad when you get in bed and you're making love and you hear the g——d—— phone ring. It interrupts arguments, it interrupts meals, but sex is the ultimate of interruptions. (10)

As the above quotation suggests, there are some doctors' wives who accommodate themselves to their husbands' work commitments and the priority of those commitments in their lives with less than cheerful acceptance. Perhaps the least happy of the medical wives are the ones who realize that the pace of their husbands' work reflects not merely the unpredictable imperatives of patient care, but the husbands' active preference to be spending time at work over and above what is required. It seems easier for many medical wives to accept the schedule of their husbands' work if they can view it as a necessity rather than a choice.

I try to make him unavailable when we go out, but if a good friend calls, he can't say no. . . . I don't think he needs to work as hard as he does. . . . Technically he's home from Friday night 'til Monday morning on the weekends he's off. It doesn't actually work that way though. . . . Last Saturday he did surgery in the morning. . . . . I sometimes feel that anyone in the city could call and he'd go. (11)

Now that he has a partner, all coverage is divided in half. Supposedly he should be able to get home earlier because of that. It hasn't seemed to work out that way though, He still goes to the hospital twice a day. (9)

Doctors themselves often invoke the hardship of medical working hours as justification for the high financial rewards of medical practice. It is interesting to note, however, that in spite of their heavy workload and the mental concentration that it requires, a study of family physicians finds these men reporting the "greatest amount of satisfaction with their jobs, low levels of anxiety and depression and irritation and few somatic disorders such as difficulty in sleeping, loss of appetite, or fast heartbeat" (Institute for Social Research, *Newsletter* 1975:3). This suggests that the internal imperatives and rewards of medical practice are equally as motivating as the external rewards and imperatives.

Doctors who devote unusually long hours to their practice earn the admiration of their patients, but their wives react more ambivalently as they are made to feel guilty and petty if they make claims on their husbands' time that detract from the lofty imperatives of medical practice. A wife, then, is left with the difficult task of reconciling her own feelings and experience of her secondary status in her husband's life with the very different experience and response that the public has toward her doctor husband.

It's a very difficult life especially for a wife because she doesn't have the calling. A good doctor is dedicated. The woman has married the man and not the doctor. She has no way of knowing what that means until they get married. The practice comes first. The wife shares her husband—he takes the call and she is expected to understand and accept with no complaint. She doesn't have the calling, though. She has to make the sacrifice; to him it's a challenge. But the wife doesn't know the person. The patient is nobody as far as she's concerned and her own plans are put into the background. This has happened many, many times. He's a superb doctor and has a fantastic relationship with patients. He gets a daily self-lifting from others. (10)

Another wife, married to an internist, recounts her vivid fantasy of offering an explosive challenge to a roomful of her husband's hero-worshippers: "This man is not Jesus Christ! He does not walk on water! Let me tell you what he's like at home!" Then she added sadly:

I don't know why I can't be happy in a marriage to a guy everybody else thinks is great. He's got everything most women say they want. But he does not fulfill me. His needs get met in his practice. Everyday he's God to somebody. (2)

The nature of academic work is such that a wife's accommodation to her husband's career in university teaching is both less self-conscious and less self-depriving than that of the doctor's wife. The academic, much more than the doctor, responds to his work as a set of internal rather than external imperatives. The inner-directed orientation toward the definition of work and accomplishments means that academic work is to some extent deferable and its schedule adjustable. Even though virtually all of the academic wives describe their husbands as adhering to a rigorous and tightly organized schedule of daily work, a wife's knowledge that her husband's schedule is potentially alterable gives rise to a complex emotion—she feels she is not a victim of his work, but at the same time she makes concessions to it.

Now being an academic does give you the flexibility—if some morning like over the summer he wanted to take off a morning to go fishing, he did that. Or if something comes up and he needs to be at home at four and he doesn't have a meeting or is in the middle of research and is not tied up he can come home. (36)

There's no one looking over his shoulder and he's only responsible to himself as far as how he spends his time. If there is a real necessity family-wise or any other time he can take an afternoon off with a free conscience and make it up sometime somewhere else. He likes the idea that he doesn't have to punch a time clock and that in many ways he is his own boss. (32)

In a sense he probably puts in more hours than other people; it's just divided differently. The work goes on seven days a week. . . . I don't think it's the ivory tower that other people think it is . . . but in a way it is a less stressful life in that you can organize it yourself. You are an independent agent. (28)

However, the inner-directedness of academic work yields not only flexibility but a particular kind of anxiety, the pervasive feeling that work is either never done or, once done, is never adequate.

During every waking hour the conscientious college professor feels driven by his inadequate preparation for teaching, by the books he has not yet read, the articles not yet written, the ideas not yet clearly formulated. Inside and outside the classroom and the laboratory he carries this guilty load, and it creates for him a sense of strain and indeed a continuity of labor not adequately reflected in the formal teaching schedule. That is why the professor often feels overworked; he may have a sense of working terribly hard when no one else can see that he is doing anything. Indeed, he *may* be working hard when no one else can see that he is working at all. It is also possible for him to mislead himself into believing that he is working hard when in fact he is only dreading it. (Stoke, as quoted in Millett 1962:74)

For many academic men the feeling of never having completed the work at hand is a constant companion to the academic commitment. That is reflected in the responses of the academic husbands to questions about their use of personal and professional time. (See table

4.1.) More than half of those answering feel that they are spending less time than they wish professionally as well as personally. In contrast to the doctors, then, few professors feel that they are meeting their own professional time requirements. Wives comment that their husbands' drivenness affects the marriage relationship both psychologically and in terms of time spent together.

Summer is just a more intense work time. We never go anywhere. Usually we take some long weekends with the children. That's the type of time off that we take. In summer we just live the kind of life we live in winter without any interference at all. We just set our own schedule, but it remains work time. He never takes time off from his research. He always has more than one project going at a time. Summer is also a time to reevaluate all the work he has done during the winter. . . . He does consider himself successful, but that's sort of irrelevant because he always is thinking in terms of what he is going to do in his work. He has a really ideal standard. (23)

My husband is meticulous, ultra, ultra conservative, careful. Every line he writes has to be checked, verified. Every line he writes has to be perfect. He's really a perfectionist and not everybody is that way and it's hard for him to work with someone whose standards are not as high as his. . . . We don't do much on weekends. My husband does not like to go places and Sunday he works all day. Saturday mornings he usually goes into the lab if he's not taking our son to soccer. He has decided to set a good example to his graduate students who he feels do not put in as much work as they should. (35)

While the pace and intensity of medical practice vary little from workday to workday or from year to year, there is a kind of ebb and flow in academic life due partly to the seasonality of the academic calendar and partly to the cyclical nature of research and writing. The essentially static quality of medical practice is reflected in a wife's feeling that she must permanently and consistently occupy an unobtrusive and subordinate position in relation to her husband's work. But because of the variation and fluctuation over time in the kind of work being done, the timetables for that work, and the particular demands of the work, the academic wife is more apt than the medical wife to feel that her husband's lengthy and unpredictable hours and her exclusion from her husband's life occur on a task-specific and therefore time-limited basis. Her accommodation to her husband's work is often experienced as either temporary or potentially changeable, rather than as permanent and fixed.

I helped him to get established in those early years by understanding about his hours and why he had to spend them. If I hadn't it would have detracted from what he had to do. (38)

We spend maybe an hour or an hour-and-a-half together in a day. It's been very bad lately because he's under a lot of pressure getting a grant ready. (33)

I used to feel sort of put upon in the early years when he was working eighteen hours a day. Since there seemed to be a sort of higher goal I understood he wasn't doing that selfishly. (27)

This year I haven't seen him since April. He's been writing and is very involved in this translation. We spent the summer together but I was really all by myself. I most definitely notice a difference when he is writing and it's coming to an end right now so that every spare minute when he is home from teaching he is up there working and I really don't see him at all. . . . It goes in cycles when he is getting a book ready to be published or a translation ready for a deadline. (26)

His schedule is more predictable now; that was not so when he was doing research around the clock. When things are growing you have to do what you have to do. It's better now in the past few years. You have more grad students who can run back and forth to the lab and do these things. When we were grad students he came home for supper and went back to work 'til ten or so and that was a four year stretch. . . . That evening lab pattern was pretty continuous from graduate student days up until a few years ago. Then he was teaching and now he is administering so he has to do other things. (36)

He took the job here as assistant head of the department and then he was on one administrative committee after another. . . . He does like it but he wants to know what it would be like to live as a professor who taught. So that in fact he suddenly has all this time he never had before. In the past he was at the university a large part of every day. Now he is essentially there for his classes and can be home by three-thirty. (21)

Whereas the medical wife most often feels that she cannot legitimately question or complain about the amount of time her husband spends at work, the academic wife knows full well that her husband's work pace is to a large degree a matter of his personal preference and satisfaction. While she may respect those as imperatives in themselves she is also freer to challenge or complain about the toll that his work commitment takes on her.

The biggest difficulty is that he is so totally absorbed in his work. I think if he were less interested in his work, he would be more interested in leisure-time activities. Those men who want to go places all the time are the ones who are not as happy with what they are doing professionally. He is very intense and wrapped up in his work and it just doesn't leave much time. (35)

He takes his work very seriously and doesn't have enough time in the routine nine-to-five hours doing what he wants to do. As a function of that he spends a lot of time outside of those hours doing academic work. He doesn't have any set vacations and on holidays quite often he will go in and work. . . . I suppose to a certain extent for a while I repressed or subdued my own life or life style and the kinds of things I enjoyed doing so that he had the time to work and I was able to do work for him. . . . The work he does is voluntary . . . it's his satisfaction. . . . (37)

By the same token the academic husband himself is probably far more likely than the medical husband to have a relative rather than absolute sense of his own importance professionally. The doctor, after all, enjoys extraordinary authority in his role, reaps considerable financial rewards from his work, and evaluates his own merits as a practitioner pretty much on the basis of his standing in the local rather than the wider medical community. The academic, in contrast, has little authority over others in ways that matter to them deeply and personally, lives on a fixed and not overly generous income, and must reckon with the modesty of his own accomplishments compared to those of the most prestigious and productive members of his discipline. The doctor's sense of success, like his work itself, is externally derived and tangibly demonstrated; for the academic, success is more often a matter of personal and inner definition. Many academic wives spoke of the process by which their husbands came to terms, so to speak, with the adequacy and scope of their professional accomplishments:

Yes, I think he does consider himself successful. He's had a moderate career—you have to be honest with yourself in your forties. You know that you are not going to be the greatest critic that ever lived and you are not going to write the last word on anything maybe. But you've written a couple of good things and you have a decent life. (30)

I think he has a good reputation in his field, but I don't think either he or I would say he is a top man with a name that is on the tip of your tongue, but he is very well regarded. He's aware of his own abilities. Maybe he could have done something more monumental but he realized that you can't do that without killing yourself. He does the work he wants to. (27)

He's well aware of the fact that he's never going to be world famous but to people who work in the same or related fields his name is known and well thought of. . . . I think he saw in his four years as a graduate student that he did not want to emulate some of the people he knew there—even though he respected them . . . he did not want that kind of life for himself. He was exposed to people who were very high caliber [scientists] and that made him aware of what quality means. . . . He had the opportunity to realize what he could do in the sense of self-assurance but the choice was his whether to follow in their footsteps or do something else. His choice was to follow something else and not follow this extremely high-pressured type of life. (32)

The language of deference and subordination which the medical wife uses to describe her noninterference with and accommodation to her husband's career seems to flow directly from the rather absolute nature of medical practice itself both as regards the imperatives of time and the status and authority of the practitioner. The academic wife sees herself not so much as having to step down but to step aside in order to accommodate the time requirements of her husband's career. As an academic husband comes to terms with a relative definition of his own success, a diminished or circumscribed time commitment often results. It also opens up for the wife the possibility of a relative pattern of accommodation—one that is chosen rather than imposed upon her—and she may come to feel that she too can lay claim to some choices for herself, similar to those her husband made earlier in his life.

Moving On

A wife's accommodation to her husband's work involves an acceptance of the career's mobility requirements, not just an accommodation to its time requirements. The successful professional career is built on the assumption that a person is free to move from one location to another, in search of the best professional opportunities, or to remain in one place if that is necessary to meet a professional commitment or to build professional standing. For both medical and academic couples geographic mobility in the early years of marriage was linked to the husbands' professional education and training. During the early training period, the husband's career needs were almost always the sole determining factor in the geography of the marriage, but those career needs did not yet reflect a husband's long-range sense of his own professionalism, nor did they involve any permanent commitment to a particular locale. When the time came to make the longer term or even permanent commitment to a teaching position or medical practice, however, the process of deciding where to move became more complex, both for the professional husband himself and at least potentially for his family as well.

Holmstrom comments that it is "advantageous for career advancement if a person can decide where to live without taking into account the interests of the other members of the family" (1973:30). Since all of the men in the study were able to search out places in which to teach or practice, free from any but their own career considerations, they can be said to have enjoyed just such an advantage. The great majority of medical and academic wives had no specifically formulated career plans or goals for themselves to bring to bear on any decision to move. Those few wives who did have more focused career aspirations for themselves fit them in and around their husbands' needs.

Yes, the second time he visited here I came too because I had reservations about the area. I said never in the world. I wanted to live in a city. . . . I wanted a place with cultural attractions . . . but considerations of my own work were not primary. The only thing I did when my husband visited here was to speak with a [physician in my field] in the community. But I wasn't looking for work. (12)

At the time he was looking for jobs it was a choosing situation. He had several job offers. It was the heyday of science in the 60s and money was available. We like New England and he was favorably impressed with the department and the people in it. We did consider possibilities for me and one of the reasons we chose this area was that if a nepotism rule existed at the university it would not necessarily stop me from finding a job since there were other institutions here. Both of us felt that when the kids were in school I would get a traditional academic job. . . . It was naive though. (34)

As far as a job for me, no such considerations were taken into account; there was a job available for him and we came here. (22)

The fact that the needs of the budding career were of primary importance in the determination of where the family was to move does not mean, however, that that decision was necessarily uncongenial to the wives themselves or that it did not take into account a variety of other interests unconnected with the career. The physician or surgeon, especially, has a fairly wide range of choice as to the location of his practice. As an entrepreneur who is in the business of delivering services that are almost everywhere in chronically short supply, the doctor knows that he is virtually guaranteed a generous income and the high status that goes with it just about anywhere he locates. Often, therefore, the young doctor is able to pick and choose from a number of possible options that might be professionally acceptable to him. Although the organizationally based academic selects from a less extensive list of available positions, at the time the academics who are part of this book were establishing their careers (in the late 1950s through the 1960s), many universities were expanding their faculty ranks in an effort to build outstanding departments. Almost every academic husband had at least two, if not more, job possibilities open to him when the time came for him to join the junior ranks of a faculty.

In such situations, where the husband was able to choose from at least a few and sometimes several professional openings, it was usually not difficult to find a teaching or practice situation that combined optimal professional advantages for the husband with a location and way of life that had general appeal for his wife and family as well. So long as a wife was looking to satisfy only general or rather diffuse interests and was not in search of highly specific career or other opportunities for herself, her requirements could be actively incorporated into her husband's search for a job. Most of the women interviewed have not been dissatisfied with the places where their husband's work has brought them.

[This,] is a nice town to raise children. We had five children by the time he had his first job. [The university] was growing then and he liked the people. He did consider other possibilities at the time, but this had everything he was looking for. He came up first and then I came with him. I would go wherever he wanted to go. He asked me if I liked the area and would not take the job until I saw it. (39)

His father was in practice here. He never considered any other location for practice. . . . I don't know if his father always expected him to be in practice with him, but [my husband] always assumed he would come back. I knew when we married that we would end up in ———. It was all right with me. I was brought up in the old-fashioned way that you went where your husband went. I have enjoyed the size of the town and the location. (11)

I'm originally from ——— and we decided that we did like the east coast, so we went out so many hundreds of miles in various directions. He was interested in an associateship rather than solo practice. He corresponded with a surgeon who then decided to retire and offered him the practice to take over. It was a very attractive offer—we liked the area and surgeons [in his speciality] were needed so we began in solo practice. (16)

He felt that he wasn't really growing that much professionally there. He wanted a more dynamic department. We wanted to be on the east coast because our families are there. . . . We felt that it was our responsibility to remain close. So New England was the ideal area. . . . It was really sheer luck that he got a call asking if he was interested in a position here at the university. So he came down for the interview and felt that the job was his after the interview . . . and fell in love with the place the first time we drove up to look for a house. We had both decided to take the job. (28)

Once the move was actually made, however, many academic wives found the initial settling-in period to be a rather difficult and lonely time for them. Precisely because the medical profession has such a strong sense of itself as a cohesive social group and sensitivity to its standing in the wider community, the medical wife whose husband was new to practice found herself immediately welcomed in a highly organized fashion into the social life of the medical community and into the other social, cultural, and civic activities of the larger community as well. As academic social life is far less extensive and cohesive, the wife was often left very much on her own when she arrived with her husband in a new place. At the same time she felt it necessary to lend support to her husband's career by not leaning too heavily on her husband for companionship at a time when his major energy should be directed toward successfully establishing himself in his new position.

It was a year of certainly hard work for him. He had classes six days a week and all new preparations. As for myself I found it very hard to adjust to a new situation. I had been in an academic surrounding for so long and suddenly here I was in this tiny little apartment not knowing anybody. (22)

Our first daughter was born two months after we moved here. I hadn't met anyone before that. That may account for the depression I felt. I had no interests in common with the neighbors and there were no social get-togethers in the department. (40)

The only thing is that we made the mistake of being in a house that was very isolated. I had a baby and I didn't know how to drive. I had always lived in the city and used public transportation. There I was in the woods and I couldn't even see the street. . . . My husband was really busy then and always had to go back to the lab at night. That was really bad because I was eager to move out and get going. . . . I've never been a clubwoman and I never really met too many people I wanted to associate with. (35)

Moving is very hard—I think it is hard for a woman. You don't have something to throw yourself into. A man throws himself into a job, buries himself in his work and doesn't have to deal with the loneliness and time on your hands. . . . Brand-new friends are not built into the day the way they are at work. I was enormously unhappy. (25)

In the medical career the peak of geographic mobility tends to be confined to the years of education and training; the establishment of a private practice typically involves permanent residence. All of the medical wives whose husbands are in private practice consider themselves to be permanently settled where they are. No wife thought it likely that her husband would ever make the effort to build another practice in another place, nor did she forsee any serious possibility that her husband would change the direction of his career altogether in a way that might require the family to move.

In the academic career, though, the potential for mobility is always present, in later as in early stages of the career. In about half of the academic families, the husband's present teaching job was not his first one, although most of the men had held only one teaching post before accepting their current university appointment. But the present teaching position is not necessarily the last. About two-thirds of all the academic wives mentioned that, for a variety of reasons, their husbands are very open to the possibility of a move in the future. Either they are dissatisfied with the present "quality of life" in the department specifically or at the university generally, or they somehow do not feel that they have completed their quest for recognition and success. The hospital-based physician also has an organizational career and the wives of those doctors sounded very like the academic wives in their discussion of the bigger and better things that might lie ahead for their husbands in another place. When the wives of all of these potentially mobile husbands were asked what their own reaction to a move would be after being settled for so many years in their present homes, their response was virtually unanimous support for the primacy of their husbands' career goals.

My feeling is that his profession is something he's worked so long for and I can pick up a job anywhere. The most difficult part would be for the children; they love it here. This community is all they've ever known. (8)

Absolutely my major concern is that [he] be happy in his work because then he's easier to live with and life in general is better if he's happy doing what he's doing. If a negative situation arose with his job here, I would not hesitate to go. But I am very happy here. (32)

On a practical level I plan to stay with [my husband] and wherever he is I will accommodate my professional interests to that place. (21)

The Wife as Advocate

As a wife a woman supports her husband's professional commitment not only by the various ways in which she more or less passively accommodates to his work, but by her active advocacy both of the kind of work he does and the way he does it. Her advocate expression seems both to underlie and justify the shape of her accommodation to her husband's career.

The wife believes in her husband's professional worth and views her husband's work—whether medical or academic—extrinsically in terms of the value or the importance of the work itself and the skill and proficiency required to do it. She sees him as a model or exemplar of superior professionalism. The pride (bordering on hero-worship among some doctors' wives) that a wife takes in her husband's competence and accomplishment undoubtedly helps to compensate for any disappointment—even anger—that she experiences as a consequence of the long hours he spends in the pursuit of his career and the loss of time together that this entails:

Medically speaking he's the greatest diagnostician in [the area]. He's a superb doctor with a fantastic relationship with patients. (10)

He is compulsive and dedicated to his work. He sweats through every case he has; he's very attentive to details and every one is different. He feels reassured knowing he is overtrained; it means his standards are very high. . . . He's the very best . . . surgeon in the whole [area]. I'm being objective of course but I'm also his wife. (20)

He saves so many people and people are so grateful they write poetry about him. . . . He's been given these abilities to serve mankind. (15)

I have respect for what he does and what he can do. I would never hesitate to say to anyone he's the best in what he does and no one is finer. (14)

I'm proud to be married to someone who is making a contribution to society. . . . Patients tell me how nice it is when he comes to see

97

them because he's never in a hurry. That's part of what makes him good, so he should be that way. If that's one of the things he does, then I'll just have to put up with it. He has no conception of time at all.(19)

He's very good on committees and good in dealing with people. He's low-key and efficient. He's just a natural, it's obvious. Anyone could look at him for just twenty minutes and see that there is a natural-born department chair. (24)

He couldn't work more hard; you can't work harder than from eight in the morning until one at night—seven days a week. . . . He subscribes to every periodical in his field. . . . He probably reads more in his field than anyone in the department. He does a lot of extra reading and is always sorting slides and preparing lectures—trying to make it easier for students to understand. . . . As far as teaching goes he is probably the best person in his department. (29)

A wife frequently advocates her husband's professionalism on intrinsic grounds as well, in terms of the personal satisfaction that he derives from his work and achievements. This style of advocacy is particularly characteristic of the academic wife. In this respect a wife's commitment to her husband's professionalism is an extension of her personal commitment to him in marriage. Although many wives mentioned that they married the man and not the professional, the distinction is really an artificial one, because at the time most of these couples met and married, who a husband was as a person was in fact inseparable from who he was becoming as a professional. When a woman married she invariably married a man with a dual identity—that of husband *and* physician, or surgeon, or scientist, or writer, or historian, and so on. Because they care about their husbands, these wives care about their husbands' work and express their understanding that work is a primary source of confirmation and validation of worth.

Yes, he could work less hard. He has tenure. He doesn't have to prove anything. He's secure and doesn't have to set foot in that lab if he doesn't wish to. But then he may as well wither away. He could but I don't think he should for his own sake. Which also means that he's content. I'm not going to have his problems to deal with if he's happy doing what he's doing. (40)

I realized that [he] would get a big kick out of his work and that that would take some time and that he would need to get a kick out of his work in order to be happy. It's not just a job for a paycheck. (38)

He's a good doctor and his rewards come from that. No matter how good you are, he's always striving to do better. He's very achievement-oriented. (8)

Medicine is incredibly gratifying to him. He gets a lot of feedback and it stimulates him to contribute. (7)

He thinks he's very good and I think he's very good. He's just had a bad setback and that is why he's working so compulsively now. He feels good when friends that he respects tell him that things are good and the published word means a great deal to him. When he's well reviewed he's happy and when he is badly reviewed it depresses him. (26)

Interestingly, though perhaps not surprisingly, the medical wife quite often describes her husband's rewards as a doctor as being inextricably bound up with his status and autonomy. It happened repeatedly that a doctor's wife would quickly shift from a discussion of the personal satisfaction her husband obtains from his private practitioner role to a defense of the status quo of the present shape of the health care system overall, and opposition to any change that threatens to make her husband less of his own boss. Her personal advocacy of the nature and source of her husband's work satisfaction amounts, therefore, to a form of political advocacy as well.

It's a difficult life and it's a life that is changing. You aren't as much your own man as you used to be. So many things are controlling him. He's been through malpractice twice. . . . That interferes with treatment. You worry that everybody you see in the office might start suing. And the bill gets higher for the patient. . . . The financial part of medicine these days is hard with Medicaid and so on. Insurance decides what they are going to pay for and it's not based on what the doctor has ordered for the patient. . . . He finally had to begin to have the patients absorb what Medicaid would't cover. It's always seen as the very rich doctor's fault. The government is giving out erroneous information about how doctors practice. (10)

The least rewarding part of his work is the lack of understanding on the part of the general public as to what medicine and doctoring are all about. People expect him to have a lot of money and talk to him about business. That bothers him. . . . He is frustrated by state interference and state requirements. . . . People don't understand what affects the statistics of health care and that's not just how doctors practice. (13)

He would rather not see his son go into medicine. He's had a very satisfying career, but it just isn't like it used to be with all the government take-over and constant fight with the insurance companies. . . . He really cares about the individual person and wants to be able to spend time with them. (18)

One of the hard things for him has been seeing the hospital hiring full-time doctors. One house officer questioned [him] about how he was treating his patient. There are frictions between the full-time hospital physician and the private practitioner—who is going to decide and control. [He] resented the interference. It's very much a concern of all doctors—it's all right to question, but he had the feeling that they were telling him how to practice medicine. (3)

Quite apart from the pride that a wife may take in her husband's professional accomplishments and the satisfaction she derives from his sense of professional well-being, a wife often feels directly rewarded by her husband's profession in ways that are themselves the basis for her support and advocacy of his career. Although a medical wife may defer to her husband's status, she clearly gains from it as well. Doctors' wives showed considerable preoccupation with the prestige and the money associated with their husbands' work. Several were quite matter-of-fact about the benefits they reap in these respects.

I have an opening. People know I'm Mrs. ———— . It gives me some standing. The woman I work with knows my husband is a doctor and that helps her out. . . . A doctor's wife can add to her business, it can add social contacts. (4)

Many places I go they ask if I'm Dr. ———— 's wife and then mention how good and kind he is. (15)

[Does he have to work as hard as he does?] I don't know how well he gears his time. . . . He could cut back his private practice but then we wouldn't have the enjoyment and the income. (19)

Absolutely not—I would not want my daughters to marry doctors.
. . . But to tell you the truth as far as my girls are concerned, if it
was a choice between that—marrying a doctor or being on food
stamps and struggling, I'd tell them to do it. Because I've done that
too. Up until three or four years ago the money didn't matter to me.
But I don't think I could go back to that. The money is important to
me. (2)

One can forget about the money issue in medicine. You take the income for granted. (12)

I enjoy knowing about happy, satisfied patients and I get a kick out
of having someone say how much they think of my husband. (11)

On the other hand, many medical wives either do not wish to
admit to the financial benefit of medical practice or genuinely lack
perspective on how high their husbands' earnings are in comparison to other occupations. More than one woman expressed her resentment of the public image of the rich doctor and insisted that her
husband had to sustain his present work pace in order to be able to
make ends meet and to provide for their children's education.
Clearly, however, these ideas of what is financially necessary for a
family are meshed with what is, in fact, financially possible in
terms of a doctor's potential earnings. These wives' expectations are
such that they are, in effect, encouraging a pace of work on their
husbands' parts that will be reflected in their incomes. What many
would define as economic privilege, the medical family regards as
economic necessity, so that the wife supports her husband's career
commitment on grounds of financial need.

Financially if we could feel that the cost of education was at a peak
we would be happy. We had thought we could figure on the
amount of $20,000 for each kid [of five]. But inflation makes things
unpredictable. And the [two boys] are bright and they might go on
to graduate school and we would have to support them. . . . The
money aspect of his practice is important only to help us live the
way we want to, not to have money to pass on to the kids. (3)

Our most difficult times financially are coming up. The three children will be in college at once and if one decided to go to graduate
school then it will be never-ending. (9)

I think he might limit his practice to have more time, but while the
children are young and then going to college he needs to maintain
his practice as it is. (7)

101

I think that he would not like to get into a much different way of living. He would like to be able to enjoy life and retire in ten years. He can't because we'll have two children in college. He never wants to be financially strained; his biggest hang-up is financial security. He wants to keep living the way we are. I'm very happy living the way we are—I don't need a lot of things. I would like my swimming pool though. (4)

Although many academic couples worry a good deal about money, or more specifically the lack of it in their lives, the academic wife does not typically advocate her husband's profession on the grounds of its financial rewards. She is much more likely to feel personally and qualitatively rewarded by the academic way of life as such and what she feels that has to offer her. Whereas most medical wives have either grudgingly or graciously accepted their husband's profession as a necessary accompaniment to the men they married, the academic wife often expressed a positive predisposition to the academic life style, quite apart from her own husband's involvement in it.

I had always known I would be an academic wife. I've spent all my life around schools. It's a very familiar kind of existence. The academic life is the only one I've ever known personally. There are just certain kinds of people I wouldn't have been drawn to. (32)

Yes, it did appeal to me that my husband was an academic. I'm sure I never would have married anyone who was not an academic. . . . I thought of people living together in a special kind of community. . . . Yes, I did look forward to helping him with his work and living in a house full of books—that sort of thing. (29)

I love being in the academic community and the chance to sit in on a variety of courses in different fields—from literature to calculus. We do enjoy the music. I love the atmosphere. (34)

It's an intellectual ghetto. . . . It has its drawbacks but it's an environment I can swim in much more easily than I can in most other environments—even the subcultures. (24)

In a large part, though, academics put me into a setting where I could then further my own interests—which had to do with painting and music. It's an intellectually energetic community and the setting offers things to me for myself. (21)

I am very happy that he chose this life; nobody in either of our families is in academic life. . . . We feel so fortunate—we have so much time together and by its very nature it's so much more rewarding than selling paper clips or ads for shoe polish or whatever. You do feel as though you are in a worth-while thing. It's a life of mind; my husband really enjoys it very much and he can't help but be happy a good deal of the time. (30)

In contrast to the quantitative rewards from her husband's career for the medical wife, the rewards for the academic wife are qualitative, reflecting the different reward structures of the two professions themselves.

The Supportive Environment of Home

The discussion so far has centered on the patterns of accommodation and advocacy that constitute a wife's generally supportive stance toward her husband's work. In addition, however, a wife may show more direct and daily support for her husband's need to be trouble-free in his work by establishing the sort of home setting and interactions that will best nourish, revitalize, and bolster his career performance.

The academic wife (the humanist's wife in particular) has a unique responsibility for providing her husband with a satisfactory setting in which to work at home. Both the scientist's wife and the doctor's wife have adjusted to the kind and schedule of work that takes their husbands away from home into the hospital, office, or laboratory for long working hours of each day. The academic humanist, though, is quite apt to feel that his teaching and scholarly pursuits are somewhat incompatible, if not mutually exclusive, with regard to work setting. Students do not carry out research for the humanist professor in the way that they do for the scientist, and the humanist usually follows a pattern, begun in his graduate-student days when office space was scarce or nonexistent, of centering his main writing activity in a home study in order to be free of the distractions and interruptions of the departmental office.

Many wives enjoy the husband's presence, if not his active company, at home during the day, but there are times when a man's work at home has also been experienced as something of an imposition and a constraint on other members of the family, whose own schedules and use of the home have been restricted in the interest of the husband's work requirements.

I think of it as he used to pamper himself. He would be writing something and we all had to tiptoe around and be considerate. . . . In graduate school with small babies around he always had to find a place to work at home. (30)

I feel somewhat restricted as to what I can do in the house when he works here. I can't listen to music in the morning. . . . Also he doesn't like baby sitters here. When he's working intensively he likes a quiet house and doesn't want to have to worry about it. . . . My husband's work needs define our routines here. (23)

The one project I remember most vividly was the book he was writing when we were [on sabbatical] because we had a new baby and he was writing in the middle of the dining room and every time I wanted to do anything I had to move him out and get rid of his papers. (27)

He works at home. . . . He has himself in what was the nursery which has its own bath and two doors between it and the rest of the house and our clarinet-playing son lives above it and he has to practice down here in the kitchen at night. Which means that any thinking I have to do in the kitchen is very difficult in the evening . . . the sound really penetrates. . . . Usually when he prepares for classes he doesn't require silence. Right now he is working every spare minute so that the children play out with their friends in the afternoon—they can't play in. This was true when the children were little too, though he wasn't working all the time. It goes in cycles. . . . But in general we have taught the children to be quiet when they are in the house. (26)

Although men require independence from the domestic setting in order to do their work, the academic husband, especially, often seems peculiarly dependent on domesticity in other respects. For medical husbands home is seen primarily as a place of leisure and respite, and by some as an arena into which they may extend their professional role as a dominant authority figure, but many academic husbands look to home as a source of nurturing. In what is a kind of "man's home is his castle" approach, they seem to draw sustenance from being able to order the flow of domestic routines around them and to count on their wives to be present and attentive in particular sorts of ways.

But if I don't talk to him he becomes very upset by this. He likes me to talk about general things—funny things an animal did or a bird I saw or something the neighbors did, which he considers to be completely superfluous and stupid remarks, utterly devoid of any intellectual content. He does not want an intellectual conversation at mealtime. . . . He told me that Greek men wanted their wives to teach them that there is something in their lives besides going to work every morning and to keep them sane. That's what he wants. He wants a conversation going that he can listen to and doesn't have to listen to if he doesn't want—like people who have the radio or TV on but don't listen. (29)

He likes to get up early in the morning together and make a fire in the fireplace and start the morning together. I go right out of my mind some mornings—the sameness bores the hell out of me. I find myself imagining I am a gypsy. He loves it—it makes him feel strong. . . . He likes blind adoration. . . . He draws his creativity from his family. (25)

He really requires a lot of attention. More attention than he gets in his view. He would like a wife who would hover a little more than I hover—be concerned about his clothes, what he eats, when he goes to bed. . . . My husband is very dependent. He doesn't like to be left alone and have to do things in the house for himself. (35)

He has a strong need to have me here. I have never experienced his going out the way he experiences my going out. (23)

Since the evidence for this dependence as a pattern of behavior is impressionistic at best, it hardly seems appropriate to try to offer any hard-and-fast explanation of it. Possibly the man who chooses to become an academic in general and a humanist in particular is less personally secure than others who seek more dominant professional roles. As a result some professors tend to draw domesticity around them as a kind of emotionally protective cloak. Also the academic role itself is lacking in authority and generalized prestige, so that the home environment is an important source of reinforcement.

The particular kinds of stress and pressure that a man experiences in his professional work are expressed in various ways at home, and over time a wife comes to learn what is the appropriate and effective response with which to ease the tensions of the day. The medical practitioner, of course, lives daily with the responsibility for the profoundly important matters of patient health and well-being—a responsibility that, depending upon his medical specialty, may also involve him in a regular confrontation with death and increasingly with the threat of malpractice as well. A few men—especially those whose wives have some medical training of their own—do bring their doubts, disappointments or general concerns they have about patient care into the family setting where a wife is called upon for direct and sympathetic support. Sometimes, then, the adjunct and supportive responses blend together.

He gets upset when he's lost a patient. . . . We breathe wrong. . . . He's not that type usually except when tension is bad. He's not the type usually that likes everything in its place, but on those days he'll come in and start cleaning things up and just picking on things. Then I'll ask him about his day and what happened. It's particularly hard if he loses a patient and doesn't know why. I try to talk about it and get it all out. There's so much criticism of doctors now and he gets more and more depressed and isn't getting much fun out of practicing medicine. (1)

He feels depressed if he feels inadequate. . . . He's under stress when he's on call. He may only get one call a day, but being on call makes him nervous. . . . He's not really so busy in that sense, but it's the worry that he's going to be called. He comes home and hangs around and doesn't know what to do. We've only had sex, for example, once or twice in all the evenings he's been on call. (13)

He shares more with me because of my nursing background and interest. . . . Six or eight years ago he was sued for malpractice by a family friend. [He] took that so badly and all four doctors involved went to court because they felt they were really not guilty as charged. . . . At the time we talked a lot about the case. I had never been in court before and used to go every day. I found it all fascinating. (6)

Most doctors, though, are less openly expressive of the kind of stress that must be the inevitable by-product of medical practice. If the wife herself lacks any medical expertise, the technical details of patient care are beyond her grasp and she is quite cut off from the actual work content of her husband's day. Furthermore, medical training is itself a training in detachment; many wives report that their husbands carry this same air of detachment into the family arena, where what they seek is not active engagement with their wives, but a respite and refuge from daily cares and problems. In these situations a wife lends support indirectly and passively (and not always happily) by not intruding and by helping her husband to relax by providing him with a smoothly run home setting and expecting little from him by way of communication or interaction.

He very seldom talks about his work. . . . He tends to come home rather tired, has dinner, watches TV, tries to read the paper and does some medical reading. We have a relatively uncommunicative relationship. (11)

I almost have to drag things out of him. . . . He's the kind of person that comes home and I wonder what I've done wrong. He seems so withdrawn and unhappy. . . . He's not a talkative person to begin with but he's less so when he's had a terrible day. . . . You know, as time goes on you stop looking. That's very cynical, but I've been through the cycle of feeling guilty.

Now if he tells me, fine, if not fine. . . . I very often feel as though he is a nonparticipant in the family. . . . He eats his food, comes and goes, he wears his clothes and makes them dirty. . . . He's very preoccupied with his work. (9)

He likes to totally relax in the evenings—read for pleasure or watch TV. He's very quiet when he's under pressure. I leave it that way. (16)

Although only a minority of medical husbands are likely to share much with their wives about the daily routines of patient care, a great many men do seek appreciation from their wives for the stress and frustration of their medical work. Physicians seem quick to anger when they feel their expertise and authority are not fully recognized or understood, and their irritation frequently extends to patients (known as "crocks") who come to them with problems that they feel are not genuinely medical and for which their technical proficiency as doctors is of little use. Upsets of these sorts are frequently carried home to a wife, who as a listener provides her husband with an outlet for his feelings. In doing so she expresses solidarity with his point of view, thereby affirming his status.

I'm just a sounding board. . . . He complains about the [minority group] patients who don't take care of his beautiful handiwork. Interpersonal relations come into it too. . . . He needs someone to run off at. Surgeons' egos need constant nourishment. I've never seen anything like it. (14)

He enjoys people depending on his ability to help them; he enjoys making obscure diagnoses. He has a little more of an intellectual approach insofar as determining a certain kind of medical therapy—it's like figuring out a puzzle. He does not enjoy inconsiderate and difficult people. He has a low tolerance for the middle-aged housewife syndrome—depressions and that kind of thing. (7)

The patients he likes least are the ones he feels might be helped psychologically. He does a fair amount of referring to psychiatry. His partner does not refer but is much kinder and nicer to people who come repeatedly and don't belong in the office. My husband will get nasty. (12)

Some encounters with problems of status and recognition seem to be embedded in the mode of practice itself. Just as the group or hospital setting of practice creates special problems of office and personnel management that are reflected in the adjunct contribution of the wife as human relations expert, the same setting generates other interactional tensions, which draw a wife into the role of acting as sympathetic sounding board. In particular, the man in group practice is often frustrated by issues of seniority and cooperation that arise among colleagues.

He might mention trouble in his relationship with his colleagues. He's the low man in the group in terms of judgment and experience. He says they listen to him but when he does feel critical of something he needs to get it off his chest. He's still trying to justify his decision to join that group. . . . He likes everything except the generation gap. He just gets put down because he's younger. . . . He feels depressed if his colleagues don't listen to his judgment or if he botches up a patient or if other people are incompetent when he is not. (13)

He talks about everything. . . . This is his first job. He is not in the
top position; he works under another M.D. who is also on salary at
the hospital. . . . He finds it a problem being under a man who has
less tact than necessary. He is very much his own man and it's hard
to let my husband do his own thing. My husband likes to be in
charge and have responsibility. He does not like having to be under
another man. (5)

The medical wife provides support primarily as ego booster
and shock absorber. The academic wife, however, serves her husband primarily as a listening post, where he can discharge the content of his day. The academic is less likely than the doctor to feel
anxious, and more likely to feel overwhelmed by the many demands on a variety of levels that are made on him in a given day,
ranging from teaching, to committee and administrative work, to
his own writing and research, and the state of affairs at the university in general. His day-end conversations with his wife, then,
amount to a kind of stocktaking and planning session in which her
response may combine both support and professional advice. In situations where he is feeling angry or personally under fire—usually
as a consequence of intradepartmental tensions—most wives respond by offering an opinion, more in the manner of a colleague
than an emotional prop.

The position he's in now has many problems and I'm a good buffer.
You can't believe the amount of politics and stress it generates. He
can reveal everything to me because I'm not going to go any further. He finds it helpful to have someone he can talk to about those
problems. Sometimes I give him feedback but not advice. If he
comes home and says the budget is terrible and we have to cut out
phones, I don't give too much sympathy. You just have to cut out a
few more phones, that's all. Basically you can't give advice—you
might give another point of view. But you're not in that situation
and can't really understand it. It helps to listen though. (36)

I play a listening role. I don't give advice or suggestions. There's a
lot of talk now about affirmative action in the department. I have
my feelings about that and will express them. I don't know whether
they are his feelings or not, but he listens. (28)

The rather casual nature of the academic wife's response to her husband's problems may not only reflect the lower intensity of academic work compared to medical work on a day-to-day basis, but the fact that the academic has access during the day to colleagues, and perhaps even students, who also serve as outlets or listening posts for him. The doctor is in the lonely position of being the top man in command where his patients are concerned; his job is to solve their problems, not to share his with them. If colleague interactions are a source of tension, he is hardly able to discuss this in the small-group work setting. His wife is really the only person he can unburden himself to. Academic departments are big enough to permit the formation of factions or friendships where a man can share his stress and tension. The academics who really have nowhere else to turn other than to their wives are also the men at the top—the departmental chairmen, and their wives report that a daily unloading does occur at home in connection with that administrative position.

Career Crises

By any objective criterion by which success in the two professions of medicine and academe is measure—income, rank, general reputation and standing—all forty men in this book are unquestionably successful. But a few of them have had times in their careers when their own subjective sense of professional success has been seriously called into question. While the ingredients of a career crisis are not so very different in kind from those that give rise to daily stress and frustration, they differ in degree and in the magnitude of the discouragement and disappointment that follow. A career crisis has the effect of calling into question in a fundamental way all of what a man thinks he stands for professionally and perhaps personally as well, since feelings of personal worth are often inextricably linked to professional accomplishment.

Career crises are of particular interest for what they reveal of the structured scources of vulnerability in the professional career and the nature of the supportive response that a wife is called upon to make in such circumstances. One academic and one medical wife made reference to career crises that are long since past, so that it is difficult to know with any precision just how the crisis was felt and expressed by the husband and what kind of supportive response was offered by the wife. In the case of the doctor it seems as though the career crisis was in part a marital crisis. For the academic, now a tenured full professor and former chairman of his present department, failure to receive tenure in an earlier teaching position on another faculty was at the heart of his crisis. Of all the teaching husbands, he is the only one who encountered any obstacles on the road to tenure and promotion.

Seven other men have more recently experienced career crises. The four doctors among them are men whose need for external recognition as a dominant authority figure seems to be unusually intense. Although all four men preside over practices thriving in income and size, they have nonetheless been deeply despondent at their failure either to maintain their status within their own medical practice or to gain the recognition in the medical community that they feel is due them. As they discussed their husbands' career crises all four of their wives emphasized their feeling that their husbands were victims of petty jealousy and competition.

His relationship [with the other specialists in his field] is very competitive. . . . They are not warm to him. He feels he practices better medicine than they do. They leave emergency room work to the residents and are not willing to take money away from their office. He will see sick patients in the emergency room. (4)

I think the big thing is that I didn't realize about the competition in the medical field. . . . In the beginning he worried if people would like him. He had a time of being really discouraged; he felt all the other surgeons were down on him and he saw everyone else busier. Surgeons are normally very aggressive and competitive. What he really has to have is recognition from his colleagues. He wants people to come up and tell him what a good job he's done. He's always the first to compliment someone else and he does it because he wishes people would do it for him. But an element of jealousy enters in. He feels himself to be better than some of the other people in town. . . . He got a special award for [doing a new surgical procedure] and gave it to the hospital but they wouldn't put it up because they thought it would hurt the others' feelings. (18).

111

Although the wives are staunchly loyal supporters of their husbands' capabilities, a couple of them did acknowledge that their husbands' own difficult personalities had contributed to the very alienation and rejection of which the husbands complained.

> The lack of recognition and stimulation is what gets him. . . . He likes to be asked to be on committees, but he's very opinionated and things are either right or wrong. He's basically very even with me, but not so much with other people. (14)

> It eats him up alive when a patient transfers. He calls up to find out why. If it's a personality problem, he works on that. . . . People don't always like him. I hope he doesn't hear this report. (4)

None of these doctors in crisis felt comfortable sharing his concerns about his professional standing with other colleagues or with a professional help source. Doctors, after all, are trained to present themselves as competent and certain, so self-doubt is difficult for them to express. And as Miles and Krell (1974) have observed, doctors are reluctant to place themselves in the "sick role" and to seek help from psychiatrically trained colleagues. The only confidantes left to them are their wives, and home is the only setting where grievances can be freely aired. The women at these times became giant sponges, absorbing a daily outpouring of resentment and frustration until in the end they themselves became saturated by it all. In any case they could offer their husbands little but temporary solace, for wives could not provide the professional affirmation their husbands sought. This is in keeping with J. B. Miller's suggestion that men are validated not by winning the affirmation of women, but by winning value in the eyes of men and by succeeding in the institutions of other men:

> There is probably a much more profound separation (for a man) between men whom they value and therefore want to love and be loved by in return and women whom they are allowed to love and be loved by. The love of a lesser being cannot mean as much, cannot be as deeply affirming and satisfying. . . . They seek a confirmation that they are worthy and desirable. But this can come to them meaningfully only if it comes from those who matter. (1972:149)

One doctor took the initiative in distancing himself from his own crisis by scaling down the subjective importance of his career commitment and finding alternative means to gratify his need for recognition by taking on various leadership positions in the local community where his authority as a physician would be unchallenged. Indeeed it is his view that his authority as a physician is the basis for his claim to his wider ranging civic and social authority. Interestingly, he is the only doctor husband in the study who indicated that career success is less important to him than other areas of life satisfactions. In the other marriages, it was the wife who finally decided to walk away from the crisis rather than to stay and be swallowed up by it. She tended to affirm her emotional separateness from her husband by stepping up the pace of her own activity outside the home.

He's not really happy, but it's not beginning to wear on me. I have a lot of other things I'm involved in. I tell him to just ride it out. (14)

Last night we all discussed the pros and cons of the young man who is being considered for the partnership in my husband's office. . . . Then this morning I had to listen to my youngest child read. . . . Then my husband asked me to make a final selection of suits he had bought and I'm wishing he would just get out of the house. You make whatever decision you want; you've had enough of my time. You're a big boy. Yet to the outside world this man comes across as cool and unflapped. But I can see him coming home in the turmoil of the day and we are very enmeshed. I have my finger in the pie of running for school committee. . . . There has to be some kind of balance between what I enjoy doing and what [he] and the kids take of my time. (3)

He wouldn't get counseling when he was going through that crisis. . . . The minute he came home there was tension all over his face. . . . I only got really mad once. I was so sick of hearing it—I have feelings too. He felt I wasn't being very realistic in my reaction since he's the one who has to work and take calls and go out at night. Well I'm the one who paces the floor till he comes home. I get up and make breakfast and carry the home. I would hear this every day—day after day—and I felt my whole life was revolving around him. It reached the point where I think I almost had a nervous breakdown. . . . As long as he comes home everyday and there's a smile on his face then I'm happy. But as soon as I see that face I'm miserable. I try to put up with it but I can't. He has to make his own decision. . . . I am now taking interior design and doing some free-lancing. (4)

One of the three academic career crises was quite similar in character to the medical crisis just described, in that the husband (who has achieved the rank of full professor in his department) felt continually devalued by his department and dissatisfied with his job responsibilities, which he regarded as a misuse of his time and capabilities. His wife described him as a self-styled nonconformist who "will rebel just for the sake of rebelling." And she, like the medical wives, listened daily to her husband's recital of his unhappiness with his lot until she could stand no more. She decided at the same time to return to school to pursue a degree of her own.

I used to become very involved and frustrated by it all because it was all so negative. It got to the point where everything was so negative that it seemed to be pushing the rest of us down into some kind of quagmire. I realized there was nothing I could do about it and it wasn't my responsibility. My worrying about it didn't have any effect and I got so sick of hearing it. . . . He's always been like this. He's a perfectionist and never would find a job he would be really happy in. (37).

The other two academic career crises are perhaps more typical of academic career difficulties in that they involved issues of disciplinary paradigms and departmental factions which affect judgments of professional worth. Both of the professors (each humanists) were caught in the crossfire of the student protest and women's movements as those made their impact felt in the department and in the classroom. Suddenly the old terms on which their standing as teachers and colleagues had always rested no longer applied, and their power and credibility diminished.

He went through a terrible crisis with his teaching and there were a few years when he was spending more time at it and being less happy about it. Those were hard years—everything was being challenged and everything going by the board. . . . I would say that was a harder time for my husband to cope with than when he first started to teach. (30)

Career crisis for these two men took essentially the form of being caught in a dispute, and as their supporters, their wives acted not so much as passive listeners but as active parties to the dispute. Although neither wife was unsympathetic to what her husband was going through, neither did she necessarily agree with his assessment of the situation either. Her own anger might occasionally rise in the course of their discussions together, but her husband's airing of the dimensions of his crisis did not have the effect of crowding her out in the process.

Oh sure, I hear it all and I say what I think which is often not what he wants me to say. But he does want me to say something. (26)

I tried to play the role of bolstering him up. We had some terrible times. My husband was doing his best to accommodate to all of this in as graceful a way as possible without hurting himself. I had very little patience. But we always had differences about the role of young people in reshaping the world. . . . My husband was much more tolerant so when it came to that point when students were demanding such sweeping changes, he was having a very difficult time. I had very little sympathy with some of the student causes and it's caused conflict between us. There were a lot of times when we just simply couldn't talk about it because we would get into a state over it. (30)

Subordination and Autonomy in the Supportive Response

The medical wife's support for her husband's career consists, in essence, of her subordination to that career and to her husband's personal and professional dominance and authority. The doctor's wife accommodates to the high status of physician by her acceptance of a nonintrusive, even secondary place for herself in marriage. Indeed the very small number of collegially based marriages among the medical couples in the study suggests that the doctor tends to marry a woman who comes prepared, in effect, to defer to her husband and his career. This is further reinforced by the fact that fully half of the medical husbands have registered a clear preference that their wives not work at the present time. In the medical division of labor the acquiescence of women is a built-in expectation of the male-dominant medical role. That expectation apparently extends to wives as well, whose willingness to acquiesce to their husbands' dominance may be why so few wives have had or have regular paid work or academic commitments of their own. Furthermore—as the nature of her advocacy for her husband's career indicates—the rewards that accrue to the medical wife as a consequence of the status of her husband's work may serve to sugarcoat her subordinate status in the marriage and further depress her own aspirations for work. These are the "vested interests of middle-class women," described by Epstein (1971:129) as a major factor in women's disinclination to seek careers of their own.

On the interactional level, the doctor's wife relates to both the stress and status dimensions of her husband's work. A practitioner's work is likely to leave him at the day's end feeling pressured, preoccupied and uncertain, and he returns home in need of recognition and appreciation. Whatever the appropriate mode of response on the wife's part, be it brow soothing, bolstering, passively listening or not intruding, it is one that has the effect of relegating the concerns and events of the wife's own day to second place, if not obscuring them altogether. This was made dramatically clear by the wives who felt pushed aside by their husbands' career crises. But even in the context of more ordinary end-of-the-day conversations together, it is seldom that the activities or stress points of the wife's day are given as much time or consideration as those of her husband's. In some cases this is because the wife herself views the content of her day as less important and therefore less worthy of attention than her husband's; in other cases the husband himself makes that judgment simply by not being a very attentive listener or active stocktaker.

I tell him anything that's happened with the children; frequently they are not up to tell him themselves. . . . I tell him about the symphony because he loves classicial music. And things that come up with the League—little things that are interesting and funny. But as for the straight volunteer work and the nitty-gritty of that—he isn't that interested. After all, he's put in a hard day and doesn't want to hear all these petty things. (19)

We talk about things with the children. We are copresidents of the PTA, but he is not involved at all. It's not a major priority for him. We talk about things in his office. (17)

We always share the things that the children do. He's interested in the things that I do, but one problem is that sometimes things don't get said. Sometimes he has a lot of things on his mind and he doesn't always focus in on what I say. I like to pride myself on my memory and I hate it when he can't remember things. (7)

I don't share too much. I don't go over too much of the mundane things of the day. (16)

I talk about everything about my day. I'm very verbal. I don't know whether he likes me to do that or not. [Is he responsive?] Well . . . sometimes. He never tells me to shut up, but I think half the time it goes in one ear and out the other. (13)

Although university teaching as a profession is certainly highly esteemed in the public eye, it does not confer the immediate and generalized personal prestige and social recognition that medicine does, nor is the academic at work an authority figure in the way that the doctor is. In addition, the time demands of academic life are less consistently rigid than medical practice. As a support, the academic wife responds more autonomously than the doctor's wife to her husband and his work, and she does not feel called upon to lend support to her husband's career by her explicit subordination to it. Of course it could be argued that she does precisely that simply by accommodating to the time and mobility requirements of his career and by not pursuing her own work in any way that would interfere with those requirements. On the other hand, the feelings of playing emotional second fiddle to her husband's career and being independent but not separate are largely absent from the academic wife's account of her relationship to her husband's work.

Then too, a sizeable proportion of the academic wives in the study actually are working or studying at the present time, and in many cases the stimulus to the present outside commitment was the very collegial standing of the marriage at the outset. The rewards to the wife of her husband's career in university teaching do not relate to status and material gain, but to opportunities for her own personal growth. The inner direction and individuality of the academic career quite probably lend encouragement to the wife to develop those same qualities in herself, and her independent achievement is in itself a form of support for the prevailing values of academic life.

The faculty wife has some chance for expression of her own ideas and opinions as she reacts to the content of her husband's day, and end-of-the-day information sharing is more likely to be a two-way flow among academic couples than medical couples. Most academic wives seem to feel that they can count on their husbands to be interested in the goings-on of their own days. On the whole then, the academic wife tends to emphasize and experience her supportive role as more collegial than status-supporting and therefore more autonomous than subordinate. To be sure, it is a role that is well tailored to the needs of her husband's career in academe, but it is a role that does not down-play her own sense of independence.

Although the distinction has been drawn *between* the two professional groups as to the relationship between the status, authority, and time demands attached to the professional role and the supportive response of the wife, similar though less pronounced distinctions appear to exist *within* the professional groups. These serve to underscore the main point. It is true that academic life tends to discourage the development of a ruggedly individualistic, highly dominant and authoritative work-role. Nonetheless, academic life does attract some men who have a minimal commitment to the teaching or colleague role and whose major or even sole preoccupation is with their own writing and research and the recognition to be gained from it. There are about half-a-dozen professors—primarily though not exclusively scientists—who fit this description both by their own and their wives' accounts of their professional work style and priorities. Such men are very like doctors in their approach to their professional role and presumably in temperament as well. Their academic commitment as described by their wives involves a set of unyielding imperatives that derive from their high striving for external confirmation of success and the absolute importance they attach to their productivity and technical mastery in their disciplines.

If he could he would get rid of all his graduate students and his post docs and go into his lab and work with his hands and with his brain and do his own research. Then he would publish something when he had something to say. He would like to have no pressures from having to teach and no administrative work for sure. His main priority is with his research. (23)

Now he is totally at work on the grant to support research. . . . His research is his biggest time commitment and it is what is most important to him. . . . He has a study at home but he does not tend to use it. He goes back to the lab because it's quieter there and he can get things done without interruption. His schedule is predictable—he works from seven to six and usually spends three evenings a week at the lab. (33)

He still hasn't realized that he's not going to get the Nobel Prize. Maybe he's still working for that. Who knows what men work for in their fields. (39)

The marriages of these men are more conventionally sex-typed and explicitly male dominant than other academic marriages, and their wives have developed their supportive roles in ways similar to those of the doctor's wives. All but one of these marriages are noncollegial and the one collegial marriage is not marked by high field relatedness between the husband and wife, so there is distance between them in that respect. The wife of the agentic academic male responds to her husband's work with a combination of noninterference and deference that places his career very much in the foreground and herself in the background. For the most part these professors' wives have kept their outside involvements to a minimum—a necessary accommodation, they feel, to the extensive and intensive time demands of their husbands' work. Like doctors' wives they go their own separate ways with their days and do not count on their husbands' availability for evening or weekend leisure time or social activities, unless that time is well planned for and scheduled in advance. In support of their husbands' career commitments, these wives make reference to prestige and their husbands' status as a breadwinner. Although the academic-style "doctor's wife" may not be called upon for active bolstering on her husband's behalf, his preoccupation with his work is often such that the wife's activities receive little attention. The following quotations give a flavor of the emphases in this version of the academic wife's supportive response:

And now he wants to make a lasting contribution. . . . When he's really writing, really working on something, it blocks out the rest of his life. That's one reason we don't have a lot of social life—to give him freedom to do his work. (23)

I don't know what time he's likely to be home on a given day. It's always been like this. He might get involved in some kind of project himself or get stopped by a student. I don't wait dinner. At one time we did, but that made everyone so irritable. He knows that if he is not here we will eat without him. . . . It would be an unusual week if he were home every weeknight. (37)

In the evenings if he goes back to the lab, then I usually have friends I go out with. I usually go to bed much earlier than he does. He often works quite late. (33)

Really we talk most about what the children are doing. He doesn't like what he calls small talk. He's really not too interested in the things that I do—that's small talk. I like to take walks in the woods and things. I'm interested in nature. He's just not interested. He'll like to know what I did but that's about it. (39)

On the medical side of things, the dominance that is inherent in the conventionally competitive, entrepreneurial male role of the private practitioner appears to be somewhat blunted in the role of the salaried hospital practitioner, who has relinquished some of the autonomy of private practice. It is probable that in contrast to private practice, hospital practice attracts a man who is less personally dominant, less concerned with the high visibility of his role and with presiding over an exclusive domain of patients who "belong" to him. In this connection it is interesting to look at the wives of the two hospital physicians in the study who function primarily as practitioners (rather than as academic researchers or administrators).

The wives of these men do not show the same pattern of supportive subordination as do other doctors' wives. The language of deference is absent, as is the focus on the prestige and status of their husbands' work. (As one wife said, "Doctors are not the gods that people think they are.") Both of these marriages are collegial marriages. One wife has worked regularly on a part-time basis for some years and has earned advanced credentials in her field during that time as well. The second wife is presently poised on the brink of deciding when and where to complete work for her Ph.D., with the full support of her husband. In the meantime she is very active in political volunteer work in which she has major leadership responsibility. These marriages are especially noteworthy among medical marriages for the amount of mutual information sharing and responsiveness to one another's day that occur between spouses. The patterns in these two medical marriages, along with those in the majority of academic marriages, suggest the existence of a general relationship between, on the one hand, a less absolutistic definition of the professional role and, on the other, a collegial marriage relationship together with a less traditionally female subordinate response to the husband's career.

In a third medical marriage, the husband (a private practitioner) has a noticeably different orientation to medical practice than other doctors in private practice, and the wife's interests and outside commitments are integrated with her husband's practice, where she has worked as a nurse for many years of his career. The features of the husband's work role and of the husband-wife relationship place this marriage in a category by itself, and the wife's supportive role cannot fairly be characterized as subordinate in the manner of most of the medical marriages in the study. This particular marriage will be examined and discussed in greater detail in the following chapter.

The organization and definition of the professional role also affect the time requirements of professional work which a wife is called upon to accomodate in her supportive response to her husband's career. This is easily seen in the case of the agentic academic male, who has clearly chosen to center his life on his research and quest for a particular kind of success. Unlike other academics, he imposes a rigid and inflexible schedule of work on himself, and his wife feels the effect of that in her own day and in the amount of time they have together.

In many respects the time demands of medical practice are also a product of the way that the work role is constructed. The medical professional role would be quite different if the autonomy of the physician were circumscribed and his authority were reduced as the supreme arbiter of how health care is to be delivered. This would require not only a transformation of the organization of health care delivery, but a redefinition of the physician's role within that organization. It is interesting to note that according to the wives in this study there is little difference between the hospital and private practice physician in the length and predictability of their working hours, despite the differences in the organization of their practices and the constrasting self-concepts associated with each work setting.

It is true that in the hospital practice the entrepreneurial base of medicine has been eliminated and an extensive back-up staff is always present, with the result that the hospital physician is less likely than the private physician to be called out after hours to attend to nonemergency cases. Also, the hospital practitioner may have somewhat more flexibility in the organization of his time during the day because there is always someone there in his unit "minding the shop." But the institutionalized authority of the physician is no less in hospital than in private practice. In each case the physician runs the show and is in charge of all decisions pertaining to the management of patient care. The hospital physician also has a great deal of responsibility for formulating hospital policy and for personnel administration and training.

Individually and collectively medical practitioners spend much of their time deciding on larger issues having to do with the social organization of health care. All of the doctors in this study spend considerable time at meetings that center on matters of health care policy, the status of the profession, or the economic aspects of their own practices. It is not only the urgency and unpredictability of patient needs, but also medicine's wide-ranging autonomy in the control of much about the mangement of patient care and the organization of the delivery of health care that make the job of

the practitioner so time-consuming. The wife of one hospital practitioner unwittingly put her finger on one example of the link between the broad-based authority of the medical role and the frequently engulfing nature of the time demands of medical practice:

If it was just dealing with the patients I have never been resentful. I
know he has to go. But he has to stay late for things like electrical
safety committee meetings. I think what the hell is the hospital en-
gineer for. Call in the ding-a-ling. Those meetings—yes, I resent
those heartily and I could scream. (1)

In a more rationalized system of health care, with greater sharing of responsibility among a variety of medical personnel for meeting patient needs and more public jurisdiction over the social organization of health care, the extent and kind of claims made on a
physician's time would undoubtedly be fewer and different from
what they are in the present system. The man who chooses to practice medicine chooses to practice it in a socially constructed way.
The institutionalized authority of the physician is purchased at the
price of a high and inflexible time commitment. It is a price paid
not only by the doctor but by his wife as well.

5

DOING DOUBLE DUTY

What is a housewife? A housewife is a woman: a housewife does housework. . . .
The synthesis of "house" and "wife" in a single term establishes the connection
between womanhood, marriage and the dwelling place of family groups.
The role of the housewife is a family role: it is a feminine role.
Yet it is also a work role. . . . A housewife is a "woman who manages or directs
the affairs of her household; the mistress of a family; the wife of a householder."
(*Oakley 1974:1*)

The domestic work of women as housewives and mothers is rarely
analyzed from the sociological perspective of its functional contribution to the career work of men. The most notable exception is
Parsons' (1954a) analysis of the "profound alteration" (presumably
dysfunctional) in family structure that would result should women
choose to pursue careers and equality of occupational opportunity
with men. His clear implication is that family solidarity, as maintained by women, is the necessary and desirable counterpart to
men's occupational achievement.

Neither have socioiologists paid much attention to the housewife's role as a social and historical construct, as a product of the occupational structure of industrial society. Oakley describes the changes in women's domestic activity that occurred with the emergence of industrial society.

> Industrialization has had these lasting consequences: the separation of the man from the intimate daily routines of domestic life; the economic dependence of women and children on men; the isolation of housework and childcare from other work. Hence, through the allocation to women of housework and childcare, through modern definitions of the role of housewife and the role of mother, industrialization has meant the restriction of the woman-housewife to the home. (1974:59)

In the typically segregationist approach to the sociological study of work and family, the domestic roles of women just *are;* they exist as a given. The assumptions seem to be that because women bear children, they must naturally rear them; because women rear children, they are naturally in the home; because women are in the home, they must naturally manage the home. Another way of looking at this, however, is that women do all these things because *somebody* has to, and in the present structure of things, men cannot because they must have time and person free and flexible for the pursuit of a career. Hochschild writes of the career system that it is "shaped by and for the man with a family who is family free" (1974:40).

Uncluttered and uninterrupted time is the valuable and necessary resource upon which the work of a career depends. It is a resource given to men by women, who as wives and mothers do double duty in the rearing of children who belong to both of them, who manage and keep the homes in which both of them live, and who organize the family and social life in which both of them engage. For all of the wives who appear in this book, their double-duty work as homemaker and mother has been at the center of their role as wife in general, and the structures and values of professional life are mirrored in just how extensively and flexibly their domestic activities have developed. This chapter focuses on the double-duty work of these wives in an examination of the ways that a woman's role as housewife has taken shape in the context of her husband's career either in university teaching or in medical practice.

Childbearing and Child Rearing

Each of the wives interviewed married with the expectation more or less clearly formulated that she would sooner or later have children; for all but one wife, who is involuntarily childless, that expectation has been realized. Upon that expectation rested still another expectation: that the major responsibilities of parenting would fall to the wife and that those responsibilities would be of central importance in organizing the shape of her days, at least until her children reached elementary school. Accordingly any possibility of work outside the home was to be subordinated to, suspended for, or supplanted by the commitment to mothering. Women articulate the relationship of their commitment to mothering with their desire for work in various ways:

I don't know that I really had specific goals. I was interested in the possibility of traveling in connection with his work. . . . No, I had no thought of a place for a career for myself. I thought I would work for awhile and then when we had children I would stop. I hadn't looked beyond the first few years of having children. (37)

Every single one of our children was an accident; I tried very hard to avoid having children, but the little gifts kept coming. Yes, children were a part of our life plan, if I ever had any plans at all at that young age. I don't think I had any plans at all. I was one of those people who never grew up until well into my adult life. I did make a very conscious decision long before we got married that I was not good enough to have a professional career in music. Anything else could come as it would. (36)

I really like research very much, but I always wanted a baby. I thought if you were going to have children you should stay home and take care of them. Not that you couldn't have a career because of being a woman but because of having to take care of a husband and children. (29)

I enjoyed my residency certainly more than my internship. Not that the work was not enjoyable but it took so much time. I don't think I had any career plans formulated when I chose medicine. I thought of it as full time when feasible. I still haven't defined my career expectations. I have added on more children and less work than I might have anticipated. I never questioned having children—at least two. His thoughts were for a higher number and my thoughts changed. Marriage was very important to me and having children was not at first. I had my first son when it seemed to be a convenient time and then I began to have rather pleasant feelings about it all. I had the baby at the end of my internship and then went into residency. I had a full-time housekeeper and she would sleep in the nights I was on call. If I hadn't had a child I would have worked harder. As it was I got out of work as soon as I could and never stayed around 'til evening. My husband's routines didn't change at all. (12)

I worked right up until the time we moved. I was pregnant when we came here. I wanted to wait to get pregnant until he was finished with his residency so I could work all the way through. We didn't want the financial strain of having a family before he finished his residency and I enjoyed working. When we knew that we were coming here I knew I wouldn't be working so I thought it would be a good time to start a family. I was thirty years old when my first son was born. But I don't think I would have gone back to work even if we had stayed in ——— . I've just enjoyed being at home with the kids. (18)

While it was undeniably the personal choice of every wife to become "parent of the first resort," so to speak, that choice is also shown to be a necessary one, when seen against the backdrop of male careers. The man who must have time and person free and flexible in order to meet the encompassing demands of his career cannot, by definition, also have time and person free and flexible to meet the equally encompassing demands of young children. The quest for career success, as it is described for the men under study here, leaves little room for any but a secondary involvement as a parent, though for some men this involvement has been more secondary than for others.

Among the medical families (see table 5.1) all but one of the first children and three-quarters of the second children were born during the time of their fathers' medical education or training, when hours were the longest and certainly the least flexible of any period in their careers. The typical schedule of work during internship and residency required that the young doctor be on call and sleep at the hospital every other night and every other weekend; in no case was he gone less than one night out of three. This regimen became a way of life, lasting anywhere from three years

TABLE 5.1   STAGE OF HUSBAND'S CAREER AT BIRTH OF FIRST, SECOND, AND
LAST CHILD
(if more than two children)

Career Stage	M.D. Children				Ph.D. Children			
	First	*Second*	*Last*	*Total*	*First*	*Second*	*Last*	*Total*
Early education	3	2	—	5	6	3	—	9
Late education	16	13	2	31	6	—	—	6
Early career	1	3	6	10	4	11	3	18
Established	—	2	8	10	3	3	5	11
	20	20	16	56	19	17	8	44
Percent of all children born during period of career education and training				64				34

NOTE: Definition of career stages
Early Education:
M.D.—through and including medical school and internship
Ph.D.—through and including master's degree, Ph.D. coursework and examinations
Late Education:
M.D.—through and including residency, other specialty training, and military service (if residency and other training still to be completed at the time)
Ph.D.—through and including dissertation research and writing, nontenure track (i.e., instructor level) teaching position, postdoctoral research
Early Career:
M.D.—in first three years of medical practice
Ph.D.—in teaching position at assistant professor level

(internship and two years of residency) to six in instances where residency training was highly specialized and prolonged. While most families experienced the shorter and more regular hours of military and public health service as a brief reprieve from the high-pressured schedule of medical training, two wives found themselves left alone with their young children while their husbands did wartime military service (one in Korea and the other in Vietnam) in places where families could not accompany them. With the arrival of their first child, many medical wives found themselves face to face with the virtual irreconcilability of their husbands' family and career roles. While the routines of medical training rolled inexorably on, the experiences both of pregnancy and infant care were borne alone and often in loneliness by the wives.

When I came home after two days in the hospital (he had been on call in the hospital on those days) there was the house just as we had left it, where my membranes had ruptured with all the towels on the floor. It sounds horrible but he couldn't help it because he was on. He did manage to find time to drive me home from the hospital but that was all. He had a very minimal involvement with my daughter during her infancy and that was too bad as far as she was concerned. (7)

He had no involvement at all with those children and their care. Every other Sunday I took the children into his office so we could have Sunday dinner together. He just about lived at the hospital during his residency. . . . When the girls were around a year old, they would look at his picture and talk about what daddy used to look like when he was here. One day he walked home after not being home for awhile and they screamed with excitement and surprise because they really didn't expect to see him. He also made a comment about the older girl's bike being outside. You know, he didn't realize that the girls had grown so that the bike now belonged to the younger girl. (20)

It was very lonely with that first child. . . . It's the only time I can truthfully say I counted the hours 'til he would be home. I just waited. I was bored and could not afford a sitter. It was hard because he was working nights and . . . I had never been away from home. I got so I would call him a few times a day. By the second year he would say "I can't help it." I knew he was working for a reason, but I couldn't stand that reason. I finally couldn't go on like that. I had to get out. I got sitters and went shopping and took courses—nothing that amounted to anything. (4)

Our first child was born at the end of his internship year. I had to drive myself to the hospital when I went into labor. The child was born deformed and did not live very long. (3)

Then he was in the army. . . . I stayed with my mother and father for six weeks after the baby was born and then flew down to meet him. There I was at the airport with a six-week-old baby and no husband there. He'd gotten involved at the hospital and showed up late. . . . He was overseas for about a year and I wandered between parents during that time. I thought I had done pretty well, but I once heard one mother say she couldn't stand it for more than a month. (11)

129

The particularly grueling routines of internship and residency do come to an end, but the years of medical practice did not bring any substantial increase in the doctor's time commitment or general availability to his family. The majority of medical husbands leave home in the morning before their children have left for school and arrive home in the evening after very young children are in bed. It is a rare doctor's family where everyone sits down for the evening meal together on any regular basis. The much more usual pattern is for the wife and children to eat together and for the husband to sit down alone to a meal that his wife has waiting for him when he arrives home later.

Only two doctors took any regular part at all in the daytime care of their pre-school-age children. (See table 5.2.) The great majority of medical husbands have participated very little in the ongoing tasks and decision making that are part of child rearing. Only three medical husbands have had any share in half or more of fifteen common and necessary responsibilities that constitute the routine management of the days of young children. (See tables 5.3 and 5.4.) Those responsibilities that occur the most frequently and require the most active planning and/or modification of a parent's own schedule—such as staying at home with a sick child, arranging for extracurricular activities, going for a doctor's appointment, buying clothing, arranging for babysitting—are the ones that have been shared by the fewest number of husbands. Those tasks that can be done either sedentarily or spontaneously—such as making a decision about a child's schooling, spending some time with a child during his or her bedtime routines—are the ones in which medical husbands have been most involved, when they have been involved

TABLE 5.2   HUSBAND'S HELP IN DAYTIME CHILDCARE

Number Who Cared for Preschool Child Once a Week or more	M.D. Husbands [a]	Ph.D. Husbands [b]
Oldest child	1	4
Youngest child	1	3

[a] N = 18 for both oldest and youngest child.
[b] N = 17 and 16, respectively.

TABLE 5.3   HUSBAND'S PARTICIPATION IN CHILD
REARING

Participation (number of tasks) [a]	M.D. Husbands (N = 18)	Ph.D. Husbands (N = 17)
Low (0–3)	11	7
Moderate (4–6)	4	3
Substantial (7–9)	3	4
High (10 or more)	0	3

[a] Number of child-rearing tasks of a total of 15 which husband has either shared with wife or assumed sole responsibility for himself. For description of specific tasks, see table 5.4.

at all. Not surprisingly, their greatest contribution to child-rearing management has been in the selection of doctors.

No academic husband made any major changes in his work routines in response to the birth of a child, but the greater fluctuation and flexibility in the use and organization of a professor's time compared to that of the physician often meant that the professor father had more time left over for parenting beyond the time required for his work. The academic husband was more regularly present on the home front when his children were born, and he tended to be a more active assistant in the routines of infant care than the doctor father. In this connection, several academic wives mentioned that the birth of a child during the summer months, when their husbands had a more relaxed pace of work, meant their husbands were more available to help in the early weeks of a baby's life.

On the other hand, the much-touted flexibility of academic work can be overemphasized. In reality (especially in the graduate school and early career years, when the majority of these men become fathers for the first and second time), it is a flexibility that pertains more to the possibility of making minor alterations in daily routines than to any shifts in the overall structure and chronology in the academic career, which requires scholarly production at a certain level on an implicit time schedule to assure academic advancement. The best jobs and the most promising reputations await the young academics who win the esteem of those who are themselves held in esteem in the departments and in the disciplines. The

TABLE 5.4   CHILD-REARING TASKS: THE ROLE OF THE HUSBAND
(Number of Families Where Task Is Either Shared by Husband and Wife or
Done by Husband Alone)

	M.D. Couples (N = 18)	Ph.D. Couples (N = 17)
Tasks that require active doing and planning *and* that typically occur or must be done during daytime hours.		
1. Going with child for a doctor's appointment	0	1
2. Staying home during the day with a sick child	0	1
3. Arranging for a child's extra-curricular activities	1	2
4. Transporting child to and from school	2	4
5. Attending conferences with a child's teacher	3	7
6. Attending child's school performances or other daytime activities	3	6
7. Seeing child off to school in the mornings	4	6
Tasks that require active doing and planning *and* that typically occur or may be done outside of daytime hours.		
1. Arranging for babysitting	1	3
2. Buying shoes and clothing for a child	0	3
3. Allocating personal and household tasks to a child	3	5
4. Buying holiday or birthday presents for a child	4	10
Tasks that may be done spontaneously or sedentarily.		
1. Getting up in the night with a crying or fussy child	5	12
2. Being with child for evening bedtime routines	6	10
3. Selecting pediatrician, dentist, or other doctors for child	15	8
4. Deciding where a child is to attend school	11	13

NOTE: Tasks are described here in the same way that they were described on the
questionnaire forms.

academic who is always on call to his work offers tangible proof of merit and seriousness of purpose. The graduate student or junior faculty member is under considerable pressure to establish himself in a favorable position within his cohort, and he does not, therefore, allow himself to be seriously detoured or interrupted by the presence of children in his life. Hochschild's assessment of the time requirements of the academic career in the making was confirmed by the experience of the academic wives:

> A reputation is an imaginary promise to the world that if one is productive young in life, one will be so later also. . . . Since age is the measure of achievement, competition often takes the peculiar form of working long hours and working harder than the next person. (Hochschild, 1974:25–26)

The time in graduate school was difficult . . . having babies and being new to the baby business. Having all the adjustments to make when you start a family and having my husband under terrific pressure with his studies. And me feeling I would have liked to be doing something too. I couldn't do very much. I did raise these things with him, but there was no way. I audited one course for the semester and that was it. He was not going to come home in the middle of the day because it just simply took him out of his element and disrupted his thinking. Of course I catered to all that. His things came first and that was all there was to it. (30)

It was kind of a question of whether I wanted to ask him to do something or of thinking that he was involved in his teaching or busy writing something and I should get a sitter instead. He did more than his share in many ways, but I think we were both oriented toward proving his career. That was the important thing, so I would usually hire a sitter. (27)

The most difficult time, the biggest thing was being married while he was a graduate student. It was an impossible situation. Married men never did as well and I was determined it wasn't going to happen in my case. I never pushed him to stay home. Maybe I should have. On the other hand, I don't think he would have had the kind of career he's had. If his career hadn't gone well he might have resented it and it might have broken things up between us. I don't know. I don't really think it's healthy for graduate students to be married. He was taking classes and went off in the morning and usually took his lunch because he was apt to have seminars in the afternoon. He came home and studied all the time except on Saturdays. We used to go to the movies on Saturday nights. He wanted to do a lot of work at home and that meant I had to get [my son] out. As soon as he learned to walk I spent about three hours every day walking around with him so he wouldn't get in [my husband's] hair. It was excellent for the baby's mental and physical development but terribly hard on me. (29)

While the academic schedule may have meshed somewhat better with the schedule of babyhood than the medical schedule, no academic husband actually adapted or modified his schedule to child care routines. His contribution was fit into and around his work commitment. In fact some men who had been used to working at home without interruption found the presence of a child too distracting and simply stayed away from home more in order to be able to do their work; others learned the art of "tuning out" the family life around them while they worked.

I don't think it was really necessary for him to modify his schedule. He spent as much time as necessary at school and as I said the kid never slept so he was up to see him at night. (32)

He's always been very much involved in day-to-day child care, but always more or less on his own schedule. (23)

Perhaps he helped more than a lot of husbands. He did help with diapers and feeding and so forth. But I think they were plainly regarded as my responsibility. . . . I think he stayed away from home more after they were born, because each of them had six-months colic. (22)

He used to talk about how he got up in the night and got the bottle and I would sit there ready to punch him. . . . It sounded as though he did all the night feeding, all the diaper changing and all the getting up early. But he was not around during the day for any routine infant care. None at all. I never had any day baby sitters. I was constantly with them. (25)

Even after we had children, he found he could work at home even with the noise of small children. He could block it out. Anyway I tended to be outside with them early in the morning. (28)

Throughout their children's elementary school years more academic husbands than medical husbands have been involved in more of the routine work of child rearing. Nonetheless it is also true that the majority of academic husbands, like medical husbands, have had only a "low" to "moderate" level of such participation. (See table 5.3.) Only four academic husbands in all assumed any responsibility for daytime child care at least once a week or more. (See table 5.2.) The specific tasks for which the greatest number of academic husbands have taken some responsibility reflect in part the academic schedule, which allows most men to be at home through the evening and nighttime hours on a regular predictable basis and permits occasional time off during the day for child-related shopping or for attending school performances or conferences. (Table 5.4.) (The willingness to participate in these ways is quite another matter; that is a point to which the discussion will return later.)

It is certainly fair to say that in each one of these forty academic and medical families, the major responsibility for the planning and organization of the day in terms of a child's needs has fallen to the wife. The use of her time has been determined by the children's use of their time at different ages and stages of their development. No wife described the timetables of her day without reference to the timetables of her children's day, although a husband's day emerges as a separate, distinct, and independent entity only occasionally affected by family time. A wife's day is intersected throughout by her children's day, and no wife—whether working or not—orders her own day except as she takes into account those intersections. Her time is what exists in between, as the following quotes illustrate in detail.

My husband usually leaves by seven-thirty he's a real early bird and can't sleep past then. My daughter leaves at eight-thirty after the usual squabbles about breakfast. Then on the days when I go to the museum I am there till noon. Then I pick up my son and try to get him to take a nap. . . . I am always here when my daughter comes home after school and then I take care of her after-school activities. (7)

The day starts around quarter to seven. My husband leaves early and then the children have to get ready to go to school. . . . The kids come home after school and I'm here then. Then they go off with friends or have activities that they might need car pooling for. I am home from then on and do keep track of the kids. My days now are very relaxed; I do my own thing. I might do impromptu things with friends who are free like I am to take off until three. (16)

The day starts between six-thirty and seven-thirty when the baby wakes up. The other children get up and get dressed. My husband is in the operating room by seven-fifteen and takes the baby in the bathroom with him if she's up. In the morning I might have a meeting or play tennis, take a public speaking course or cross-country ski. Only the baby is home for lunch and then I put her in for a nap. I have cleaning help three days a week and I use that time to do errands then or things around the house. Then the other children come home. I have a sitter then who spends time with the baby and then I can spend time with the older children if I need to or get them to activities. (17)

The times have really changed for me now that the children are no longer babies and toddlers. . . . I realize that now I have a block of time from nine to two-thirty most days. During the morning or afternoon period I have to get dinner ready. I don't have the time after two-thirty to get dinner any more—that's shot because of chauffeuring and after-school activities. I try to paint every day. If I start in the morning then I will usually continue right on through. . . . I really like painting on the weekends. I can paint all day Saturday and Sunday because nobody has to go anywhere. (25)

I have a class every weekday. That's been true for the last two years. . . . The thing that really depresses me and I get so mad is the chauffeuring thing—music, ice skating, gymnastics. When the weather is rotten outside I just don't want to do more. I like being here. So my life changes after three. The day begins at six-thirty so my son can be at the bus stop by seven-fifteen. (32)

I stay until the kids leave by eight-thirty and I try to get going shortly after that. Ideally I would work from eighty-forty-five until two-forty-five except on Wednesday when the kids get home early. . . . I'm the one who still comes home to be with the children after school. I'd say we have a fairly traditional pattern. (34)

There is more to the hard work of parenting, however, than task performance and time scheduling. As far as family relationships are concerned the doctor's child is the product of a single-parent family to a much greater extent than is the academic child.

The pace and intensity of medical work is marked by sharp divisions of either being hard at work or hard at play, either being "off" or "on," and this is mirrored in the kind and amount of time that a medical husband spends with his children. He may coast along for days or even weeks being almost entirely preoccupied with his work and having only the most minimal or offhand interaction with his children, and then on a weekend off or a vacation period initiate a burst of child-centered activity of the "special treat" variety. Then he may retreat back to his work again, to emerge at some later date for another round of leisure-time parenting. On a day-to-day basis, the physician husband is far from being either a steady or active presence in the lives of his children:

I don't think he did anything with them when they were little. Now that they are older we talk about the importance of doing things together as a family so they will have memories of daddy. It isn't that he hasn't enjoyed them, he just doesn't have time. . . . He takes two weeks of a possible six for vacation. We do everything as a family on vacation because the children see so little of him and I don't want to remove him from them. (19)

He loves to swim and loves tennis and does a little bit of duck hunting in the fall with our son. . . . Whatever he's done outside of medicine he has tried to gear it to do with the family. He has four weeks vacation a year and they are all family vacations. (15)

He didn't take any part when the kids were born and still doesn't. He has no real involvement with them. . . . We've bought a little beachhouse and we go there for a few weeks in the summer and on weekends. That's been great and with the boat there we've done more things together. (14)

It's difficult for us when he's not around and we'd like to have him home, but this is what he's spent all these years learning about. . . . I think there are things that we do as a family where I end up being the only parent that goes with them—to the movies, ice skating and so on. I would like to see a lot more of the family doing something. . . . His big goal in a couple of years is to get a camper and to go across country. (8)

As his children grow and the particularly frantic pace of the early career years subsides, the academic husband is more likely to arrive home in the evening in time to enjoy real interaction with his children, rather than merely "catch up" on them, as the physician does. In addition, the pervasiveness of academic work, coupled with its generally lower intensity, and a fairly high degree of overlap between home setting and work setting (in the case of the humanist, especially) often leads to a less sharp demarcation of family time and work time. The result is that children and their activities are fairly easily integrated into the ordinary course of a day, instead of saved up for a special occasion.

My husband gives the children a tremendous amount of support in the area of athletics; he attends all of my daughter's field hockey games. . . . This is the first year he's been going. Three afternoons a week he gets to their school and watches their games. (25)

Early evenings are spent with the kids and we try to have music sessions with them. We all play instruments together and I have to get after them to practice. My husband plays an instrument and the first thing he does when he walks in the house is to play it to relax. (32)

He's fantastic about that—he'll be typing in the middle of a sentence and a youngster will come in and he will stop doing what he is doing and pay attention to that and go back to what he's doing. . . . He's had a very good relationship with the children and he's always accessible. They feel very comfortable about going to him and asking him for help or to do something with them and he has taken them to do specific activities with him. (27)

My husband has been very good with the children. He would get up with them at night and get up in the morning and get the day started with them. He loves to do things with them and play with them. They play soccer and he watches their games. He stays the whole time and watches. With the older boys—on top of everything else—he ran a scout troop last year for the whole year. (36)

Many academics also overlap their professional and parent roles in a way that breaks down the barriers separating the world of work from the world of home, thereby developing a more integral rather than peripheral role for themselves in the family. It is not uncommon for an academic father to share something of his own disciplinary interests with his children and to acquaint them in a casual way with the subject matter of his field. He often takes a special interest in his children's academic achievements in areas that relate to his own professional competence. Whether he uses travel, special activities, recreation, homework, or just ordinary conversation as the vehicle for bringing his children in touch with his field, the academic father frequently makes a positive and active contribution to his parenting role based on his professional role.

Yes I think he has had a professional role with the children. My husband has gone into the school and talked about genetics, and he does try to interest them in his field. One son is our nature boy. They all do well in school and enjoy different things about nature. (34)

Yes he has had a professional role in the family in a very nice way. Both of us have an interest in science and we take the same approach to the children. He feels that there is nothing that can't be explained to a child at any age. They know about molecules and atoms and so on. They have visited his lab some and they do enjoy that. . . . We have emphasized education and learning—that it's healthy to understand yourself and to know about the world. (40)

Yes he certainly has brought it home. It's the kind of field that can be discussed at home. The children are very interested in Shakespeare and have gone to the theater with us and are really up on it. We discuss things at the dinner table. Yes, he does take a particular interest in their writing and work in literature in school. (28)

Our children are fully versed in the Odyssey and in tales of ancient Greece. We tend to make an effort to bring them into things they can share more with their peers. Both of them have a terrific thirst for knowledge and share our thirst for literature and history. My husband also has a background in science and was once pre-med. . . . We do tend to be oriented to talking about things and doing something with them. (23)

The medical husband stands in sharp contrast to the academic husband in the presentation of his professional self in the family setting. The technical content of his work or the workings of his day do not seem to be subjects of conversation between a doctor father and his children. It is also rare for a physician to assume the doctor role within the family; when he does it is with his professional rather than personal self forward—he is calm, detached, and impersonal. Such behavior, while clearly appropriate to his professional role on the outside, must inevitably be experienced by small children as aloof—even rejecting—coming from their father. Certainly many wives have felt this to be the case:

Anybody who is sick goes to see him and that was true when the kids were little too. We did have a pediatrician and my husband didn't get involved in the nursing care as such. That was my job. Once my son had a problem with his testicles and he was in terrible pain. I called [my husband] at the office. He's very stable about sickness. Or if he gets in a flap he doesn't show it. My son had to go in for surgery and I was very concerned about how he would react to that kind of surgery as an adolescent and [my husband] hadn't explained it to him. He didn't think through what that experience might mean for the kid. When I mentioned this he went running back and explained it to him. (9)

My youngest was operated on when she was two. . . . My husband was a fellow in that hospital. When I get nervous I get antagonistic and obnoxious. Her arm was all done up and she hadn't had the operation yet and she was having trouble breathing. I got upset and he didn't explain anything to me and kept telling me I was being a bitch. Finally they put her in a croup tent because they found she had a swollen larynx and even the croup tent didn't work. But he remained super cool. He says it's because he's so afraid. . . . (2)

Most doctors, though, prefer not to have an active medical role in the family, and most doctors' wives prefer it that way, because they feel that their husbands tend to minimize any medical problems that they or the children might have. As the second of the two quotes above suggests, a doctor's fear that his own family might be vulnerable and frail often leads him to bring that fear under control by distancing himself. Perhaps for the same reason, doctors tend to assume that anything that ails the family is minor and insignificant compared to the more complex and serious conditions that they are trained to deal with. A number of wives have averted a family medical crisis at the eleventh hour because their husbands paid little heed to earlier complaints and symptoms.

I have to push him—he doesn't like to see illness in the family. I had a thyroid problem for a long time before it was diagnosed because he was afraid of what it was. (10)

The older child was very sick and almost died once. . . . That was a crisis point. Up to that point I had always relied on his medical judgment and he would always say "no, they're not sick" and they would always be sick. But this time my son had an infection on his epiglottis and couldn't get air into his windpipe. I had called my husband, but I finally took the boy to the doctor who took one look at him and turned white. He rushed him to the hospital and inserted a tube in him so he could breathe. From that point on I just acted like a normal wife and when the kids get sick I call a doctor. He's not much involved with taking care of them now. (13)

My membranes ruptured when I was six months pregnant and she was premature and when she was born she was full of infection. . . . When the membranes ruptured, I told him I was really wet and he told me it was just a discharge. By evening I was really soaking and I called a sitter and a friend took me to the hospital. (17)

Even with problems that are genuinely of a more ordinary sort, the doctor is prone to overlook the very real discomfort and distress that accompany a routine health problem, precisely because it is routine. Medical talent and sympathy are reserved for the exotic and unusual, and in any case the emphasis is on the technical details of a problem rather than on its possible emotional component.

As a doctor my husband often has less of an interest in his family's health. He tends to know when things are not serious and pays no attention. He gets really upset with us when we are sick. That's been hard on me. When you're sick you're sick, and you don't like to have someone mad at you for being sick. (5)

His response is to say take an aspirin and put your feet up. When my father was ill he was there and very helpful. He took it seriously because it was a real crisis. He deals with things that are so much more serious than a splinter in a finger. (19)

In many ways, then, the medical professional role conflicts with or is separate from the husband-father role and does not harmonize with family life as easily as the academic role, either temporally or substantively. In many physician families, however, the interpersonal distance that typically exists between father and child appears to be a function of the personality of the doctor and not simply of the time demands and constraints of the doctoring role per se. A man who feels most comfortable with certain kinds of professional roles and relationships is likely to express himself in similar ways in the context of personal relationships. In many ways the choice to practice medicine is indicative of a preference for emotional distance. The structure of medicine is such that the instrumental and affective roles are essentially mutually exclusive. The practitioner role—the male role—of medicine places heavy emphasis on technical proficiency and is invested with dominance and authority. In the development of that role there is little if any room left over for the development of psychological sensitivity or interpersonal skills. It is the "women's work" of medicine to provide the affective component—the nurturing and empathy of patient care.

In the family setting physicians are described as "professionally competent and successful, but rigid, interpersonally distant and covertly or overtly controlling. They are extremely uncomfortable with feelings, whether of love or tenderness or hostility" (Miles, Krell, and Lin 1975:2). As a physician, the medical husband is not predisposed toward mutuality, cooperation, or sharing, and in his relationships with his children he tends to express himself in the professional mode—either authoritatively or disinterestedly. The job of forging bonds of closeness and understanding falls to the woman of the family.

He tries to handle everybody—he's the "charger on the white horse." The boys don't want him handing down orders. Their reaction is where do you get away with that? It can be really something to deal with, the interpersonal in the family. Any wife who doesn't have to deal with this is not doing her job. It happens to everyone, especially when he is used to being an authority. (3)

He's a demanding kind of person. . . . He expects us all to achieve in our particular roles. . . . He would tend to be very strict with the kids and I'm more relaxed and have more understanding. I sort of let go before he does and I eventually get him to see my way of thinking. . . . They all adore him; he's stern. . . . They are all real workers and achievers and it's important to them that they please him. (15)

He's had very little of a father role. When they were small there would be days that he would go without seeing them. In those days he was on every other weekend. He would leave before they awoke and get home after they were asleep. . . . Yet he likes kids in his work and I've had more people comment on how good he is with kids and how much he enjoys them. Somehow ours are the last ones he gets to. . . . I feel I've carried a lot of bringing up the kids. He knows it and has been appreciative. (11)

[He's] not the taking-care-of-baby type. We may have a conflict about the amount of his involvement with the children. He doesn't begrudge me any amount of help I hire and he would not have wanted me to put off my own residency. Having a housekeeper was considered a necessary expense. . . . He helped me more in the first few weeks with the youngest child—not because of her, but because I had difficulty with the delivery and I was weak. He was concerned about me and once he saw that I was all right, then he left. (12)

I have forced him to pay attention to what happens with the kids. . . . As the years have gone on I think he has taken less responsibility. With teenage kids, I have often felt myself really up against the wall and have wanted his help. (9)

More than medical life, academic life places a premium on a man's ability to cooperate and interact effectively with students and colleagues alike. The academic role itself is not invested with a high degree of authority and dominance; indeed close colleagueship is often synonymous with friendship and the teacher-student relationship is neither as formally defined nor as circumscribed as the doctor-patient relationship. The relative distance that may exist between undergraduate and teacher is often counterbalanced by the intensity (often containing elements of intimacy) of the graduate student-mentor relationship. Furthermore, as a commitment to the "life of the mind," as it is often referred to, academic life does not evoke a highly masculine image, and probably attracts men to it who are somewhat deviant by conventional standards of masculinity. This may be more true of the "soft" cultural, expressive disciplines of the humanities than of the "hard" technical disciplines of the sciences. However, the interpersonal communication of the teaching role cuts across all disciplines, and one scientist's wife had this to say about the basis of her initial attraction to her husband:

It had nothing to do with his field, but I was searching for a person with a certain kind of inner strength. I was trying to disbelieve the masculine stereotype. I had known men who were only interested in masculine things and were not expressive emotionally. I felt that it must be possible for a man to be an understanding and loving person and still maintain his identity and strength. I also didn't want to marry a fawning Cocker Spaniel puppy type. (38)

The academic role has high potential for the integration of a strong affective component, and in general the man who chooses a career in university teaching is undoubtedly more comfortable with the expression of feelings and the presence of mutuality in a relationship than the man who chooses a career in medicine. The academic is also more likely than the doctor to make an active commitment to family life. Of course this commitment is frequently more qualitative than quantitative and as noted earlier, even in academic families, the majority of the actual tasks of child rearing have fallen to the wife. Indeed the wife quoted above went on to say that in spite of her ideas about the kind of relationship she wanted with her husband, her expectation of how the roles would take shape and what the division of labor would be was "really quite stereotyped."

But whereas in the doctor's family a husband's generally low level of participation in the tasks of child-rearing seems to be synonymous with or indicative of a more pervasive diffidence toward family relationships as such, this is not necessarily true of the academic father. The number of professor fathers compared to doctor fathers who have taken the time to attend conferences with a child's teacher or to buy birthday and holiday presents or get up at night with an unhappy child surely points to a greater interest in fathering on the part of the academic husband. (Table 5.4.) The schedule of academic work may facilitate participation in family life, but it does not motivate that participation. By the same token, the schedule of work need not be an insurmountable barrier to participation in family life. It is interesting to note that, despite the demanding schedules of their work, a few medical husbands have involved themselves in tasks that bespeak a high level of personal interest in their children.

Even though he may have participated only slightly or moderately in the actual work of child rearing, the academic father has

frequently brought to his role as father a level of interest, enthusiasm, and nurturing that is noticeably absent on the part of most
medical fathers. The skills needed for teaching are similar in many
respects to the skills needed for parenting; the two roles place a
common emphasis on stirring curiosity, inducing interest in learning, and guiding to maturity, with the result that the roles reinforce
one another. The academic husband's style of parenting is perhaps
best summed up by the remarks of one wife, whose husband, it
should be noted, has assumed almost no responsibility for the day-
to-day tasks of child rearing.

He was not much involved when they were newborns. He's been
more and more involved with them as they have grown up. That's
not to say he didn't play with them. He taught them to play ball
and would draw things for them. He started telling them Greek
myths as preschoolers, and he has nurtured an interest in various
things that they have developed on their own now. He thoroughly
enjoys their athletic events. He used to be athletic and goes fishing
now. He tries to get them involved and talks to them about their
reading and any theater they go to. In the summer we go swimming
together. In the past couple of months he's been taking our oldest
son around looking at colleges. (30)

In either professional group, it is invariably the wife who takes
the initiative when it comes to emotional stocktaking or problem
solving within the family. But the academic husband is more likely
than the medical husband to be interested and actively supportive
and helpful when it comes to responding to or dealing with any
emotional, academic, or other difficulties that might accompany the
growing up process. A comparison of the first three quotations with
the second three that follow should make clear the dividing line between professor and doctor fathers in that respect.

Physicians' wives:

We have a son who is difficult and I'm thinking of sending him to
prep school. [Is that your decision?] I wouldn't say it in front of
him, but it is. I've been going to a child psychologist. It's not my
husband's idea at all and when I go now, I go alone. My husband
went once for the first session and we talked about the whole family

history. The psychologist was very analytic and told my husband that some of the problems were because he had been away for the whole first year of my son's life. He didn't like that. When I go now I go alone. He thinks things will take care of themselves. I have taken action and made decisions about how to handle the child. (14)

It was my idea to take the kids to see a psychologist. It was [my daughter]—she was having trouble sleeping and was afraid. I don't think my husband saw a thing and now I am having trouble with my son. He thinks of women as bitches. His . . . teacher told me he was surly and that she had come close to slapping him. I told her my husband was overeducated and wouldn't help me with him. My son and my husband are kind of allies. . . . My daughter said about a week ago that she felt like committing suicide. Both girls saw the psychologist for a while, but I can't get anywhere with my son.(2)

Our oldest boy is dyslexic. It's not a big concern for my husband. I've been more concerned than he was. My husband has always done well in school and can't relate to the idea that the children won't too. He's not upset and he is interested when I tell him what the tutors have to say. (5)

Professors' wives:

Our oldest child had always been a problem because he was extremely active. As he got older he was more and more difficult to manage. . . . Then the next year his teacher left partway through the school year and his behavior got progressively worse, so we did decide to get some help. We had no conflicts about going into therapy. . . . My husband was a little reluctant to do it because of the time commitment but he was willing to try it. It was obvious we needed help. I was the one who said I think we should do this. . . . Part of what the psychologist said was that in some ways we hadn't communicated enough about how to deal with specific episodes of behavior. . . . So now we try to talk more about the children. Any kind of stocktaking about the children or any relationships has been my function. My husband made a decision to go into therapy for himself partly to get us out of the one-sidedness. (23)

He's involved in their academic career almost to a fault. . . . He got the principal of the school to agree that our son should be in situations where he learns what he wants to learn. And then our next oldest son wanted very much to make a certain English course and my husband got involved in that and called the teacher over the phone. . . . He is concerned that they are having problems in school because they are exceptionally bright children and he wants to see them fulfill themselves. (26)

Our daughter is now in college again. She doesn't know what she wants to do. . . . There was a time when she decided to go to Europe and educate herself. . . . Then she went off to — and we had no idea how to get hold of her and were just about to set out tracing her when we learned she was alive and well. . . . At the time she occupied most of our thought and conversation during this period. . . . When she returned she saw a psychiatrist who told us we were the problem not her. We talked that over for awhile and decided we didn't want to get into that situation. We realize we have problems in the family but we will muddle through. The conversations between my husband and me were beneficial—it did open up some avenues that neither of us had thought about and then things began to fall into place. . . . We suggested to her that we would support her if she wanted psychotherapeutic help of some sort. (27)

The dividing lines between the two professional groups as to their fathering style is not always so clear-cut, though. Those academics (described in the preceding chapter) who have deemphasized the teaching component of their professional role and place the highest premium on their research and scholarship and the recognition they earn from that are very like doctors in their tendency to dominate or distance themselves from their family roles. Their depersonalization of the academic work role and preoccupation with technical mastery through research translate into aloofness in the family. As fathers they have involved themselves in their children's lives only indifferently or sporadically.

Mostly he sees our son just to put him to bed and possibly briefly in the morning. Sometimes he takes him out camping. (33)

He just doesn't understand young children and had nothing to do with them literally. (39)

He has not really had a great deal of involvement with the children. They were both difficult children. The second one is allergic to all sorts of dietary things. Until she was fifteen months old she woke every night. Mostly I got up. When it was obvious it was going to go on for a long time he did get up occasionally. . . . He doesn't

147

talk much about his work to them. He finds it difficult to put technical facts into the kind of language they can understand. I don't think it bothers him whether they take an interest in his work. I don't know if it's because they are both girls or that he can see they have different kinds of interests. (37)

Here again, there is an obvious correlation between the structure and style of professional roles and family roles.

Homemaking and Housekeeping

Child rearing is only one part of home and family life. In any household there are a great many domestic and social details to attend to. There are meals to be shopped for, prepared, cleaned up after; clothing to be cleaned and pressed; houses to be decorated, refurbished, repaired, and cleaned; bills to be paid; kinship ties to be maintained; social and leisure life to be planned and organized.

As a general rule the division of labor in household management is arranged along highly sex-typed lines in both the medical and the academic families. Although considerably more academic than medical husbands have made a "substantial" or "high" contribution to household management (see table 5.5), the responsibility for most daily, routine, and repetitive chores of homemaking and housekeeping has fallen overwhelmingly to the wives in both professional groups. A task-by-task elaboration of the shape of the household division of labor (table 5.6) shows quite clearly that very

TABLE 5.5   HUSBAND'S PARTICIPATION IN HOUSEHOLD
DIVISION OF LABOR

Participation (number of tasks)[a]	M.D. Husbands (N = 18)	Ph.D. Husbands (N = 18)
Low (0–3)	5	2
Moderate (4–6)	10	7
Substantial (7–9)	3	6
High (10 or more)	0	3

[a]Number of household tasks of a total of 15 that husband either shares with wife or assumes sole responsibility for. For description of tasks, see table 5.6.

TABLE 5.6   HOUSEHOLD AND FAMILY MANAGEMENT: THE ROLE OF THE
HUSBAND

(Number of Families Where Task Is Either Shared by Husband and Wife or
Done by Husband Alone)

	M.D. Couples (N = 18)	Ph.D. Couples (N = 18)
Household chores that are typically done daily or regularly throughout the week.		
1. Meal preparation	0	2
2. Routine housekeeping	0	1
3. Grocery shopping	0	3
4. Keeping clothes, linens washed, cleaned, pressed	0	2
5. After-meal clean-up	2	9
Household chores that are typically done less often than once a week.		
1. Paying household bills	9	10
2. Arranging for car repairs	13	12
3. General home maintenance—minor repairs, yard work, etc.	13	16
4. Major or seasonal housecleaning—rug cleaning, closet clean out, etc.	1	4
5. Purchasing, replacing small household items	0	1
Social and leisure life and planning.		
1. Accepting social invitations	8	14
2. Arranging for family get-togethers	17	13
3. Making travel and vacation plans	18	16
4. Sending holiday and special occasion cards and gifts to family and friends	3	7
5. Extending social invitations to your home	10	13

NOTE: Items are described here in the same way that they were described on questionnaire forms for wives. In instances where someone outside the family is paid or hired to do a particular job, wives were asked to indicate which spouse actually carries responsibility for the supervision or management of that task.

few, if any, husbands in either profession have taken part in the basic and nondeferrable areas of home maintenance—meals, laundry, cleaning, and restocking. The academic husband is more apt than the medical husband to be at home with his family for the evening meal; this probably accounts for the fact that half of the professors do help with after-meal clean-up.

Husbands have taken the most responsibility for those tasks that are conventionally thought of as male, i.e., bill paying, home repairs or yard work, and car repairs. None of these, it should be added, occur with the same regularity or frequency as the more ordinary chores of housekeeping. Perhaps it is in keeping with their greater indifference to interpersonal ties and communication that fewer doctors than academics participate in the maintenance of kinship and social ties—at least in the form of special occasion correspondence and the acceptance of social invitations. While the majority of men in each group do participate with their wives in making plans for home entertaining, it is invariably the case that the actual work of planning and preparing for an evening's socializing is carried out by the wife.

The tables reveal the broad contours of the household division of labor as it has taken shape within the medical and academic family, but they provide only a partial picture of what has been involved for the academic or medical wife in her double-duty role as housekeeper and homemaker. A fuller understanding of the scope and definition of that role is to be found behind the scenes, inside the homes and in the words and experiences of the women themselves.

It is a time-honored practice of sociology to regard the physical setting and appearance of a house as a major indicator of the social universe in which its occupants live and move. Indeed it does not take a great deal of traveling back and forth between academic and medical residences to realize that home for the doctor and his family is a rather different place than it is for the academic and his family, and some of those differences were described in an earlier chapter. The difference between the two is not merely that doctors' houses are more expensive than professors' houses, but that they are far more elaborate. With its sweeping, wooded, landscaped yard, matched suites of period furniture, color-coordinated, draped and chandeliered rooms, cheerful matched print or plaid family room, lavishly equipped kitchen, spotless powder room, polished antiques and endless array of accent pieces—the lamps or pictures or other "objects" designed to complete the effect—the average suburban doctor's house, immaculately maintained, is the house of TV commercials and women's magazines.

In contrast, the academic house is a far less glamourous and perfected place; it is smaller and plainer both inside and out; it often sits in the midst of a modest, look-alike subdivision or on a small in-town lot. Furnishings and appointments are casual, eclectic, and often downright shabby, giving no evidence of any planned decor. Its general state of repair bears the stamp of the home handyman or do-it-yourselfer. And overall the prevailing standards of cleanliness, neatness and order in the academic home fall far below those of the medical home.

These houses themselves and the differences between them tell us at a glance much about the housewife's role that is not revealed by a mere description and enumeration of tasks performed. The doctor's wife presides over a high-status domain, the creation and maintenance of which requires considerably more time, energy, planning, and organization than its less elaborate academic counterpart. The academic home is such that for many women housekeeping can be reduced to the basics of keeping beds made, dishes washed, floors mopped or vacuumed, and maintaining some, but not necessarily a high, degree of order and cleanliness. For many medical wives those chores are only the beginning, for a good deal of their time goes into the planning and shopping and consulting required by the "doing" and "redoing" of their homes. In addition, academic wives rely on outside household help to a far lesser extent than medical wives. (Table 5.7.)

Housewifery expands to fill not only the time available, as Frie-

TABLE 5.7   PATTERNS OF OUTSIDE HOUSEHOLD HELP (EXCLUDING CHILD CARE) AT PRESENT TIME

Amount of Help	M.D. Families (N = 18)	Ph.D. Families (N = 18)
No help	5	14
Less than 10 hours a week of help	8	3
10 to 24 hours a week of help	5	1

dan suggests (1963:224), but the life style as well. Of course it is to a large extent a woman's own choice to maintain her home to standards that qualify it to serve as a domestic outpost of her husband's occupational status. The five medical wives who have not hired any domestic help despite a generous income have imposed even heavier demands on themselves in their housekeeping role than most doctors' wives. On the other hand it is also clear that the medical husband himself often has his own vested interest in maintaining the status quo where his wife's homemaking role is concerned, and in many specific ways her role is much more directly and authoritatively shaped by her husband's expectations and preferences than the housekeeping role of the academic wife. Far more than the academic, the doctor expects to be personally serviced by his wife in her domestic role in ways that not only convenience him directly but that also do not inconvenience him. The boundary lines between what pleases him and displeases him, between what he will and will not do tend to be quite sharply and permanently drawn, and whatever the parameters of a wife's own day, it is clearly her job to maintain those boundaries in place and intact.

No, he doesn't have specific expectations for the house. He's very good about that. I'm not organized, but he doesn't like to come home and find a sitter here and he doesn't like to come home and not have dinner ready. I manage the house as I want. . . . He took his Boards the summer we moved into this house. I was painting all the woodwork in the house and was overseeing the papering. He really wouldn't help me. He didn't study all that much, but he would have felt terrible if he had taken the time to paint. I told him if he failed his Boards he would have to get a new wife when he studied next time. It was very pressured. He took three weeks off to study. I was moving and had the children who were then two and four. I had four days to do all the papering and painting before we moved in. (17)

OK that would be interesting if I made demands on him for his time around here. He would say do whatever you want, just as long as . . . . But I'm the one who handles the finances and I could get someone to come in full time and I don't think he'd object. But he wants a good dinner and he's very fussy. He doesn't like any prepared things. And he wants the house to be clean. (14)

He's demanding of me. He expects the house to be running smoothly and not to have any problems with the kids. (15)

He's not enthusiastic about my working full time. He's quite accustomed to being catered to. He doesn't demand it but has come to expect it. He's concerned about coming home and finding dinner not ready. (9)

As long as I'm home when he's home and home when the kids are home and I'm able to shop and run the household then he doesn't care what I do. (4)

This house is a bugaboo too. I have someone clean twice a week. . . . My husband begrudges her that $12 every time I pay her to clean. He told someone I was the laziest, most self-centered person he'd ever met. He thinks I won't make myself do it, so he shouldn't have to pay. . . . My house is never dirty—it's just not always picked up. He can't stand the clutter. He couldn't come in and sit down and relax without picking up. (2)

In her response to questionnaire items about her husband's participation in the household division of labor, one surgeon's wife actually checked off all the items as belonging in the "not applicable" column. She wrote a note in the margin explaining that in her marriage there is no question or choice as to who does what in the home, because it is "simply assumed that all of these chores will be done by a woman." It is hard to escape the impression that in many medical marriages a doctor's investment in his wife's domestic role has as much to do with the reinforcement of his status as with his comfort and convenience per se. If that be so, the meaning assigned by Veblen to the performance of housekeeping services in the "leisure class" remains pertinent:

But much of the services classed as household cares in modern everyday life, and many of the "utilities" required for a comfortable existence by civilized man, are of a ceremonial character. . . . These occupations are chiefly useful as a method of imputing pecuniary reputability to the master or to the household on the ground that a given amount of time and effort is conspicuously wasted in that behalf. . . . The servant or the wife should not only perform certain offices and show a servile disposition, but it is quite as imperative that they should show an acquired facility in the tactic of subservience. . . . Even today it is this aptitude and acquired skill in the formal manifes-

153

tation of the servile relation that constitutes one of the chief ornaments of the well-bred housewife. (1934:58–60)

Many doctors also draw lines between their own work and "women's work" in the area of household finances. More than a third of the medical wives are placed on allowances or budgets by their husbands—an arrangement not found in any academic family. The woman who runs the home on a predetermined budget or allowance is not permitted even the illusion of independence and self-sufficiency in her domestic role; her husband is her patron and her benefactor and for her part, she is like a child who is not wise in the ways of the world.

If he sees an article in *Medical Economics* that I should read he'll give it to me. He thinks I should know what other doctors are making and what their wives are spending. He placed me on a budget because he knows I would never ask for more than he gives me. I find that other doctors' wives spend a lot more on themselves than I do. Sometimes I will complain about this. It's more in jest. I'm not deprived. *(15)*

He brings home a check weekly and I take care of all the bills here at home. I get a certain amount of money every week and it's up to me to budget. I'm responsible for everything with the house and kids. *(4)*

He handles the investments. . . . I decide on food and clothing and so on and I handle the household finances. I do not buy any jewelry for myself. He usually picks that out for me. *(16)*

No financial area is solely his own, though the final decisions are his because he doesn't think I'm that good a manager. *(5)*

My husband gives me an allowance. I take care of everything connected with the house and he takes care of the big things. *(3)*

The academic husband is not in the habit of handing down such rigid and permanent directives about the shape of the household division of labor and the terms of his participation and nonparticipation in it. And academics, after all, have participated more in household work than doctors—they are three times more apt to show "substantial" and "high" levels of household participation than doctors (table 5.5). Although the pattern of work in the academic household may have settled into place along conventional sex-typed lines, the academic husband does not seem to have a specific investment in enforcing his dominance and insisting on a set order of things. The professor husband tends to be less exacting in his expectations of how the household should be run, and he is more amenable to an impromptu or temporary or occasionally even permanent renegotiation of his own household role. Then too the faculty wife herself, perhaps encouraged by the positive valuation placed on personal development and self-expression in the academic setting, has felt far freer than the medical wife to challenge or even circumvent her husband's customary expectations in the interests of pursuing her own goals. While the physician's family has remained pretty much set in its ways over time so far as the division of labor is concerned, many professors' families have made substantial changes along the way.

Yes, absolutely his routines changed when I took the job. . . . I had been responsible for not only the cooking and cleaning and most of the children's activities, but also for a large number of chores that go with a family—banking, dry cleaning, and home repairmen. Once I took this job my husband took over a large part of this of his own accord and he simply just does these things which need doing. . . . There was a great deal of tension before I took the job. . . . Since I had never worked full time he was very apprehensive. But once I started working and got into the business of it, he apparently made up his mind he was going to do the best he could to help me out. I will never understand why. (30)

Oh yes, I was very traditional. . . . I was going to stay home and make life lovely and cook lots of yummy dinners—all that stuff. I was looking forward to having my own little home and *Ladies Home Journal* decorations in it. I never, ever got there and I more and more decided that wasn't what I wanted. But he expected the same thing. I was going to lay myself down on the floor for him. I was going to be the perfect wife, be very efficient and well organized. That's what I thought I was going to do. Actually I got quite a bit more selfish as time went on. As I have demanded more he has done more. At first we had these little roles . . . and as I got bored with that particular role and moved over here, he just moved over too. He still doesn't do things like the dishes or anything material of that sort, but I would say one has only to ask and he'll certainly do whatever is needed—even the dishes. In fact he made a bed the other day. (26)

We had a very traditional set-up until the first time that I taught. So [his] contribution was to fix breakfast—he started on Tuesdays and Thursdays and then it quickly went over to the whole week. Then he discovered he liked making breakfast and has continued doing it since then. . . . Yes, he likes things in the house neat. I'm not a slob but I'm not as fastidious as he is. We have compromised and he does realize it may be a bit of a fetish with him. He's never complained about how the house is and I don't feel guilty because I think I do pretty well. There are times when he would like to have clean socks and for a few days he may have to wash out his own socks. But he's not a complainer. (34)

Housekeeping has become less of a priority since I began in school. The house isn't as well kept as previously and things like darning socks tend to be put off and so does sewing for the girls. . . . My husband would prefer to see the home somewhat better organized and better kept. There are certain things that I could do more of if I were at home. . . . He likes things to be clean and to look neat and be tidy. But if it gets bad enough he'll do something about it, although he'll make a comment about it first. I feel very upset that all that responsibility should be mine. He has done a lot more since I've been going to school, though I think possibly he has begrudged the time he's felt he's had to spend. I do think it can be shared and it's important to me to go to school. (37)

There's been a major reorganization around here. I don't do as much at home. [He] does the groceries now. We divide up differently than before. We talked about it seriously for about a semester. We saw the physical obstacle—the problem of how to get things done. [He] was not delighted to suddenly have more responsibilities—on the other hand he wanted me to get a degree. (21)

The academic work role itself undergoes many changes in scope, orientation and content during the life of the academic career. A professor's courses and research and writing projects vary from year to year, as do the extent and kind of his administrative responsibilities. Furthermore he is often called upon to rethink the content of his roles and the quality of his relationships with colleagues and students. He is accustomed to rearrangement in his professional life and is perhaps less likely than the doctor to be disconcerted when that occurs in his personal life. The doctor who is used to a set order of things in his practice and who seldom encounters challenges to his professional role, carries these expectations into his home setting.

The two doctors' wives who have defined their housekeeping role most flexibly and least elaborately are married to the two hospital-based practitioners described in the previous chapter. For these physicians, the hospital setting is not the usual scene of rugged individualism and dominance that characterizes the world of private medical practice; neither is there evidence of subordination to high status housekeeping by their wives. What was particularly outstanding about these two medical households was their extraordinary clutter and disarray, a product of the wives' avowed disinterest in housekeeping or in interior furnishings and decoration. In both homes the decor was very plain and well used. The husbands have been highly tolerant of the general household disorder that results from their wives' heavy outside involvements and have borne up quite well to challenges either to increase the amount of their own participation or to lower their own expectations.

The hospital takes the blame for everything. He blames medicine for his ineptness at doing something else. And I scream back, "the hospital doesn't put out the trash!" We fight about the division of labor when medical practice and I disagree. I had a tendency when I was first married to think the doctor had to be freed up to be a doctor. That lasted until we had our first baby. Then I said "wait a minute, the doctor wants a family, the doctor wants a wife, the doctor can participate." It took me a while. I came from a family where they are all in awe of "my son-in-law the doctor." He walks on water according to my mother. She gives me a lot of flak about what I do to him. He told her his halo was getting heavy. (1)

He's very flexible and whatever I want to do is fine. We sit down and think it through—where are you going and what are the implications for the family. . . . I'm not a real house person. I like my time alone at home to get my head together, but I knew I would never be just a housewife. My husband knew that after one messy week of living with me. The minimum gets done. I don't clean to clean. It took adjusting on his part. (8)

157

More than other doctors' wives, these two wives have defined their double-duty work in terms of their own standards and expectations, and they are terms that their husbands respect and agree to.

Social and Community Life

The social and public participation of the wife is an aspect of and is contained in her domestic as well as her adjunct activity. Her social and community commitments benefit the establishment and mobility of her husband's career, but in addition her husband stands to gain from those activities in his personal and family life as well. Professional life, whether medical or academic, can be relentlessly one-sided, and many husbands are rescued from a life that would be all work and no play by wives who see to it that they take some regular time off for socializing and entertaining. Most of the wives interviewed described themselves as far more outgoing and socially gregarious than their husbands and report that they provide their husbands with a social life that they would not otherwise seek for themselves and indeed do not need to learn how to seek because they can rely on their wives' competence in that area.

He will go to the lab on Saturday and Sunday unless I plan something and say "let's do this." It's up to me to initiate it. (39)

A wife does more than provide her husband with recreation through her social and community activities; she also provides him with a window on the world around him. She brings him in touch with a diversity of people and experiences that are not found in the homogeneous world of work. In many ways her world is bigger and more varied than his, precisely because it is less focused. The academic is perhaps more easily led into the political and cultural life either of the wider university community or his residential community by virtue of the subject matter and values of his work than the doctor, whose workday life is narrowly bounded and cut off from any but the medical community. The medical husband, therefore, is especially dependent on his wife to keep him informed, to broaden his horizons, and to expand his range of social acquaintances.

We might talk about my frustrations with the town. We talk about politics. I keep him posted on news that he doesn't get to follow. He has no involvement in community activities. He has very little spare time. (17)

I've been trying to branch out and meet people with the same interests as ours but not in medicine. . . . It's the first time in our lives we've had people over to dinner who are not friends of my husband's. He enjoys meeting the people I've met. When we were first married I was always a little ill at ease with his associates . . . and now when he is with my friends he is a bit ill at ease with people that he doesn't have a work bond in common with. I can feel him groping around—I think it's good for him. He can get so involved in medicine it could be his whole life. Prior to becoming a doctor he was a very interesting person. I can see him growing more inward. (7)

I tell him the tidbits I have learned outside. He is interested in this and likes what I do. He does get the total community picture talking to me. . . . Sometimes my identity is so attractive that he resents that I've got the freedom to do it. (1)

At the same time that a woman represents the community to her family and to her husband in particular, she also represents her family to the community. The idea that the more privileged classes have an obligation to give back something to the community in order to establish the moral basis of their economic worth is deeply woven into the fabric of American life. Since men are frequently too busy working to earn the money on which their families' affluence rests to uphold their civic responsibilities in any active way, the job of tending to the poor and maintaining high standards of citizenship and culture and has been a traditional responsibility of their more leisured wives. Most of the doctors' wives and some of the academic wives have been active and enthusiastic participants in the "service cliques" of their community, thereby paying their families' social debt to the educational, political, and cultural institutions of the towns where they live and work.

It is easy to be skeptical about both the motivation behind and the long-term impact of the volunteer role. Gold, for example, interprets the volunteer role as a product of the loneliness and emptiness in women's lives and as a way of satisfying women's need for achievement while maintaining intact the traditional female role, including the powerlessness associated with it. She describes volunteer work as a "hybrid of work and role playing, more closely linked to occupational therapy than to work accomplished in the economic sense" (1971:393). On the other hand the equally persuasive argument may be made that a woman's altruism does for the community what her social outgoingness does for her husband—it mitigates the harshness of a purely economic and work-oriented approach to the world.

Freedom and Constraint in
Doing Double Duty

Of all of the many and varied ways that wives support and contribute to their husbands' professional attainments, their commitments as homemakers and mothers are the ones that have been most deeply and continuously etched into the lives of these women. It is also in doing double duty that they have been most indispensable to their husbands' career success. It is never considered an extraordinary feat for a man to have both a family and a career for the simple reason that the double-duty work of his wife absolves him of much, if not all, of the tasks and responsibilities associated with parenting and household management. He is therefore a free agent to pursue his career on whatever terms he or others deem necessary, and that is, indeed, exactly what those terms assume. Rossi summarizes the central importance of women's work as mothers and homemakers to the pursuit of high-ranking occupational careers.

> The life that men have led in these strata has been possible only because their own wives were leading traditional lives as homemakers, doing double parent and household duty, and carrying the major burden of civic responsibilities. If it were not for their wives in the background, successful men in American society would have to be single or childless. (1972a:351)

Like most professional men, of course, the doctors and professors whose wives are speaking in this book are neither single nor childless. And like most professional men, they live in the best of both worlds. They have had the time and independence to develop their intellectual capacities and talents to the fullest, and to pursue high-level and challenging work while enjoying the comfort of home and the companionship of family. It has not fallen to them to reconcile the conflicting demands of family and work, and for this they have their wives to thank. The twofold advantage that these men have enjoyed in their lives is ingenuously depicted by one surgeon's wife:

I have wondered did his profession change me? He has worked so hard and has a really fine reputation. Many places I go they ask if I'm his wife and will say such nice things about him. It's made a better person of me. I have tried to live up to him. I think there's a stigma about being a doctor's wife. People talk about being a "typical doctor's wife" and I wonder what they mean—better dressed, Junior League and all that. I don't know how I fit in. I think I've pleased my husband whatever I've become. When you said you were interested in learning about the relationship between professional life and family life, I asked him if I and the children had had any effect on his practice and he said quite succinctly, "No." He said, "You've made my life easier and pleasant, but I would have been the same doctor without it." (15)

And that is precisely the point.

To examine the amount of freedom and constraint involved in doing double duty is also potentially to raise some complex questions about the psychology and socialization of women and about the evolution of a subjective sense of self that predisposes women to make certain choices and to seek certain rewards and gratifications rather than others. It also runs the risk of steering a course that arrives at the essentially sexist stance concerning subjective happiness and limits to options that underlies the question that is so commonly asked and answered all in one breath: "If she's happy and that's her choice, then why shouldn't a woman be at home?" That, however, is not the issue at hand here. The intent is rather to draw some general conclusions about the structure of a wife's double-duty work as it has evolved in relation to her husband's work and about the amount and fixity of the space that doing double duty occupies in a woman's life.

The major difference between doing double duty as a medical wife and as an academic wife is plainly that the domestic roles of homemaking and parenting are bigger and less yielding for the physician's wife than for the professor's wife. This seems to be a function of the professional dominance of the medical role and its intrusion into the family life and life style of the medical family. The doctor's wife tailors her double duty commitment to the status, as that is personally and professionally expressed, of her husband's position as a physician. Emotional distance and absence from home are bred into the doctor by a profession that officially leaves the business of nurturing to women, to nurses at work and wives at home; by a profession that removes men almost entirely from family life and opportunities for personal growth throughout a very long and demanding training period; by a profession that jealously safeguards its autonomy, with the result that the doctor hoards patients who then hoard his time. As a consequence, the medical wife is not only the primary manager of childrearing, but the emotional mainstay in her children's lives as well. This is true to such a great extent that a wife's choice to have substantial outside commitments of her own might run the serious risk of emotional desertion for children in medical families.

There is good reason to believe, however, that the doctor's wife holds tight to her mothering role as a way of meeting her own needs for intimacy as well as her children's. Often doctors seem to be no better at satisfying their wives' needs for intimacy than their children's. One doctor's wife—an acquaintance, not a research subject—suggested in casual conversation that the women who hold up best in their roles as doctors' wives are the ones who are comfortable with a great deal of distance in their relationships. There may be some truth in this, and women who pride themselves on needing little attention from their husbands (or "T.L.C." as one wife put it) may be good examples. It is clear, though, that many of the doctors' wives who were interviewed had hoped for a more communicative relationship with their husbands, and for these wives, coming to terms with their husbands' general lack of responsiveness has been both painful and disappointing. With great consistency these wives described their husbands as calm, logical, unruffled—qualities which the women found exasperating precisely because of their lack of emotional engagement. When confronted with such control, a wife is often made to feel silly or somehow inferior when giving expression to her own feelings, and over time learns to adjust to the tone he sets.

I get irritable about very small things. . . . He's much more easy-going than I am. He doesn't lose patience and is good natured. We have learned what was important very early in our lives and we don't get involved with little things. (17)

It's hard to get him stirred up to confront his feelings. . . . But I think I talk too much. [He] is very logical. He goes to the john every single day at exactly the same time. He wanted to make an appointment with me every Thursday to have sex. Can you believe it? But he can be kind. I feel that I'm too much for him to handle. (2)

He's unbelievably calm to the point of being exasperating to me. It's difficult to get him angry. He's very even tempered. That's all right but he doesn't appreciate the fact that other people are not that way. He just lets me blow off steam if I need to, but he doesn't get angry and sometimes I want him to. His calmness makes me angry. But I think a lot of emotional reactions of women are really hormonal. He knows that sometimes I get really bitchy for no emotional reason. (7)

The hardest time was the period of my sterility. We had applied to adopt a third child and were refused because of my emotional hang-ups. I had had a stillbirth and [he] was new in practice and gone a lot. Usually I made a scene about every six months. [And how did he respond?] He's an excellent doctor—he just listens. [And was that what you were looking for?] NO! That's not what I was looking for, but that's what I got. There's nowhere to go. A wife is stuck. . . . There are lots of periods where you have to get over your problems in the interests of everyone else. [He] would always say to me "count your blessings." Sometimes they were hard to count—hard to see them. . . . We didn't argue until about four years ago because he wouldn't answer me. Once he answered me back. (10)

He thinks I'm too critical of everything and I get irritated because I think he's too easy-going. We don't argue very much—he's a very calm person. I'm more apt to flare up. But I've learned not to over the years. . . . He withdraws when there are too many ups and downs. *(19)*

The medical wife is further constrained by the sheer magnitude and elaboration of maintaining a home to the high-status life style that prevails in medical communities. More importantly, however, the dominance of the physician's role and personality is matched by a dominance in the home setting through the doctor's unwavering nonparticipation in the "women's work" of the household and in the specification of certain requirements to be met by that work as well. Furthermore the doctor's social standing and that of his family impose additional civic responsibilities on the wife in her double-duty activities.

For all of these reasons it is not surprising that so few medical wives have found it possible to make any substantial commitments outside the family other than on a volunteer, or otherwise highly time-limited and deferrable basis. Most of these women had only a tentative and slender history of and commitment to work earlier in their lives; they entered into marriage with their own interests only vaguely or stereotypically developed. Over time their double-duty work has the effect of further attenuating any motivation to work outside the home or of diffusing the interests that might once have been there, so that focusing becomes difficult. One young doctor's wife might well have been speaking for all medical wives when she spoke of the freedom-limiting aspects of doing double duty as she has known it.

He would never tell me I couldn't work, but I'm more insightful about what a total involvement on my part would mean than he is. He has his job and his commitments. As far as the family is concerned, what attention he gives to us and the few things he does around the house are really his total involvement. I completely run the entire house, manage the billing and even mow the lawn. I really do a lot of stuff and he wouldn't be able to share that. . . . Right now I have no definite goal to work toward. I have a lot of varied interests but I don't have any one thing that interests me. When [my son] gets into school all day I would not have any guilt feelings about pursuing my own interests but not to the neglect of the children. I really do feel a great obligation to them right now.

I'm the only stable person in the family. If his job obligations were half of what they were and he could share in the responsibility I would not have the same feeling of obligation. But because of his position I feel as if it's been dumped on me. I may not like it but it was my decision—our decision—to have children and I don't feel as though I can go back on that. (7)

The double-duty contribution of the academic wife has typically been both more scaled down and less iron-clad in its boundaries than the medical version. The academic husband is more predisposed by his own professional role at least to share occupancy in his household and with his family than the medical husband, who so often seems like a visiting dignitary in his own home. It is true that a half-dozen or so of the professors have built regular or prolonged periods of travel away from home into their schedule of work, and their wives have felt the heavy burden of their husbands' periodic absences. "Those were always the times when the children got into trouble."

But the structure and values, and possibly even the subject matter, of academic life encourage an emphasis on process, communication, collegiality, and cooperation that are similar to the manner in which the teaching-committed academic husband involves himself with the world of home and family. He does have considerable input into the relationships with his children, if not into the management of the work and schedules that they generate. And he is far less inclined than the doctor to leave the stamp of male dominance on the household division of labor, either in terms of his own expectations, patterns of participation and willingness to change, or toleration of some rearrangement in those patterns of participation. In any case, housekeeping in the academic home is a relatively modest affair, geared more toward amenities than status, and need not therefore loom as a major occupation or preoccupation for either spouse.

There are, therefore, more doors opening outward in the academic than in the medical double-duty role and this difference is reflected in the much higher proportion of academic wives who have engaged in some paid work or study commitment throughout the years of their marriage and who are doing so in the present.

Undoubtedly the academic environment itself has served both to stimulate interest in and provide opportunities for achievement in a way that the more limited and isolated environment of medical suburbia does not. Then too, many more academic than medical wives brought specific credentials or interests to marriage on which to build—these wives probably invested less than doctors' wives in the elaboration of the housekeeping aspects of the double-duty role to begin with.

Relative to medical wives, academic wives show a rather impressive record of accomplishments. Relative to the accomplishments of their high-ranking, well-published academic husbands, however, the achievements of academic wives are considerably diminished in size. The academic husband is no more constrained than the doctor by the responsibilities of home and family as he travels the road to career success, though he may be more able and more inclined to make contributions in those areas along the way. Double-duty responsibility falls to academic and medical wives alike, and for the wives of each group, the freedom to achieve is the freedom that is to be found within that role, not outside it. While the academic wife has indeed found greater freedom than the doctor's wife within the double-duty role, her record of accomplishments is also a record of deferrments, holding actions, interruptions, substitutions, dead ends, and making do's in the interest of being true to her domestic roles as she has felt it necessary and desirable. As a result they are also accomplishments which, when measured against the level of pay, recognition, education and credentials, status, and rank that attach to the successful professional career, are distinctly secondary to her husband's. One wife with a Ph.D. of her own, who has yet to achieve tenure in the department in which her husband is a full professor of long standing, reveals in microcosm the inevitable and inherent tension between her double duty and her professional commitment:

He writes at home and is grumpy when he is interrupted. He has a facility that I don't have and perhaps it's because I'm responsible in a more direct way for the running of the household. He can close out all sorts of extraneous sights and sounds and become really unaware of his surroundings. This means of course that if some disas-

ter happens he isn't as aware. But it's also an advantage because
you can concentrate a lot better. He doesn't interfere with the
household routine, but he's not as available either. Even with the
two of us working together, I don't tune out the way he does. . . . I
would probably work better if I were totally removed from household distractions. I think oh gee, it's 3:35 and I really ought to get
the roast in or forget about it. But that's it, I can't. If I'm not there to
do it it doesn't get done. (22)

Then too, dominance is not an altogether absent feature of the
professional and personal role of the academic male and some academic wives have been nearly as much constrained as any doctor's
wife in their double-duty role by the impact of their husbands' professionalism on domestic roles and relationships. Those academics
who are concerned primarily with their own productivity and recognition as researchers and scholars have been the smallest contributors among the academic husbands to the work of their households. The same men have been the least active and involved
fathers. In keeping with their agentic and conventionally male approach to their work role, the division of labor in these academic
homes is rigidly sex-typed and it is understood that housework is
exclusively and unalterably a woman's domain.

I take care of the home and the children. My husband does nothing
at home. He earns the money and I spend it. That's what it amounts
to. I pay all the bills. I keep the house running. I paint, I wallpaper
and look after the furnace. He has no particular expectation of how
he wants these things done, as long as it doesn't interfere with him.
As long as he doesn't have to think about it. He isn't interested in
that and he doesn't want to have to worry about it. (39)

For these wives, as for most medical wives, the noninterference
and deference that constitute their supportive response to the primacy of their husbands' work turns into the inflexibly drawn com-
prehensiveness of doing double duty. Together their contributions
impose great constraint on their time and inclination to pursue
their own independent activities. To the extent that academic wives
in this group do have outside work or study commitments, they are
tentative and highly time-limited—they stay well within the limits

of what the women consider to be manageable and still meet the obligations of their double-duty commitment.

> My first obligation is to the house and to the children. If I can work in the other fine. Otherwise I'll drop it and not worry about it. (36)

> I could have been full time this year. . . . I immediately said "no, my children are still young." Actually I think my children are old enough to come home and let themselves into an empty house for an hour or two before I come home, but my husband is very reluctant and even on Wednesday it has rankled with him that I couldn't be here any earlier than I am. (35)

The few wives in this group who have made somewhat more enduring and substantial work commitments than other wives have lowered their standards of housekeeping, with the result that they have met with their husbands' active displeasure. The choice for these wives then is either to keep their own work within the narrow limits of what is possible inside the housewife-mother role as that has been structured by their husbands' dominant personal and professional roles, or to push beyond those limits and to risk major strain in the marriage itself.

In each professional group the men who are most noteworthy for the amount and kind of their cooperation, interest, and participation in their home and family lives are those men whose wives have been active partners in their husbands' professional careers throughout their marriage. There are four couples who fit this description—the husbands are a hospital physician, a private practitioner, a humanist, and a scientist. In each of these marriages the wife has lent her own skills and training to her husband's work to the extent that her adjunct activity has practically constituted a career in its own right. Though the two academic wives have had part-time work of their own in addition, the content of their work is closely related to their husbands' fields. In these four marriages, the lines between work and family are blurred, and family, like career, comes close to being a joint enterprise shared by husband and wife.

The other side of the two-person career then, is the two-person family, in some respects a latter-day version of the preindustrial family where "work and family structures tend to be linked as parts of an integrated whole" (Oakley 1974:10), except of course in these cases the career actually belongs to the husband and his work takes him away from home, leaving the daytime management of home and children to the wife by necessity if not in principle. Nonetheless these families, far more than the other families in the study, convey a strong sense of the mutuality that lies behind the arrangements of their domestic lives and work.

I get up late in the morning—around ten. He gets up with the children and sends my son off to school and I spend the rest of the morning with my daughter. Then while she is in school the afternoon is mine. I might work on the upkeep of the house, spend an hour on the violin, do some carpentry or home repair, do some reading or needlepoint or work on illustrations if I have an assignment. . . . I don't know if his evenings are work-oriented or if his work is sort of interest-oriented. In this case they overlap. I do his multiple-choice exams and record grades. He works on his research and writes papers or lectures. He plays several instruments and listens to records. . . . The amount of time we spend together in a given day is pretty good. We may be doing different things. He is in his study and I'm in mine, but we stay up together from about nine to two. . . . We have done a lot of work together, and still do some for the [nature] sanctuary. He has given lectures and I have done posters. . . . He does give me feedback on my illustrations and we both made a substantial time commitment to his book. I did chapter illustrations and a lot of wash drawings. My daughter's life style changed a lot—she would get up at ten and stay awake 'til ten. (31)

My husband has always been involved with them since infancy. He's changed diapers and given bottles. Each stage with them is nicer than the one we've left. . . . My husband used to take the kids into the hospital on Sunday nights when he had dictation to do. When they were in the office the kids used to color and hang pictures on the wall. Patients would come in and contribute to the gallery too. . . . He would go grocery shopping on Wednesday afternoons and take the kids with him . . . and he picks up bread and school lunch desserts on the way home. . . . He doesn't show stress. I think that's why we could have ten children. I always managed to have something on the table for supper—maybe it was only peanut butter. When he came home the kids would climb all over him. . . . His practice has been a joint venture. . . . I love medicine. I have always liked doing nursing in his office. I enjoy the satisfaction of doing things for people. The rewards are the same for him. (6)

In two of these four families the presence of a strong religious commitment yields a combination of altruism and privatism that is manifested in a kind of special dedication that the husbands bring to both their professional and family life. The devout and observant academic Jew and the Catholic doctor are much alike in the commitment to service they bring to their work; in the case of the academic this is evident in the very high priority attached to the teaching role; in the case of the doctor it is shown by a lifetime of practice in a working-class setting (which has earned him a very modest income indeed, by the usual standards of medical income) and residence in an unassuming neighborhood inside the central city where he works. That these men are also notably family-centered is not the result of any androgynous ideal. Quite the contrary, it is their religious conservatism that leads them to value traditional family relationships and to invest the kind of time in family life that will ensure the preservation of that value and those relationships. This religiously constructed version of the male role attaches equal importance to a man's work and to his family responsibilities.

Of course he's very involved with the boys. Their upbringing has been a fifty-fifty deal all the way. In fact our sons don't know that there are other fathers that have nine-to-five jobs and don't see their kids. . . . We decided to go to Israel on his sabbatical because we're Jewish. It was a choice between England, which is his field of work in literature, and Israel, where our hearts are. It was a good place to spend a year because of the children. We thought that a year in Israel could do more than thirty years of Sunday School. It helped them learn Hebrew and prepare for our oldest son's bar mitzvah. (28)

In their relationships with their wives, these two men are devoted husbands in the old fashioned sense that the phrase implies.

He calls home a couple of times during the day. At noon when he's eating lunch just to say hello, and then just before coming home to see if I need anything. He has always done that all these years. He's a real family man. (6)

Usually he will spend the mornings on his own work, and after he's had a morning at work we will do something together—take a walk or go to lunch. The afternoon is just for us. I couldn't think of a better profession for our kind of life. . . . We have something very special and have tried to center our lives within ourselves. We are a very close family. (28)

Writing about the fate of community in modern society from his vantage point in the nineteenth century, Durkheim anticipated that the morality and cohesion of modern society would derive from professional rather than from religious life. In his study of suicide, he expressed his hope for the social potential of occupations in the following manner:

> But when once they have so many things in common, when the relations between themselves and the groups to which they belong are thus close and continuous, sentiments of solidarity as yet almost unknown will spring up, and the present cold moral temperature of this occupational environment, still so external to its members, would necessarily rise. . . . Thus the social fabric, the meshes of which are so dangerously relaxed, would tighten and be strengthened throughout its entire extent. [1951, p. 381]

It is clear though, that at least for the two families just described, it is religion that supplies the morality and cohesion to professional and personal life alike.

6

STOCKTAKING

The inquiry on which this book was founded began with only two givens: the fact of the professional accomplishments of each of forty men and the fact that each of these men has, at the present time, a wife. It has been the aim of the preceding chapters to examine the many-faceted relationship between the two by detailing the features of the wife's role as those are intertwined with professional career structures and values and by capturing something of the quality of the various experiences that these women have had throughout the years as wives of men now successfully established in their careers as university professors and practising physicians.

It is time now for stocktaking. In part this means shifting from an emphasis on the fine points of connectedness between one or another aspect of professional life and a particular nuance or characteristic of the wife's role to a more comprehensive analysis of the interdependency of professional life and married life, of the relationship between the social structure of work and the social structure of family. Another, though not unrelated, kind of stocktaking has to do with being a wife and what that means and has meant, personally and sociologically, for these wives of doctors and professors. These two kinds of inventories yield a particular kind of understanding of the structure of professional life with implications in turn for understanding patterns of career participation that the future may hold for both men and women.

Women's Roles and Male Careers: Patterns of Interdependency

There are many ways in which family life takes its shape from and is contained by professional structures. Marriage is timed and children are born to fit career calendars; the geographical history of a family is the history of career mobility; social relationships overlap with and enhance occupational relationships; the rhythms of private and leisure time are set by the rhythms of work time; the expression of intimacy is cued to the pressures and stress of work. The wives of this book offer indisputable proof of their contributions to their husbands' careers and of the integration of their roles with the requirements of professional life. As a group they have helped to promote their husbands' careers and have asisted in the content and management of professional work. They have actively and passively supported and encouraged their husbands' career commitments. They have provided their husbands with the valuable and necessary time in which to acquire professional education and training and to build successful careers by assuming the major responsibility for the management of home and family life.

The most visible and central contributions that wives make to male careers is in fulfilling double-duty roles as parents, homemakers, and directors of family life. This is as true in academic life as it is in medical life. The picture of the greater mutuality of the academic marriage and of the more participatory and flexible academic husband and father is no doubt reassuringly "nicer" and dearer to the hearts of well-meaning humanistic liberals than is the picture of the more hierarchical medical marriage and the more authoritarian and remote physician husband. The academic wife is less alone in her domestic role than the medical wife, but every professor, like every doctor, has made compliance with career structures the first order of business in his life, and in both professional groups the wives have been the mainstay of family routines and relationships.

The functions of the double-duty contribution are obvious; their very triviality and dailyness are what make them so invaluable. It is difficult to imagine men living the kind of professional lives to which they are accustomed if they were also responsible for grocery lists, kindergarten car pools, after-school play groups and birthday parties, dentist appointments, sick children and the evening roast and so on. However, women's double-duty work is pivotal in the system of male careers not only because of its great importance in its own right, but because it contributes to the development of a wife's adjunct and supportive contributions. The latent function of women's roles as homemakers and mothers is that of acting as a deterrent to the career aspirations of women, and this works to the advantage of men. A man with a career-free wife at home faces no interference with the expected mobility patterns or timetables of his career; nor does he have to cope with competing claims for time in which to do the day-to-day work of his career; neither does he come home to a partner at the end of the day whose activities outside the home take up and demand equal time with his own. The wife who is free to give her best in lending support is the wife who is free from major or serious preoccupations with her own work and who feels herself qualitatively or quantitatively rewarded by her husband's career and the life style it entails.

Even women who have worked for a substantial part of their marriage and/or who now have regular work or academic commitments of their own, found their own achievements at their lowest ebb during the years when their children were very young. These were invariably the same years when their husbands were doing the crucially important work of laying the foundations of their careers as assistant professors or new practitioners. The timing of these combined circumstances was fortuitous, for it was then that the often newly located and housebound wife was most motivated to perform the social functions as an adjunct to her husband's career. A wife's participation in the social life and activities that helped her husband to become well-thought-of among those who mattered to his reputation was also an opportunity for her to make her way into the community and groups of people where she could find friends of her own. Her presence at home during those years also made her available for certain helpmate tasks, such as typing or editing or record keeping, which she could work in and around the routines of young children. These ways of assisting a husband's budding career often served as outlets for a wife and gave her a sense of accomplishment and participation outside the strictly domestic sphere.

The variations in the ways that these forty wives have developed their roles on behalf of their husbands' careers reveal a complex interplay between professional life and family life, between career structures and personality. The marriages of the people in this book are made in the image of the occupational world: the role definitions and relationships of professional work are mirrored in the role definitions and relationships of husbands and wives. The husband's role in the family is fundamentally an extension of his professional role, and the role of the wife simultaneously takes its shape from and reinforces the structure and values of her husband's professional commitment.

The agentic professional role—the role that is dominant, authoritative, oriented toward technical mastery and external recognition—is a stereotypically male role that usually has its counterpart in a conventionally sex-typed marriage, status inequality between partners, and a wife's role that is associated with deference and subordination and the clear delineation of "women's work" inside the home. Thus the doctor in private practice, whose work role is intrinsically agentic in emphasis, and those academic professors (more often the scientist than the humanist) whose major commitment is to their research and scholarly productivity and prestige, are typically married to women who have built few, if any, self-based interests and activities into their marriages, and whose roles are tailored in traditional female ways to their husbands' dominant and depersonalized professional roles.

The professional role that is less ruggedly individualistic, more

175

cooperative, more committed to interpersonal communication and service, is most often accompanied by a marriage that is less conventionally sex-typed and has some flexibility in the domestic division of labor and greater mutuality in the parenting role. The role of the wife in this marriage is more collegial than subordinate, and she is more likely to respond to the content of her husband's work than to its status. The wife herself usually sustains some outside commitment of her own, and the marriage relationship is built on some degree of status equality between partners. This particular mesh of family and career roles is found primarily among academics, particularly those for whom commitment to colleague relationships, the process and communication of teaching, and the life of the academic department is as strong if not stronger than the commitment to the product and prestige of research and scholarship. A similar pattern is evident among physicians whose work roles are less dominant and entrepreneurial than the usual medical role: the doctor whose religious values underpin a strong commitment to service in his medical practice and two physicians who are in full-time salaried hospital practice. Neither pattern of professional-marital interdependency, it should be noted, is "better" than the other. Each is serviceable and appropriate to the particular profession in question.

It is obvious that these differences in "fit" between male professional roles and women's roles in the family have not been fashioned out of the whole cloth of professional life alone. It seems quite evident that the control, mastery, and status of the agentic medical professional and academic research role is more attractive to conventionally dominant males. These men marry traditionally female women, who seek their main satisfactions in the nonoccupational world of family, and derive gratification from looking up to their husbands, living through their hubands' professional status, accomplishments and rewards. Similarly, the less traditionally defined male, who seeks a more expressive, less dominant, and less depersonalized professional role has contracted a marriage tht embodies more mutuality, cooperation, and status equality between spouses. Occupational roles and subcultures, then, act to reinforce the personality traits underlying the choices of both occupational specialty and marriage partner.

There are undoubtedly important differences in the emotional make-up of the would-be doctor compared to the professor, or the agentically oriented professional compared to the collegially oriented. More than the teaching-committed academic, the doctor appears to have a well-developed sense of his own importance that requires continual nourishment in the form of the devotion of others: he is more inclined, therefore, toward hierarchical roles and relationships in which he is at the top of the hierarchy. (Coker, Greenberg and Kosa, for example, refer to the "authoritarianism of general practice and the 'Machiavellianism' of internal medicine and psychiatric practice" [Mumford, 1970:76].)

A variety of social and psychological variables must certainly underlie these personality differences of professional men and their consequent preferences for occupational and marriage roles. One probable factor is that academics typically come from more socially marginal backgrounds than do physicians and are less likely to have internalized a strong sense of their special personal worth that would encourage them to seek out or feel comfortable in highly dominant professional and personal roles. Veblen's thesis of the relationship between the social marginality of the Jews and their intellectual preeminence (1934:221–24) speaks to this point, as does Lipset and Ladd's commentary on "Intellectuality and Social Background" (1975:149–67). S. M. Miller, himself a professor, provides some insight into the link between personal psychology and his own predisposition to reject status inequality in the marriage relationship:

> Looking back, I don't believe that I could accept a woman who would center her life completely on me and devote herself to making me happy. At one level, the intellectual, how could one individual be worthy of such dedication by another? At the deeper, and I suspect now, more significant level, I rejected or stayed away from easily giving or male centered women because I did not consider myself worthy of another person's total devotion or capable of evoking the sentiments which would sustain it beyond the initial impulse. Furthermore, it

demanded an emotional response that I possibly could not make. In short, I did not think so well of myself that I could live with (over-whelming) devotion. As a consequence, I was usually involved with young women with strong career goals who were seeking their identity through work and not through family. (1972:247)

Notwithstanding the variations in work roles and wife roles that cut across the two professions, certain features of work are unique to each profession. These are reflected in some pronounced differences between medical and academic wives in the emphasis and the content of their roles overall. In particular the organization of medical work and the nature of the medical task lend added weight to the role of the doctor's wife that is absent from the role of the academic wife, regardless of her husband's orientation toward his work.

Medicine has a stronger sense of itself as a profession than ei-ther university teaching or the individual disciplines of academe. Medical training encourages the development of a cohesive and en-compassing professional identity in response to rigid and externally imposed structures of work. During medical education and train-ing, not only the doctor but the doctor's wife is socialized to an ex-plicit awareness and acceptance of the fixed structures of medical work and a professional commitment that is mutually exclusive of and takes precedence over personal commitments. Nolen's autobio-graphical *The Making of a Surgeon* (1970), for example, contains only one chapter on marriage and family; it is tellingly entitled "Life on the Outside." From early marriage on, the doctor's wife develops her supportive and double-duty responses in ways that accommo-date to the non-deferrable imperatives of patient care and the ex-traordinary time demands that grow out of the institutionalized au-thority of the medical role, in which major responsibility for the management of patient care is in the hands of the doctor alone. To a much greater extent than the academic wife, the medical wife learns to tolerate frequent inconvenience and disruption to her own life as a result of her husband's work. She is often called upon for active bolstering of her husband's personal sense of his professional au-thority as well.

The entrepreneurial and community base of medical practice requires that the doctor be highly attuned to his standing in local lay and colleague groups. As a result, social and public participation is much more formalized and comprehensive for the medical wife than for the academic wife, whose husband works in a smaller socially salient professional community and does not have to conscript a clientele or establish rapport with other colleagues in order to work effectively with his students. The economic autonomy of the medical profession is reflected in the doctor's high socioeconomic status, which involves his family in a high-status suburban life style, and impels his wife to high-status housekeeping.

Not only is the role of the doctor's wife more clearly and self-consciously drawn than the role of the faculty wife, but it also changes less over time. In both professional groups, the need for certain of a wife's adjunct contributions falls away once the career is well launched. For the doctor, once that point is past, the pace and intensity of medical work is essentially invariant and the problem-solving, client-centered work of the practitioner repeats itself from month to month and year to year. Furthermore, the financial rewards of medical practice are undoubtedly a powerful incentive to continue on with an undiminished time commitment to work. The wife maintains her double-duty and supportive roles to a similarly steady beat.

In keeping with the fluctuations in the content and calendar of academic work, the faculty wife finds more flexibility in her roles. The professor is not motivated to prove his success repeatedly by his income; once he attains the rank of full professor, his success is established and permanent, and he is likely to feel comfortable with a rearrangement of his professional time commitment, which allows his wife some rearrangement in her own role. In any event the academic wife knows that she can do no real damage to her husband's career by a shift of emphasis in her role at this point. The time span of the double-duty commitment of the medical wife is also likely to be longer than for the academic wife, because the doctor, because of the structure of medical practice, may be virtually unavailable to his family throughout his career.

One final comment remains concerning the interdependency of

women's roles and male careers: the patterns described in this book emerge with especial clarity and cohesiveness because the focus has been only on marriages that have survived all the years of husbands' career development. Presumably the integration of the roles of wives with their husbands' professional roles is strengthened by the sheer passage of time spent in the marriage and the occupational subculture, and reinforced by exposure to other husbands and wives who share that subculture. On the other hand, research reported on here, by definition, deals only with enduring marriages. A very different picture, perhaps one with a lack of integration of marriages and careers, might emerge from a study that included women divorced from their physician and professor husbands. It would be worthwhile in the future to study marriages that were not successful. The findings reported here, of the interdependency of women's roles and male careers, would be strengthened if such a study showed incompatibility and strain between occupation and family roles in medical and academic marriages that ended in divorce.

Changing Structures of Family and Work

To be sure, the patterns of interdependency between family and career roles that are described and analyzed in this book pertain to the lives and work of only forty couples, captured at one point in time, in the late nineteen-seventies. It is possible though, even within this microworld, to catch glimpses of larger structures beyond and behind, as well as some sense of patterns of change that may be occurring in family structure that are related to changes in the workplace.

While academic marriages are described in this book as more egalitarian, flexible, and home-centered at the present time than most medical marriages, it is probably true that academic marriages of a generation or so ago were more like medical marriages in the present than they are today. Some of the older academic wives quoted in this book have alluded to an earlier time in their lives when participation in a cohesive faculty-wife network and well-organized set of women's activities on behalf of their husbands' careers figured much more prominently in their lives than they do now or than they ever have for younger faculty wives.

Kohn (1978) suggests that changes in the structure of work are reflected in changes in personal value orientations and, specifically, that the substantive complexity of work directly affects a man's intellectual flexibility in nonwork situations. There can be little doubt that there has been a pronounced increase in the substantive complexity of academic work, according to Kohn's own criteria, in recent decades. Colleges and universities are now marked by far more organizational elaboration than in earlier decades, and the individual academic's accountability to colleagues and administrators outside his department, to students, and to his field of scholarship is more far-reaching than ever before. It is also true that the increased competition of academic life and the relative difficulty of obtaining tenure and promotion now compared to twenty years ago has resulted in a deemphasis on personal ties and friendships, and a concentration on explicit kinds and levels of achievement and productivity as the basis for academic success. All of this adds up to a picture of a man whose work requires considerable intellectual flexibility, which is then carried over into the home setting. Then too, as the tightly knit residential and social communities which once characterized much of academic life give way to less personal and more bureaucratic ones, academic couples are simply freer to go their own ways personally and socially.

The fact that the few hospital-based physicians who appeared in this book behave in their marriages in ways similar to academic husbands suggests that a convergence between the two types of professional families may be in the offing, to the extent that medical practice becomes more organizationally (therefore more substantively) complex. However, doctors are much further away from being organizationally bound-in in the way that academics are. Medical practice is still private practice for the most part and the trend toward group practice has done little to mitigate the dominant role of the physician or to intensify his responsiveness or increase his interpersonal accountability.

Even in an organizational setting, the medical role remains a highly dominant one with respect to the medical division of labor,

181

and the physician even continues to control the organization of ancillary or related services, such as social work. A main point of Freidson's study (1961) of physicians in group practice is that by establishing a virtual monopoly on services and strong solidarity with other physicians in the practice, the group practitioner tends to become more remote from and less responsive to patients than the solo practitioner. The new breed of doctor tends to be preoccupied with his technical proficiency, on the one hand, and the convenience of his schedule and the profitability of his practice, on the other.

As a future trend, it is likely that physicians will be more concerned with their leisure and family time and with the enjoyment of the fruits of their labor than with seeking gratification in the god-like status of the solo practitioner. Certainly a number of the young wives who have spoken in this book have emphasized the importance of the good life to them and their husbands.

Medicine is changing. Most men are going into partnerships and groups so they won't have to work so hard. As of next week he'll be incorporated with his partner. He never wants to be financially strained. His biggest hang-up is financial security. He wants to keep living the way we are—to take vacations, live in this house and educate the children. Two years ago just the two of us went to Italy and we hope to be able to travel, especially to Israel. One vacation during the year is a meeting. Last year we took several breaks away either for a week or a weekend. It was refreshing and it helped him to get away from the practice. (4)

One afternoon a week he is off and we plan to do things together. He really does take it off and on days when he has no surgery, he might take the whole day off after doing rounds in the morning. The worst would be coming home by two-thirty. That we consider not taking the day off at all. We used to go to New York for the opera. We would go down and back in one day, but that's very tiring. We do go to Boston and the things we do together are without the children. He's off every other weekend and when he's off he doesn't do rounds. On the weekends off we usually go somewhere. This weekend we are taking the two oldest children and going to the mountains to hike. His vacation may be in pieces. He gets close to six weeks a year. Last year, we took one week during the children's winter vacation, then we went to Europe alone for two weeks in the spring. This fall we are planning to go to England for one week and then we'll take about five days at another time.

When he was looking for a practice he decided to look for a situation with a partner. It's too impossible to be alone. I think the amount of free time was a bigger thing to me than to him. But he also doesn't want to live too hard. (12)

It is hard to know whether these changes in the medical work orientation will be reflected in changes in role structure at home. It is a safe guess that the doctor's wife of the future will have more of her husband's company than she has had in the past. The security, financially and collegially, of the group practice situation may well diminish the doctor husband's reliance on his wife's supportive and adjunct activities to some extent. Whether or not these changes will also be accompanied by greater egalitarianism between marriage partners and a greater contribution by the doctor to family and household affairs is more difficult to predict. What is most interesting is to speculate on the kinds of changes that would occur in the kinds of persons who elect to practice medicine and in the structure of medical marriages and family life were the profession to be fully bureaucratized—in a publicly controlled and subsidized system of health care—and the medical division of labor reorganized so that the physician became partner and colleague to persons working in a wide array of health related fields, instead of being professionally dominant over them as is presently the case.

While the status and authority of the physician remain fundamentally unaltered in the work settings either of group or hospital practice, it is true that the actual work task in those settings has become more specialized, more circumscribed, and more dependent upon informal cooperation with others compared to the old style of solo practice. In this respect medicine, like academe, reflects the general trend in modern occupational life toward a highly differentiated division of labor. "Tasks are divided into specialized roles that demand a high degree of competence in a narrow rather than broad spectrum of activities" (Giele 1978:354). Giele suggests further that one important result of this trend is that "sex, which is an ascribed status defining a broad range of tasks, should become less important as a mechanism for assigning roles in modern society and should be replaced by standards that put greater reliance on achieved characteristics such as the person's ability to perform a specific task" (1978:355). Specialization of tasks, she concludes, will diminish the distinction between family functions and productive functions and will put the primary emphasis on role definition, which may require a combination of instrumental and expressive skills and behaviors.

It is asking a lot of forty couples to confirm this trend, although there is enough evidence of a convergence between work and family roles among those academics and doctors whose work task is similarly delimited, organizationally cooperative, and service-oriented not to disconfirm it. Certainly as occupational categories, professions are similar in many respects, and as they are affected in common ways by overarching trends in the workplace, we may expect to see some general convergence between professions as to the characteristic structures of family and work associated with them. It is not likely, though, that the individual professions will lose certain of their distinctive features, and it is to be expected that professions will continue to exist as occupational subcultures which embody the different values, contents, and role definitions of the various professional endeavors.

Insofar as there remain some fundamental differences between the nature of medical and academic work roles, as there is every reason to assume will be the case, there will remain fundamental differences between the kinds of people and spouses attracted to those roles. Just what the points of commonality and distinction are and are likely to be generally between structures of work and family in the lives of professionals are best discovered by further study over time of patterns of interdependency between work and family in elite occupations in addition to medicine and university teaching. (See, for example, Kanter's recent work, *Men and Women of the Corporation*). The study of the two professions offered here constitutes merely a beginning, not the end, of the analysis of patterns of change and stability in family work roles.

To Be a Wife

Although there is a sizeable literature that deals with the social and psychological factors that influence male occupational choice, there is no comparable literature that examines the socialization patterns that would predispose a female to marry into one occupational setting rather than another and, accordingly, into one or another set of wife roles. The wives in this study are by and large much better educated than most women in their age group. Nonetheless, they have gone in very different directions in the kinds of marriages they have made and in the kinds of roles they have played in those marriages.

The different content of the educational and work background of medical and academic wives suggests that academic wives are products of a socialization process that urged them in two directions at once—toward the self-expression and independence of an adult work role on the one hand, and toward conventional marriage and family roles on the other. The academic marriage in a sense represents a compromise between those two directions in that it holds open the possibility of the pursuit of personal achievement and gives rise to a degree of flexibility in domestic arrangements that provides a wife with some time and space for her own outside work or education. Clearly the social and psychological factors that reside in the past histories of doctors' wives overrode the possible influence of education on the development of any substantial commitment to work or other self-directed activities. These wives traveled along one path only in their socialization, and it was a path that led them straight into very conventionally defined marriage and family roles.

It has been clearly shown in this book how each of these different role definitions and sets of life choices on the part of wives has meshed with and served the needs of their husbands' careers in medicine and university teaching. But what of the needs of the wives themselves? How well have their own expectations been met in their roles and what has been the effect of being a wife on their own growth and development?

For those women, most especially doctors' wives, who have chosen to be in conventionally sex-typed, male-dominant marriages, there has frequently turned out to be a painful irony in their choice. The sort of man whom the very traditionally defined female is most emotionally predisposed to marry is, it seems, often the sort of man who is most likely to let her down in the very relationship in which she seeks her greatest satisfaction and rewards. The woman who marries with the idea of giving *her* all to a man is usually inclined to marry a dominant, authoritative male, who is usually inclined to give *his* all to a highly instrumental professional role, who is far better at receiving than returning devotion. Doctors' wives told the tale over and over, sometimes explicitly, sometimes implicitly, of marriages entered into with an eager and sure expectation that total self-fulfillment awaited them exclusively within family roles, only to find those roles bereft of the affection and intimacy they sought in them, and to discover that their husbands, heroes in the workplace, were distant, remote, even absent at home.

I had very realistic ideas when we married that it would all be romantic and lovely. I got married with the notion that I was going to change him, take this quiet guy and make him into a great lover. . . . I thought, I'm going to love him so much that he will love me back and come home everyday with a bouquet of roses. I thought it would be all violins. There's not a lot of give-and-take in his personality and you sort of learn to live with someone who doesn't talk too much. You don't change people, life goes on. . . . I would like a guy who would work from nine to five and come home and spend the rest of his time adoring me. (9)

The hardest part about being a doctor's wife is sharing him. No, I would not want my daughter to marry a doctor. Most wives have problems with husbands as far as feeling that their husbands don't pay enough attention to them as to whatever business they're in. Then double or quadruple that for a doctor. If you had asked me some years ago or even now on a bad day what I would change about his work, I would have some suggestions. I've gotten into his routines and I make my life around his. It's an alone life. I have let him know of my resentment of his practice. I resent it that I am not the only [naked] woman he has seen. It's another bit of sand on the pile of resentment. It's another thing I have to share that most wives don't. He gives me a very good life as a human. He's all the things women say they want, but I don't have quite as much of them as I would wish. I get very greedy. I've got a good thing and I'd just as soon have more of it. (4)

Of course not every woman who has lived inside a traditional marriage relationship gives voice to or has experienced such a keen sense of disappointment as the two women just quoted. Many express the gratifications to them of a lifetime spent in service to their husbands and families; others take pride in looking on the bright side and not complaining about a situation or relationship they feel unable to change.

Someone asked me the other day, "If you could live your life again changing nothing, would you do it?" I said, "No, who would want to go through all that again." [What would you change about his work if you could?] I used to think the hours. But what can you do? I wish he were more involved with the family around here. But you know, there's good and bad with everyone. (14)

After dating him for four years, I knew he was all-important. I wanted more than anything to be a good wife to him and to be a mother. I wanted a large family. I never thought of myself with any career goal. . . . Well, I wish he were home everyday at six and we could plan our lives a little easier. People call and want us there, and I have to say I don't know. Yes, I'd like to be able to plan a little bit better, but that will never happen so I put it out of my mind. (15)

It only took me a short time to realize that being a doctor's wife wasn't too pleasant. I knew about the training period, but I didn't know how bad it was. I thought I would see more of him after his training but that hasn't been the case. But he's happy when he's working and I'm happy when he's happy. (6)

For the last twenty years I have been a housewife and mother, geared to keeping [my husband] happy so he could do a good job. Maybe a lot of women's libbers wouldn't like that but that's what I do best. I'm a good mother and a good wife and a good home-maker. I do a damn good job at it. (39)

Quite apart from a woman's own subjective assessment of the rewards and costs to her in being a wife in the traditional mode, there is also an objective case to be made that the woman who centers her life primarily on meeting the needs of others and on being needed by others does so at considerable expense to her own maturity and selfhood. This is meant neither as a personal nor as an ideological judgment, but as a sociological observation. For it is only true in one sense that a woman *chooses* to enter into a relationship of ongoing inequality and to spend her life in the service of someone whom she regards as her "better"; in another sense she makes no choice at all, but is impelled into that role as a consequence of certain feelings about herself and her proper place that she has been assigned and assigns herself as a woman. These feelings are then reinforced by the marriage relationship itself:

> In a situation of inequality the woman is not encouraged to take her own needs seriously, to explore them, to try to act on them as a separate individual. She is enjoined from engaging all of her own resources and thereby prevented from developing some reliable and valid sense of her own worth. Instead the woman is encouraged to concentrate on the needs and development of the man. (J. B. Miller 1977:18)

Years spent inside the undeniably demanding and valuable to others, but nonetheless low-risk and often formless role of traditional mother and homemaker serve to erode further a woman's capacity for independence and self-determination. What is striking about so many of the most traditional of the medical and academic wives is that despite the competency and sensitivity with which they have reared children and managed households, they are nonetheless afraid, uncertain, unfocused, simultaneously self-deprecating and self-indulgent in their assessment of their potential for and interest in participating in the larger world of work and achievement.

[What are your goals for yourself in the next ten years?] Gee, I'm sorry you asked that. First I'd like to see the girls getting through their difficult teenage years. I don't combine going to school and doing anything else very well. My husband has said he'd be happy to see me audit something but not to take anything for credit. So I really don't have any immediate plans in the future for a really demanding full-time job or for going back to graduate school. I really can't project that far. Volunteer work does contribute to society, but I'm not doing the kind of thinking I did in graduate school. But I don't think I could put out all that effort for a job or going to school and do what I'm doing now. When the children are gone I'll have to do something. I'm not the type to sit around and play golf. Maybe I can write on my own. Lots of little things interest me—decorating, travel. But those are not substantial involvement. It has to be more intellectual. I do enjoy the volunteering and how do I find the ideal job that goes from nine to three and gives me the summers off and the flexibility to travel with him to a conference abroad if one comes up and one that's also kind of challenging and a little bit creative? (19)

I was ill prepared for marriage. I don't even know why I got married. I thought it would be nice not to work and to be married to a man who would support me. I guess I had the image of a fairy princess living in a tower. . . . Why should I worry about ten years from now? I think about a lot of things and my husband tells me I'm like Don Quixote tilting at windmills. You know I had started thinking about a lot of things in my life and then I got pregnant and breathed a sigh of relief because then I didn't have to think about them for awhile. (20)

I ask what it will be like ten years from now when I am not so wanted. I am a lazy girl and have only studied to get by. To go back and finish up my B.A. doesn't interest me very much. Perhaps I could get a certificate in school health and do something I enjoy doing and help with college expenses. I have also thought of our working with a UN agency for a few months together. There always has to be a plan or alternative. This is how we should be thinking. We do look forward to doing more camping. (3)

I'm still confused about my role as a wife. The confusion starts when you become a mother and then continues. If I were required to work for money I would be much more motivated and the only motivation I have now is my own need and sense of fulfillment. Like all mothers I have guilt feelings about a dual role and dual responsibilities to a job and the family. It's hard to get up the gumption and go to work. (13)

I don't like the idea of losing the children, but there's no way of hanging on. I have thought of going back to school, but I don't want to go back to school and read about social problems. I think I want to do something fun, so yesterday I signed up for an extension course in interior decorating. I'm willing to try to fool around with it. I just don't want to go back to school and get into that heavy stuff. (15)

I've been wondering about what goals I might have for myself. I still have two kids at home. I really don't know. I have a lot of friends going back to school, getting degrees and going to work. It really doesn't appeal to me. I don't know what does. I've wondered about doing something further with my sewing. I've done a lot of things in the arts and crafts field that I would like to try. In the hospital now I'm making up crafts kits for children and other patients. I have needlepoint kits sitting there to make up and just haven't found the time for it. I've done a little kitchen consulting work for friends. Maybe I could expand on some of these things I've enjoyed doing. Looking back I would say it's been basically a satisfactory but not overly exciting life. On the other hand we've done a great deal of traveling. *(11)*

The occasional doctor's wife who is more purposeful about her own goals and pursuits is handicapped by the lack of vocational and educational resources available to her in the suburban medical subculture, in contrast to the academic wife who finds considerable support as well as opportunity in the academic environment for putting together some outside commitments for herself. Then, too, the medical wife is victimized by the status of her husband's work should she seek a job or educational program. It is possible for an academic's wife to work as a sales clerk or attend the local community college, as some of those interviewed have done, but a doctor's wife is unlikely to want to be in a job or academic setting that does not befit her husband's status. Others may not want to take her in either. A number of doctors' wives mentioned that they felt certain jobs would be closed to them because of employers' attitudes that doctors' wives do not "need" the money and are not, therefore, worthwhile applicants for various positions.

It looks, then, as though academic wives are the "winners" in the contest for self-determination, insofar as they are typically less submerged in their marriage relationships and have a greater investment in their own independence and achievements and more options open to them than doctors' wives. As is often true, however, appearances are deceiving. For academic wives (along with the one or two medical wives) who now have or are working toward modest careers of their own do not measure their accomplishments and opportunities against a standard of the relative absence of those in the lives of other women. Wives who have wanted little for themselves have, by their own reckoning, lost little in that respect by being wives. Wives who once wanted more or have come to want more for themselves are frequently frustrated, angry, regretful at the realization of what might have been, of the toll taken by the years on the development of their own career potential as a consequence of deferring to the primacy of their husbands' careers and assuming the major responsibility for home and family life. The struggle of these wives to find and assert themselves has taken a further toll in the form of personal despair and storminess in the marriage relationship itself.

When he was a graduate student I never questioned myself about any alternative to what I was doing. It sounds very naive, but I felt you do the things that are expected of you and, then, that's that. And if I felt discontent—and I did feel discontent—that was not to say that I wanted things to be different, but simply to register the discontent along with everything else. I see a lot of the change in the marriage as reflective of my dissatisfaction over the years. Yes, it did get to the point where it was either/or; either change the marriage or get out. Looking back now I'm wondering if I wasn't more content when I decided I could not tolerate the life I'd been living. When I was most verbal about my discontent with our relationship, then I had grown to a point of being more accepting about my own attitudes and evaluations about myself. I felt more strongly that I had these rights and did not intend to be subordinated. (21)

I suppose to a certain extent for awhile I repressed or subdued my own life or life style and the kinds of things I enjoyed doing so that he had the time to work and I was able to do work for him. I think there have probably been quite a lot of adjustments I have had to make because of his being an academic and spending so much time on his work. Probably at this point I'm doing some more readjusting because I realize that I'm important too. And I have one passage through this life just like he does, so that what I do with my life has become important too—not just secondary to his. (37)

I was originally hired to teach because they had expanded the program in the department and had more students and wanted cheap labor without any commitment of a lasting nature. I taught several discussion sections of a large lecture course. I had a series of one-year contracts. [Looking back on it, then, you are rather cynical?] Cynical is not really the word. It was much worse than that. Of course I'm cynical about motivations and opportunities. No, I was glad to have a connection with the academic community, but I was not unaware that it was a lot of work for very little money. Also it was the least exciting of work. [And your husband's reaction to this?] If you mean did I cry on his shoulder, I guess I did to a certain extent. On the other hand, there was never any question of his abandoning his job so we could go elsewhere. I had to be sensible. He at least had a job. I was the one who basically didn't. I suppose I felt his sympathy was more of an intellectual sort. He understood when I said it bothered me. I don't really think he had any empathy. He had never been in that situation. (22)

I did go to work and my husband didn't object at all provided I kept it in a small range so he did not have to be imposed on to babysit or anything else. I went through a very bitter period for a few years when I felt why did I have to keep my own activities so small. Provided the children were taken care of and the house and there was no infringement on my husband, I could do it. But if I hadn't been so limited I could have finished school ten years ago. I could have had an M.A. or a Ph.D. I could have earned a great deal of money all those years, which would have been nice. His attitude was always, "You want to do that. Can you get a sitter? Are you going to be able to manage?" He was so involved in his own career. . . . I've gotten over that. You can't remake your life. But I was very bitter for awhile. (30)

Yes, he really needs me and these terrible blow-ups and these affairs are the only way I've learned that. If I go on a painting binge or play the violin, he'll come home and say, "Couldn't you at least put the violin down?" I feel as though he's gone for years like that. I feel as though I've become stronger because I've carved out my life. I can live alone. I deal with loneliness all day long, every day. . . . I work in the bedroom, that's my studio. I'm not interested in showing in this area, but I am ambitious in a sense, not for a lot of money but for real true appreciation of my work. . . . My husband tells me he feels left out of my life with all that I do. We had this discussion the other day, and I said, "God, you're the one who's had everything. You're famous, at the top of your career. You've had awards. You have books coming out. People respect you. Everyone knows who you are." (25)

I thought that I would be married eventually and be a traditional mother for part of my life and by the time the kids were in school I was really interested in going back to professional work. My husband was agreeable, but what we were innocent about was the whole business of entering the academic world again after a ten-year delay. I don't see how I could have been so naive. In my own graduate department, even though 40 percent of the graduate students were women, I never looked around and realized there was only one female faculty member in the department and none in [my field]. And that one woman was unmarried. And when I was in college the two females in the sciences were either unmarried or married with no children. I never made the connection and asked what happened to all those women, where did they go?

It was a difficult time for me the year after I finished my degree. It was such an exhausting thing to go through and when it was all over, nothing was different. I had three kids and there was a constant mess. It was the usual harried housewife thing and it was a real let-down. And then it was beginning to dawn on me that things were not going to work out quite as I thought and I wondered what it was all for. I thought maybe I should just have thrown in the towel. I had to work my way through that. . . . If I had it to do again, the biggest mistake of my life was not having continued on and finished my degree before having the kids. But I don't regret having children and I couldn't conceive of trading off children for a career. (34)

In all, the experiences of these forty doctors' wives and professors' wives have been more alike than different. They tell a common story of lives lived inside a role which has all too often closed them off from themselves, from the world, from their husbands. In each situation there has been a measure of deprivation and in each response—whether accommodation, resignation, or assertion—a measure of pain.

The Structure of Professional Participation: Prospects for the Two-Career Family and Women in the Professions

Almost certainly there will be those who raise questions about timeliness of the subject matter of this book and of the relevance of researching the wives of professional men instead of professional women themselves. The argument seems plausible enough: times are changing, barriers to women's professional participation have been dramatically reduced and there is little to gain, therefore, from a study of male career participation alone and the equation of career success with male success. Without doubt the decade of the 1970s has witnessed a great upsurge in the numbers of women determined to combine family and career and a dramatic increase in the numbers of women enrolled in graduate and professional schools. Both the socialization process and the law are more supportive than ever before of expanding professional options and opportunities for women.

For the most part, though, it is yet to be seen whether today's aspiring women professionals will become tomorrow's successful professional women, not only in numbers equal to men, but on equal terms, as family members and career participants both. To date studies have shown that the two-career family is more an ideal than a reality, and the established elite occupations continue to be heavily male dominated. In their studies of two-career families, for example, Holmstrom (1973) and Poloma (1970) found few marriages in which the wife's career was considered as important as her husband's and where the husband and wife had actually attained equal career success. "On the one hand, the two-career couples deviated a great deal from middle-class norms. On the other hand they were still a long way from equality between the sexes" (Holmstrom, 1973, p. 155).

Prospects for the actualization of the two-career family—one in which both partners have equally successful careers in the mainstream of professional life—are best understood, not in terms of wishes about what might be nor of ideologies of what should be, but in terms of the structures of professional work and the conditions of professional participation. The careers of the men in this book and the roles of the women who are their wives are important, therefore, for what they reveal about the organization of professional work and the ingredients of successful professional careers. Presumably the terms of their participation and success in professional life are the same ones that today's young professional hopefuls will be expected to adhere to. The point made early on in this book bears repeating here—the road to career success is not paved anew by each career aspirant nor by each generation of would-be professionals. It is, rather, a well-worn route that must be traveled in the proper way if one is to arrive safely at the hoped-for destination. A commitment to a career is a commitment not only to the substantive work of that career but to its characteristic structures, norms, chronologies—that is to say, modes—of work as well. It may well be that the main barrier to women's professional participation is not located outside or on the periphery of professional life, in women's attitudes or admissions and hiring practices, as it so commonly thought, but is inherent in the very assumptions about professional work that have evolved from the male dominance of professional life.

Those assumptions have been revealed in the career patterns of the doctors and professors in this book, who are now the mentors of students in training for or beginning careers in university teaching and medicine, who will guide a younger generation to follow in their professional footsteps according to their standards of professionalism. These now successful professional men followed the prescribed regimen and chronology of professional training; they were productive and mobile in the ways that were necessary for their career potential to be recognized; they maintained the pace of work and forged the relationships and contacts with colleagues needed in order for their careers to become fully established. That they have been successful, however, is the result not only of their own diligence and attentiveness to their careers but of their wives as well. Indeed it is hard to see how it could have been otherwise, because men have created the structures of professional work and they are structures that assume above all the freedom of the male role, which assumes in turn freedom from family roles, which are assumed to be the responsibility of women.

In light of the contributions made by wives to male careers, the notion of male professional achievements as meritocratic and independent is clearly a half-truth. So too, the notion that the present structures of professional work are intrinsically more professional than alternative career modes is open to question. The fact is that the organization of professional work and rewards is far from a rational, efficient and inevitable development, but a socially constructed phenomenon that reflects the predominatly male incumbence of professional life. Yet the present standards and structures of professional work stand as the virtually unalterable givens of professional life and dictate the terms of professional participation for men and women alike. For the two-career family those terms appear to be essentially no-win terms. It is very difficult to imagine how, as a generalized social pattern, couples will be able to combine full and equal career participation along with family life, when the structures of career participation have been built by persons who are family-free for persons who are not family-free.

Sooner or later either career or family is likely to be compromised in the life of the two-career family. It is easier to change families than careers, since families are formed as individual and private choices, while careers are defined by external requirements. A not infrequent choice of many two-career couples is to remain childless, thereby avoiding some of the dilemmas and difficulties faced by the two-career family. For the extremely privileged there is the choice to hire others to take on the major burden and responsibility of parenting and homemaking, but, as Hochschild notes, this is a partial solution at best "since tending the sick, caring for the old, writing Christmas cards, and just being there for people in bad moments—that is, all that wives do—still would need doing" (1974:46).

Implicit in either of these choices is the acceptance of the need for women to make their lives as much like the lives of traditional professional men as possible in order to conform to prevailing standards of professionalism; implicit in that acceptance, in turn, are the assumptions that the world of intimate personal relationships *should* be of only secondary importance compared to the instrumental world of career achievements and that family life can be dispensed with as a mere problem of management. For the organizing value of career structures as men have constructed them is that only a soft-headed, undedicated, and therefore inadequate professional person would allow family life and responsibilities to compete for time and attention in any way. An academic wife who sought admission to a graduate program was confronted firsthand with the judgment that her professional potential was inversely related to how much she cared for her children:

I went in for the interview and was turned down flat by the person interviewing for the program. It was one of the most demolishing things that ever happened to me. He asked if I had children and I said, "Yes." Then he said to me, "The people we take into this program have to be totally committed to art. Would you put your children before your art?" (25)

Clearly the criteria used to determine what constitutes acceptable professional experience and productivity are highly arbitrary and reflect the instrumental bias of the male value system. Surely professional life in general would be greatly enriched—and clients and students better served—by a view of training and expertise that is not restricted to relationships with academic mentors and the accomplishments of classroom and laboratory, and the size of one's publication list and practice, but takes into consideration and legitimizes major life experiences as professionally relevant and worthwhile. Current forms of professional socialization may actually be professionally dysfunctional. The regimen of medical training, for example, is poor preparation for a profession supposedly dedicated to caring as well as curing, since it precludes the opportunity for a doctor's personal growth and time to spend in caring for persons as intimately connected with him as his own wife and children.

Even in the academic world, as the wife quoted above discovered, there is a tendency to cordon off close human relationships and creativity from one another. Although the academic professional role is in some ways less agentic and more flexible than that of other professions, there is nonetheless a great deal of rigidity in the way that academic career timetables are constructed and in the standards of judgment brought to bear on one's productivity and worth as a scholar. The apparently pliable form of academic life is deceptive, for academic life has a solid core as well; the present tight job market in university teaching is likely to lead to increasing rigidity as the condition for professional success comes to depend more and more exclusively on research and publications. Although many of the academic husbands on view in this book have managed some involvement in the world of home and family and their wives some participation in the world of work, there has remained between them a fundamental inequality in the home and in the marriage and an imbalance between husbands and wives in their respective work achievements. Despite the fact that many of the academic marriages were favorably predisposed toward acceptance of the ideal of the two-career family by virtue of the mutuality built into the marriage relationship and the credentials of the wives, that ideal was realized by none of them.

The most frequent solution to the dilemma faced by the two-career family is for a wife to scale down or put aside her own career aspirations during the heavy years of childrearing. This arrangement allows a husband to pursue his career without compromise and to reap the advantages of his wife's contributions to his career. At the point when a woman feels able to let go of some of her childrearing responsibilities and to explore the possibilities for her own work and development, her husband's career is usually well established and the need for certain of the supportive and adjunct contributions of the wife has concomitantly diminished. A wife, for her part, may launch or resume her career at this juncture in her life, creating what gives the appearance of the two-career family, but the wife's accomplishments are likely to lag behind and fall far short of those of her successful husband. Women who pick up where they left off usually find they are out of date so far as the substance of the work they put aside and, because of their age, out of phase with career ladders which men are able to climb without interruption. Continuing education notwithstanding, major careers are rarely built if they begin in mid-life. No matter how able a student a thirty-five or forty-year-old woman proves to be, her professional potential will almost certainly be viewed less favorably than that of her twenty-five-year-old counterpart.

It is possible, of course, to choose career tracks and goals other than the ones that the husbands in this study have chosen. In academe, for example, there are opportunities for teaching in nonuniversity settings, where there are no graduate students to be trained and expectations for scholarly work are lower than in university settings. In medicine there are practices in fields like psychiatry, radiology, anesthesiology, public health, college medicine, hospital emergency-room work, that seldom involve irregular hours or visits to hospitalized patients. Work in these practices is more easily scheduled and routinized than in the private practice of surgery and primary care, where time demands are unpredictable and patient care is divided between hospital and office. And in almost any profession there is the option to work part time.

While these choices are worthwhile in themselves and offer many gratifications to individual professionals, they hardly constitute a triumph for the two-career family. Rather they have the effect of removing the two-career family, and women in particular, from the high-prestige tracks in the mainstream of professional life. As long as two-career families find it necessary to remain on the edges of professional life in order to function at all, the core structures of professional life, and the power conferred on those who work in them to order the values and organization of work in the professions overall, will still be reserved for those who are best able to fit into them, namely traditional men with career-free wives at home.

At first glance it would appear that single women are in the most favorable competitive position with men in the quest for professional success. Unencumbered by ties either to spouse or children, the unmarried woman seems to have replicated the freedom of the male role, thereby laying claim to the fundamental condition of career success. However it is precisely because professional roles and family roles are not mutually exclusive but interdependent that the single professional woman remains at a disadvantage compared to her married professional male counterpart.

The man with the career-free wife is not only unfettered in the pursuit of his career, he is also supported and assisted in that pursuit in ways that the unmarried woman is not. While a married man busies himself with his professional commitment, his wife is buying and cooking his food, cleaning his home, doing his laundry, overseeing home repairs and perhaps even doing some of the work of his profession as well. Because she is simultaneously managing her domestic and professional life, the single woman suffers a drain on her time and energy which is not experienced by the married professional man.

Also whatever the nature of her personal social-sexual relationships, the unmarried career woman is unlikely to be able to build on them in a way that allows her to be accepted as a social unit and to reap the career gains attendant upon married couple socializing. To the extent that the single woman's personal social world does not harmonize with or flow easily into her work world she may experience a strain unknown to the married man in sustaining and/or reconciling the two kinds of commitments. Absent too in her life is a built-in source of daily support and companionship to provide her with both a refuge from the workplace as well as with a revitalization of professional energy.

Of course some examples of genuinely successful two-career families (in the sense described earlier) and of individually success-ful professional women do exist. It would certainly be well worth-while to study such persons and families in depth in order to dis-cover whether there are common or merely idiosyncratic factors that enable them to survive and thrive. In this it would be important to pay attention to any adjustments that husbands in two-career families have made either to their own professional roles or in their expectations of their wives compared to the husbands described in this book. And it would be especially important to discover if these two-career husbands and wives, as well as successful single profes-sional women, have managed to develop enduring and satisfactory alternatives (either in their own relationships together with spouses or lovers, or with friends, colleagues, kin) to the traditional wife role—alternatives that provide the necessary adjunct, supportive, and homemaking resources and services that enable them to sustain dual commitments to career and domestic and personal life without undue stress.

For what the male careers and wives of this book show above all is that existing models of careers reflect, even assume, the inter-dependency rather than the equality of family and career roles. Male professional participation is propped up at every turn by the roles that women play as wives of professional men, and we may well ask who and what structures will prop up either the members of the two-career family or the single professional woman in the absence of a career-free wife at home? Seen in the light of current definitions, standards, and values of professionalism, the prospects for the eventual success of the two-career family, the full participa-tion of women in professional life, and the eradication of prevailing patterns of male dominance in the professions appear very dim indeed. It is no wonder that so many women who are now trying to travel the road to professional success so often claim, with a hollow laugh, that what they really need is a good wife.

APPENDIX:
RESEARCH METHODS

The main purpose of doing the research that is central to this book was to examine the roles of the wives of professional men for what those roles might reveal about the organization of professional work and the ingredients of successful careers. The general definition of the research task is set out in chapter 1, in the first two sections. The logic of the sample selection was guided by the concept of the "theoretically relevant" sample as discussed by Glaser and Strauss:

> The basic criterion governing the selection of comparison groups for discovering theory is their *theoretical* relevance for furthering the development of emerging categories. The researcher chooses any groups that will help generate, to the fullest extent, as many properties of the categories as possible, and that will help relate categories to each other and their properties. (1973:49)

Holmstrom offers a similar, though more lucid, formulation:

The question a researcher asks is "what group of people can I study whose experiences will highlight the issues that I am trying to understand?" The rule for selecting a group is to choose one that will give you insight into the problem. (1973:7)

In chapter 2 these ideas are specifically defined and applied, and there the notion of what is meant by the successful professional career in the context of the questions posed in this book is elaborated on and the criteria spelled out according to which academic and medical professional men and their wives were selected for study. This Appendix describes the actual procedures followed in selecting the sample and the techniques used in data-gathering and analysis.

The Sample

The size of the sample was determined by a combination of methodological and practical considerations. To the best of my knowledge, the kinds of questions I wanted to ask had not been addressed in other studies. At the outset there was no way of knowing whether the initial classification of women's roles would in fact prove a useful avenue of inquiry into the interrelationship of family and career. In any case, it was essential that the classification be used only as a guide and not as a predetermined static construct. Questions loomed large about possible contrasts, variation and change—and the sources of those—in the profiles of roles played by women in the context of male careers. For all of these reasons it seemed far more desirable to obtain information from a small sample from which relevant variables would emerge, than to try to order the variables ahead of time. These considerations dictated the choice of intensive in-depth interviews as the primary research mode. In anticipation of the time demands on one researcher conducting in-depth interviews, a workable sample size of forty cases was chosen, a size that could reasonably be expected to provide some basis for comparisons within and across the two professions. Of the forty cases, ten were chosen from each of the four subfields within the two professions of medicine and university teaching.

I realize that since sociological research is currently dominated by quantitative methods and large-scale samples, it is common to offer an *apologia* whenever a study deviates from those prevailing norms of research. However, I will offer no such defense here, because to do so would, I believe, amount to an implicit acknowledgment and acceptance of the assumption that what predominates—by virtue of the fact that it predominates—is somehow better or more worthwhile than what does not. My own thinking is that methodology should logically follow from the kinds of questions asked and the problems to be explored. Certain questions and problems lend themselves better to one research approach than another, and there are advantages and disadvantages to any approach taken.

I chose to do the research for this study in the ways that seem to me to offer the best understanding—of a particular sort—of the problems posed by the questions that framed the study. I would be less than honest if I did not also admit that doing in-depth interviews with a small number of people rather than administering survey questionnaires to large numbers of people is the approach to research with which I am most at ease and from which I derive the greatest amount of pleasure. Most social scientists, after all, go about their research in the way with which they are most at home and best equipped to do. Unfortunately, though, they usually feel obliged to justify their methodology on grounds other than their own preferences and competencies, which then appear, after the fact, only as coincidentally underpinning the research.

The specific individuals who became the actual research subjects were drawn from two lists. The first list was drawn (from information provided by the university's personnel office) of tenured full and some high-ranking associate professors in the natural sciences and humanities, most of whom had been promoted to their rank within the past five years. Only persons from the academic disciplines as distinct from the professional schools of the university were considered; scientists in mathematics and the strictly physical sciences were not included on the initial list, nor were humanists in the various language disciplines. From the *Directory of Medical Specialists* another list was drawn of Board Certified doctors in the fields of internal medicine and surgery (and one or two in pediatrics) who were presently practicing in the particular city I was interested in as a medical setting.

Both the *Directory of Medical Specialists* and the graduate school catalog of the university contained some biographical information about the careers of the men who might be candidates for inclusion in the sample base. From these sources I was able to learn a man's age and some information on his educational background and the course of his career generally, which made it possible to select men who were nearing or at the peak of their careers, (roughly between the ages of thirty-five to fifty) and whose careers seemed to have developed in customary career tracks for their professions. However, no men from either profession who were natives of and fully educated in other countries were included in the initial lists of those who might be approached in the study, because of the likely possibility that both their careers and marriages would have been shaped in major ways by the values of another culture. In this way I obtained lists of about thirty men in each profession and the subfields within them, who appeared eligible for inclusion in the sample base. This list of sixty came very close to exhausting the total number of people supplied by the two sources who seemed to fit the guidelines of the sample. The reason for beginning with a list of sixty rather than forty was to allow for the possibility that some people might not be married, could not be located, or would not be willing to participate in the study.

At that point it became necessary to ascertain whether a wife "went with" each one of these men and if so, how she might be reached. Since women typically travel in disguise so far as their telephone listings are concerned (and in the case of many doctors' wives, are not to be found at all except among the "unlisted"), discovering whether a man had a wife and how to contact her proved to be no small task. So far as the medical wives were concerned, a helpful "informant" (herself the wife of a doctor in practice in the city from which the medical sample base was being drawn) provided information about the marital status of doctors whose names were on the list, as well as their home addresses and telephone numbers. For the academics it was necessary to phone the various departments and ask whether professor so-and-so was married and what his home telephone and address was. Three of the academics about whom I inquired in this fashion were at that time unmarried and another two were away on sabbatical with their wives and so could not be included in the study. None of the doctors was unmarried.

Once their marital status had been verified, potential subjects were approached in batches of ten. Each group of ten women was contacted by personal letters that explained the purpose of the study and the general arrangement of the interview. A few days after the letters were mailed, each woman who had received a mailing was contacted by telephone and asked if she would be willing to schedule a time and place for an interview. When the interviews for the first group were coming to an end, another batch of letters was sent out to the next group of women on the list, who were contacted and scheduled for interviews, and so on, until the full quota of forty women was contacted and interviewed during the six-week period of field work.

In all, forty-six wives were contacted and asked if they would be willing to participate in the study; six persons refused—two medical wives and four academic wives. In general academic wives showed more wariness toward and skepticism about the study in the initial telephone contact than did the medical wives. Possibly the idea of one academic peering inside the domestic and family lives of other academics was coming a little too close for comfort for some faculty wives, and possibly academic wives are more knowledgeable about (and jaded by) the research process itself. The medical wives clearly regarded the study as something of a novelty and seemed for the most part pleased and flattered to be asked to participate. In fact some of them mentioned during the interviews that their friends had heard about the study and wondered if they too could be included in it. None of these volunteer offers was followed up, but they did confirm my overall sense of friendly acceptance toward the project among the wider community of medical wives. (Indeed this was my first clue to the social cohesiveness of the medical community). Two of the doctors' wives admitted during the interviews that their husbands had expressed some objections to their participation in the study and were distrustful of the legitimacy of and motivation behind the study. As it turned out, these were the most actively unhappy marriages of the medical sample.

Data Gathering

One woman was interviewed inadvertently by telephone. In the course of turning down the invitation to participate in the study because of the busy-ness and unpredictability imposed on her life by a newborn baby, her obvious interest in and curiosity about the study turned the conversation into an interview, with the researcher furiously scribbling notes on the other end. Except for one woman who scheduled an appointment in her office, all other wives were interviewed in their homes. Given the particular focuses of this study, it was a great advantage to see a person in her home setting and to catch a glimpse (or in the case of the doctors' wives, more than a glimpse) of the general life style represented by that setting. All of the interviews were tape-recorded, and although the ethics of social science research would naturally guarantee confidentiality and anonymity, it was surprising how few women—no more than half-a-dozen—raised questions about this on their own.

The advantage of the personal interview as a data-gathering technique is that it can combine structure and standardization with open-endedness and flexibility. Although the same basic ground was covered in all the interviews, each one was also tailor-made to the individual woman in the sense that she was allowed to respond to questions in her own way, at her own pace, with feelings and attitudes as well as facts. Many of the interviews were self-starting, and preliminary casual conversation over a cup of coffee often turned quite easily to areas relevant to the study. New topics or questions were introduced when responses to preceding ones had run their course or were in danger of veering in directions well away from the central interests of the study. Most of the questions asked were not about the features of the wife role as such, but probed into the more general areas in which those features might be revealed—the marriage relationship over time, the different periods of the husband's career, the wife's activities throughout the marriage, the organization of work time, family time and leisure time, the wife's attitude toward the husband's career, her sense of her goals for herself past and present, and so on. At the end of the interview the wife was asked if she was satisfied, in light of her own experience, with the kind of ground that had been covered and how it had been covered, and if there were any further points that she would like to raise or elaborate upon.

On the whole the interviews presented no unusual problems. Many women commented that they found the questions very interesting and enjoyed the chance to think about various aspects of their lives in the particular ways presented to them by the interviews. Certainly the rapport of the interview situation was enhanced by the fact that I too—as the wife of a "professional" man and a mother—could lay claim to the same roles about which they were being questioned and that we shared some common understandings in spite of the inevitable and necessary role distance between us that the interview situation imposed. Nonetheless, it is my feeling that methodological discussions of interview techniques often overestimate the extent to which the interview is a product of the role and skills of the interviewer alone. This emphasis masks the fact that the role of the interviewee has its own intrinsic rewards and gratifications that predispose an interview toward success. Most people enjoy talking about themselves and find it flattering to be requested to do so, especially in situations where they are fully accepted and not susceptible to judgment or criticism. The real expert of the interview situation is the informant, not the researcher, and it is precisely that feeling of expertise that sustains a high level of enthusiasm and participation on a respondent's part. How often, after all, do the wives of successful professional men have the chance to be experts in their own right, in their roles as wives?

It very quickly became apparent that each wife saw the interview as a chance to make a statement about her life and as an opportunity to be heard and understood in the way that she wanted to be. It seemed important that she be allowed to make that statement, if she was not to feel frustrated and cut off by an interview that satisfied only the needs and motives of the interviewer and not her own. Some interviews involved considerable pain and distress for the wife, but intense, deeply personal soul-searching or revelation was not a necessary condition of response to the kinds of questions posed in the interviews. The interview questions themselves were not designed to create intensity of feeling; when that occurred it was a consequence of the content of a woman's own life and the way that she chose to articulate it. In fact my own personal ethics as a researcher incline me to stay away from very private emotions and experiences, even at the risk of losing some potentially valuable data.

The interviews lasted anywhere from one and a half to four hours, with an average length of between two and two and a half hours. This included the time spent at the beginning or end of each interview recording in writing some basic facts pertaining to education, career history, personal background and marital history of the couple. At the end of each interview the wife was presented with two sets of questionnaire forms, one for her and one for her husband. The questionnaire for the wife was designed to elicit information about the specific norms and behavior of the husband's and wife's roles, the facts of her own marriage as to the division of labor in household and child care tasks, the use of outside household and child care help, income, areas of life satisfaction, and finally a few questions touching on feelings of self-esteem, frustration and dissatisfaction. The husband's questionnaire was a somewhat abbreviated version of the wife's, with additional questions that referred specifically to the importance attached to various aspects of professional career involvement and feelings about the use of time overall in the spheres of work and personal life. A covering letter was attached to the husband's questionnaire to provide him directly with information about the study and to encourage his response to the questionnaire.

Of the forty women who were interviewed, thirty-six returned the questionnaire forms. Of the four nonresponses, two were the wives of academic humanists, one a surgeon's wife, and one an internist's wife. Nine out of ten scientist husbands returned the forms. The two academic humanists whose wives did not return the forms also did not themselves return them; a third husband from this group was out of the country for the duration of the semester in which the interview took place and was not available to complete the forms. Three surgeon and four internist husbands were nonrespondents, including the husbands of the two medical wives who failed to return the questionnaires. In all then, twenty-nine of the forty husbands completed and returned the questionnaires, making a total of sixty-five husbands and wives who were questionnaire respondents of a possible eighty, and twenty-nine couples of a possible forty.

Data Analysis

From my own vantage point as a researcher, the great advantage of the in-depth interview is the sheer enjoyment of the personal encounter that it entails. The great disadvantage is the overwhelming amount of data that it generates. This was a particular problem in this study because so little work had been done in the areas in which I was interested that it seemed wise to cast a very wide net in both the interviews and the questionnaires in order to pull in as much potentially pertinent information as possible.

The first step in the chronology of data analysis was the codification and tabulation of information obtained from the questionnaires. Although this process took a great deal of time, the questionnaire findings ultimately proved useful primarily as supplements to or lead-ins to the interview material. Except for certain descriptive factual material, little of the questionnaire material stands or is reported on its own in the study. In part this is because cross-tabulations with such a small sample and even smaller subsamples do not yield very sturdy patterns that are conclusive in their own right, and in part because many of the questions dealing with personal attitudes and valuations proved in retrospect not to have been well worded or had clearly been answered normatively, from the respondent's perspective of what he or she thought one *should* feel or think. Then too, certain sets of questions, such as those dealing with self-esteem and incidence of stress, yielded no real patterns or contrasts at all, probably because they were too abbreviated or dealt with issues that do not lend themselves well to itemized responses.

Organization of the questionnaire data, therefore, amounted only to taking baby steps in the process of data analysis; the first giant step occurred with the transcription of the tapes themselves. Though I balked at the magnitude of the job and frequently bemoaned the lack of the financial wherewithal to hire someone else to do the job, the process of relistening to and transcribing the tapes proved to be enormously helpful as a way of simultaneously generating, confirming, and discarding various hypotheses. While it had been clear to me during the interviews themselves that the general notion of a threefold classification of the wife's role was relevant to understanding the lives of the women interviewed and would eventually clarify that role, the interviews themselves were organized around substantive areas and not along the lines of that specific classification, which remained submerged and in the background while the interviews were going on. It was only when I was typing transcripts that I began to sense the fit between the classification as I had originally conceived it and the interview material, and to see with some clarity both the general contours of the wife's role and its specific features, some of which were quite unanticipated. The supportive contribution, for example, turned out to be far more diffuse and complex in scope than I had first imagined it might be. The idea of the classification of the wife's role was only an angle of vision; the shape and content of the role were defined by the data themselves.

Transcribing the tapes also helped me to get back onto a sociological track in thinking about my research subjects. For I found that while I was actually doing the interviews I tended to become immersed in the richly varied and unique details of the lives of each woman to the point where I was struck much more by the individuality of the wives than by the similarities or patterned differences among them. It was a proverbial case of not being able to see the forest for the trees. Only by listening to tape after tape (in two groups of the twenty wives in each profession), now disassociated from the need to create the interview and make it work, did I begin to experience the cumulative effect of the data. I realized that the women were talking not only about what they had *done* in their roles as wives, but about the quality of the marriage relationship itself. With that I began to see that the patterns of interdependency between family and career roles were far more complex and multilayered than I had first imagined.

In the end each transcript (which averaged about ten typewritten pages in length) was duplicated, cut up, and reorganized in terms of the classification of the wife's role—adjunct, supportive, double duty. From that point on the process of data analysis really defies methodical description. As any researcher knows, there is a turning point when the research process becomes not simply a set of procedures but a total experience of daily living and breathing of the data, of playing hunches, of exploring new pathways, of turning back from blind alleys. It is a lonely, tedious, and frustrating journey—an odyssey that often holds less adventure than punishment. One presses on, sustained by the hope—and thrill—of discovery along the way.

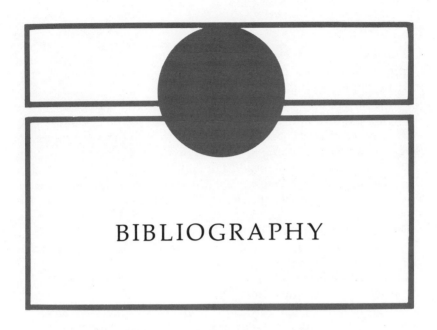

BIBLIOGRAPHY

Ariès, Philippe. 1962. *Centuries of Childhood: A Social History of Family Life.* Translated by Robert Baldick. New York: Random House.

Bakan, David. 1966. *The Duality of Human Existence.* Chicago: Rand McNally.

Becker, Howard S. and Anselm L. Strauss. 1956. "Careers, Personality and Adult Socialization." *The American Journal of Sociology,* 62:253–63.

Becker, Howard S., Blanche Geer, and Anselm L. Strauss. 1961. *Boys in White.* Chicago: University of Chicago Press.

Bernard, Jessie. 1971. *Women and the Public Interest.* Chicago: Aldine-Atherton.

—— 1973. "My Four Revolutions: An Autobiographical History of the ASA." In Joan Huber, ed., *Changing Women in a Changing Society,* pp. 11–29. Chicago: University of Chicago Press.

Davis, Fred and Virginia L. Olesen. 1972. "The Career Outlook of Professionally Educated Women: The Case of Collegiate Student

Nurses." In Fred Davis, ed., *Illness, Interaction, and the Self*, pp. 56–76. Belmont, Calif.: Wadsworth Publishing. Originally published in *Psychiatry* (1965), 28:334.

Durkheim, Emile. 1951. *Suicide*. New York: Free Press.

Epstein, Cynthia Fuchs. 1971. *Woman's Place: Options and Limits in Professional Careers*. Berkeley: University of California Press.

Fogarty, Michael P., and Rhona Rapoport, and Robert Rapoport. 1971. *Sex, Career, and Family*. London: Allen & Unwin.

Fox, Renée C. 1957. "Training for Uncertainty." In Robert Merton, George G. Reader, and Patricia L. Kendall, eds., *The Student Physician: Introductory Studies in the Sociology of Medical Education*, pp. 207–41. Cambridge, Mass.: Harvard University Press.

Freidson, Eliot. 1961. *Patients' Views of Medical Practice*. New York: Russell Sage Foundation.

—— 1970a. *Profession of Medicine: A Study in the Sociology of Applied Knowledge*. New York: Dodd, Mead.

—— 1970b. *Professional Dominance*. New York: Atherton Press.

Friedan, Betty. 1963. *The Feminine Mystique*. New York: Dell.

Garland, Thomas N. 1971. *Husbands of Professional Women: The Forgotten Men*. Ann Arbor, Mich: University Microfilms.

Giele, Janet Zollinger. 1978. *Women and the Future: Changing Sex Roles in Modern America*. New York: Free Press.

Ginzberg, Eli et al. 1951. *Occupational Choice*. New York: Columbia University Press.

Glaser, Barney G. and Anselm L. Strauss. 1973. *The Discovery of Grounded Theory: Strategies for Qualitative Research*. Chicago: Aldine.

Gold, Doris. 1971. "Women and Voluntarism." In Vivian Gornick and B. K. Moran, eds., *Woman in Sexist Society*, pp. 384–400. New York: Basic Books.

Goode, William J. 1960. "Encroachment, Charlatanism and the Emerging Profession: Psychology, Medicine and Sociology." *American Sociological Review*, 25:902–14.

Hacker, Helen M. 1972. "Women as a Minority Group." In Hamida and Haig Bosmajian eds., *This Great Argument: The Rights of Women*, pp. 127–44. Reading, Mass.: Addison-Wesley. Originally published in *Social Forces* (1951), pp. 60–69.

Hochschild, Arlie Russell. 1969. "The Role of the Ambassador's Wife." *Journal of Marriage and the Family*, 31:73–87.

—— 1974. "Making It or Making It Better: Notes on Women in the

Clockwork of Male Careers." Unpublished essay prepared for the Carnegie Commission on the Future of Higher Education.

Holmstrom, Lynda Lytle. 1973. *The Two-Career Family.* Cambridge, Mass.: Schenkman.

Hughes, Everett C. 1958. *Men and Their Work.* Glencoe, Ill.: Free Press, 1958.

—— 1971a. *The Sociological Eye: Selected Papers on Work, Self, and the Study of Society.* Chicago: Aldine-Atherton.

—— 1971b. "Personality Types and the Division of Labor." In E. C. Hughes, *The Sociological Eye,* pp. 326–37. Originally published in the *American Journal of Sociology* (1928), vol. 33.

—— 1971c. "Professions." In E. C. Hughes, *The Sociological Eye,* pp. 374–86. Originally published in *Daedalus,* 92(4):655–68.

Institute for Social Research. 1975. "Job Demands and Psychological Strain," *Newsletter* (Spring), pp. 3–4. Ann Arbor: University of Michigan.

Kanter, Rosabeth Moss. 1977. *Men and Women of the Corporation.* New York: Basic Books.

Knudsin, Ruth, ed. 1974. *Women and Success: The Anatomy of Achievement.* New York: Morrow.

Kohn, Melvin. 1978. "The Reciprocal Effects of the Substantial Complexity of Work and Intellectual Flexibility." *American Journal of Sociology* (1978) 84(1):24–53.

Laws, Judith Long. 1976. "Work Aspiration of Women: False Leads and New Starts." In M. Blaxall and B. Reagan, eds., *Women and the Workplace.* Chicago: University of Chicago Press.

Lipset, Seymour Martin and Everett Carll Ladd, Jr. 1975. *The Divided Academy: Professors and Politics.* New York: McGraw-Hill.

MacPherson, Myra. 1975. *The Power Lovers: An Intimate Look at Politicians and their Marriages.* New York: Putnam.

Mauksch, Hans O. 1972. "Nursing: Churning for a Change?" In Howard E. Freeman, eds., *Handbook of Medical Sociology,* pp. 206–30. Englewood Cliffs, N.J.: Prentice-Hall.

Merton, Robert K. 1972. "Insiders and Outsiders: A Chapter in the Sociology of Knowledge." *American Journal of Sociology* 78(1):9–47.

Merton, Robert K., George Reader, Patricia L. Kendall, eds. 1957. *The Student Physician: Introductory Studies in the Sociology of Medical Education.* Cambridge, Mass.: Harvard University Press.

Miles, James E. and Robert Krell. 1974. "Marital Therapy in Couples in Which the Husband is a Physician." Unpublished report, Department of Psychiatry, Faculty of Medicine, University of British Columbia, Vancouver.

Miles, James E., Robert Krell, and Tsung-Yi Lin. 1975. "The Doctor's Wife: Mental Illness and Marital Pattern." Unpublished report, Department of Psychiatry, Faculty of Medicine, University of British Columbia, Vancouver.

Miller, Jean B. 1972. "Sexual Inequality: Men's Dilemma." *American Journal of Psychoanalysis*, 32:147–54.

—— 1977. *Toward a New Psychology of Women*. Boston: Beacon Press.

Miller, S. M. 1972. "The Making of a Confused, Middle-Aged Husband." In Constantina Safilios-Rothschild, ed., *Toward a Sociology of Women*, pp. 245–53. Lexington, Mass.: Xerox College Publishing. Originally published in *Social Policy* (1971), 2(2):33–39.

Millett, John D. 1962. *The Academic Community*. New York: McGraw-Hill.

Moore, Wilbert E. 1970. *The Professions: Roles and Rules*. New York: Russell Sage Foundation.

Mumford, Emily. 1970. *Interns From Students to Physicians*. Cambridge, Mass.: Harvard University Press.

Myrdal, Alva and Viola Klein. 1968. *Women's Two Roles*. London: Routledge & Kegan Paul.

Nolen, William A. 1970. *The Making of a Surgeon*. New York: Random House.

Oakley, Ann. 1974. *Woman's Work: The Housewife Past and Present*. New York: Random House.

Pahl, J. M. and R. E. Pahl. 1971. *Managers and Their Wives*. Middlesex, U.K.: Penguin Books.

Papanek, Hanna. 1973. "Men, Women, and Work: Reflections on the Two-Person Career." In Joan Huber, ed., *Changing Women in a Changing Society*, pp. 90–110. Chicago: University of Chicago Press.

Parsons, Talcott. 1951. *The Social System*. New York: Free Press.

—— 1954a. "Age and Sex in the Social Structure of the United States." In Talcott Parsons, ed., *Essays in Sociological Theory*, pp. 89–104. New York: Free Press.

—— 1954b. "The Professions and Social Structure." In Talcott Parsons, ed., *Essays in Sociological Theory*, pp. 34–50. New York: Free Press.

Poloma, Margaret. 1970. *The Married Professional Woman: An Empirical Examination of Three Myths.* Ann Arbor, Mich.: University Microfilms.

Rapoport, Rhona and Robert Rapoport. 1971. *The Dual Career Family.* Baltimore: Penguin Books.

Rosenberg, Morris. 1957. *Occupations and Values.* Glencoe, Ill.: Free Press.

Rossi, Alice S. 1972a. "Sex Equality: The Beginnings of Ideology." In Constantina Safilios-Rothschild, ed., *Toward a Sociology of Women,* pp. 344–53. Lexington, Mass.: Xerox College Publishing. Originally published in *The Humanist* (1969), 29:3.

—— 1972b. "Women in Science, Why So Few?" In Constantina Safilios-Rothschild, ed., *Toward a Sociology of Women,* pp. 141–53. Lexington, Mass.: Xerox College Publishing. Originally published in *Science* (1965), 148:1196–1202.

—— 1973. "Comment" on "Minorities and Women in Sociology." *American Sociologist* (1973), 8(3):126–28.

Seidenberg, Robert. 1975. *Corporate Wives—Corporate Casualties?* Garden City, N.Y.: Doubleday.

Slater, Philip E. 1970. *The Pursuit of Loneliness.* Boston: Beacon Press.

Smelser, Neil. 1959. *Social Change and the Industrial Revolution.* Chicago: University of Chicago Press.

Veblen, Thorstein. 1931. *The Theory of the Leisure Class.* New York: Modern Library.

—— 1934. *Essays on Our Changing Order.* New York: Viking.

Whyte, William H., Jr. 1971. "The Wife Problem." In Cynthia Fuchs Epstein and William J. Goode, eds., *The Other Half,* pp. 79–86. Englewood Cliffs, N.J.: Prentice-Hall. Originally published in *Life,* Jan. 7, 1952, pp. 32–48.

219

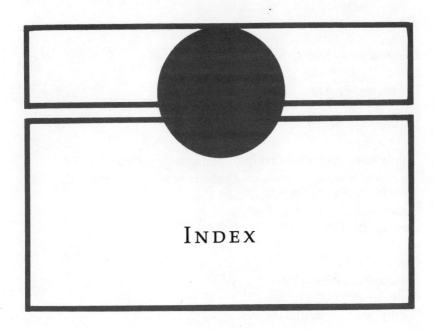

INDEX